カバー・表紙イラスト／野原　茂
Cover Illustration／Shigeru Nohara

GW01466514

Photo/S.Nohara

CONTENTS

Me163コメート（彗星）が生まれるきっかけとなったのは、航空機の理想的形態として無尾翼機を信奉するアレクサンダー・リピッシュ博士が、新しいヴァルターHWK-R1ロケット・モーターを、自身が設計した無尾翼機に搭載し、ロケット機のテストを行いたいと空軍に申し出てきたことに端を発する。1938年のことである。

この申し出は空軍に認可され、DFS（ドイツ滑空飛行研究所）194の型式名で製作発注が出された。

リピッシュ博士はフリーな設計者の立場にあったから、機体製作能力がなかったので、1939年1月部下10人を率いてメッサーシュミット社に入社し、特別に"L"部門を設けてもらい、DFS194の製作に専念した。

DFS194は、全幅9.3m、全長5.3mの小型無尾翼機で、胴体は金属製、主翼は木製だった。1939年末に初飛行し、最高速度500km/hの高速（HWK-R1の低推力に比較して）と、素晴らしい上昇力を見せつけた。

その結果、空軍はさらに発達型試作機としてリピッシュP.01V1～V3の名称（のちにMe163A V1～V3と改称）で3機を発注し、実用機としてその可能性をテストすることにした。

Me163Aは、ロケット・モーターを推力750kgにアップしたHWK-RII-203に更新し、機体全体のフォルムをさらに洗練したものに改めた。

1941年10月、Me163A V3は、ハイニ・ディットマーの操縦により高度3,965mにおいて、実に623.85m.p.h.（1,011.26km/h）もの超高速度を出し、空軍側の度肝を抜いた。もちろん、世界速度記録樹立だったが、すでに大戦が始まっていたため極秘扱いとされた。

当時のレシプロ戦闘機が600km/h程度の最高速度だったことを思えば、1,011km/hは確かに夢のような超高速には違いない。空軍省は、ロケット・モーターの燃焼時間が5分程度に過ぎず、燃料の確保、取り扱いの困難さなど、様々な問題はさておいて、Me163の迎撃戦闘機としての実用化を決定した。

実用型は、実戦機としての諸装備を施さねばならないから、再び大幅な設計変更が行われ、胴体は比較にならぬほど太くなり、主翼前縁の屈折はなくなり直線に変わった。ロケット・モーターもさらに推力を増したHWK109-509A（1,700kg）を予定した。

Me163B-0と呼ばれた先行量産型が、1943年8月から動力飛行テストを開始し、1944年1月には最初の装備部隊I./JG400が編成された。しかし、生産型Me163B-1aの就役は予定より大幅に遅れ、5月にはたったの1機、6月は3機、7月に入ってようやく12機まとまって配備され、はじめて中隊編成が可能になった。

そして、8月5日、I./JG400の3機がマグデブルク上空においてP-51Dを3機撃墜し、Me163による初戦果を記録した。さらに24日にはB-17を3機撃墜して、その驚異的な上昇力と高速の威力を示した。

確かに、レシプロ戦闘機では攻撃態勢に入ったMe163を捕捉するのは不可能であり、その出現はアメリカ軍側に大きな衝撃をもたらしたが、やがてロケット・モーターの燃焼時間が極めて短く、行動半径も50km程度に限定されることを見抜いたアメリカ軍は、JG400の基地ブランディス上空を避けて飛行するようになり、それ以後、Me163による戦果もパッタリ止まってしまった。

いかに驚異の上昇力、高速を持っていても、敵機と遭遇しなければ話にならない。かといって、基地を移動することは不可能だった。Me163の離着陸は、整備されたコンクリート滑走路でなければ不可能だったし、当時のこととて

それを有する基地は数えるほどしかない。まして、取り扱いの難しいロケット燃料は、特定の基地でしか保管できないのである。

ここに至って、Me163は根本的な問題が露呈し、兵器としての存在価値が薄れてしまった。秋にかけて、ひき続きチャンスをみて迎撃出動したものの、燃料の爆発、悪天候による離着陸事故などで損害ばかりが目立ち、戦果はまったくあがらなかった。

11月にはII./JG400も編成されたが、もはや実戦活動は停止状態に近く、敗戦を待たずに1945年4月にはI./JG400は解散して、事実上ロケット戦闘機隊は幕を閉じた。

いっぽうでは、Me163の欠点である滞空時間の短さ、地上における移動の不自由さを改善するため、Me163D（Me263）が計画され、1944年12月には最優先大量生産機に指定されたものの、たとえ本機が一定数配備されたところで、すでに状況が好転する可能性はほとんどなくなっていた。

Me163は、航空史上唯一の実用ロケット戦闘機となったが、また戦争という特殊な条件のもとで生まれた航空史上の異端児でもあったといえる。

（Me163B-1a データ Data）
全幅　Width：9.30m
全長　Length：5.92m
全高　Height：3.06m
主翼面積　Wing area：19.60㎡
自重　Empty weight：1,505kg
全備重量　Full loaded weight：3,885kg
エンジン　Powerplant：
Walter HWK109-509A-2X1
推力　Thrust：1,700kg
ロケットモーター作動時間：7分30秒
最大速度　Max speed：950km/h
着陸速度　Landing speed：160km/h
実用上昇限度　Service ceiling：15,500m
武装　Armament：MK108X2
乗員　Crew：1

ME-163　169442 USAF

Me163B-1a

写真／野原　茂、塩飽昌嗣
Photos by Shigeru Nohara,
Masatsugu Shiwaku

ドイツ博物館

DEUTSCHES MUSEUM

住所　Address：Museumsinsel 1, 8000 München 22, Germany
TEL：089-2179258
開館時間　Admission hours：9：00～17：00

ドイツ敗戦と前後して、連合軍が最も熱心に捕獲に精を出したのがMe163。実際の兵器としての成否はともかく、ロケット戦闘機という〝肩書〟は相当のインパクトがあった。イギリスは、なんとMe262、He162の倍以上に及ぶ計25機のMe163を捕獲して本国に運び、徹底した調査、テストを行った。

その中の1機、元7./JG400所属機（W.Nr、機番号は不明）が、用済み後西ドイツに返還されることとなり、1964年11月28日に引渡された。マンヒンクのメッサーシュミット社において、ヴィリー・ラ

ーディンガー技師の指揮下に、保存、展示のための復元が行われ、翌1965年7月2日からミュンヘンのドイツ博物館で一般公開され現在に至っている。

コクピット内部は照準器など欠落部品があるものの、コンディションはまずまずで、Me262と同様に外板の一部を切り欠いて、内部構造がわかるようにしてあるが、天井からの吊り下げ展示法のため、見る角度に制限がある。

オリジナル塗装が不明で、推定の塗装、マーキングにしてあるのが残念。

The Me163 was easily the one aircraft model the Allies were most anxious to capture from the Germans in the closing months of WWII in Europe. It wasn't so much the plane's actual accomplishments in battle (and they were few), but its label as "rocket fighter" which had the most impact. The British ultimately acquired no fewer than 25 Komets, twice the number of jet Me262s and He162s, and took them back to England for thorough testing.

One of these planes, originally assigned to 7./JG 400 (W.Nr. and aircraft number unknown) was eventually returned to Germany after testing, being handed over on November 28, 1964. The aircraft was restored under the direction of Willy Lerdinger, an engineer at Messerschmitt's Manching facility, and put on permanent public display at the Deutsches Museum in Munich on July 2, 1965, where it remains.

While the cockpit is missing some equipment, including the gunsight, the plane is in relatively good condition. Like the Me262 in the museum, some panels have been removed to provide views of the internal mechanism.

The plane's original markings are unknown. It is painted in a typical scheme of the period.

Me163B-1a W.Nr191316

写真／岡崎宣彦
Photos by
Nobuhiko Okazaki

科学博物館

THE SCIENCE MUSEUM

住所　Address：Exhibition Road, South Kensington, London SW7 2DD, U.K
TEL：01-589-3456
開館時間　Admission hours：月～土　10：00～18：00，日　14：30～18：00　From Mon. to Sat. 10：00 ～18：00, Sun. 14：30～18：00　Closed Bank Holidays

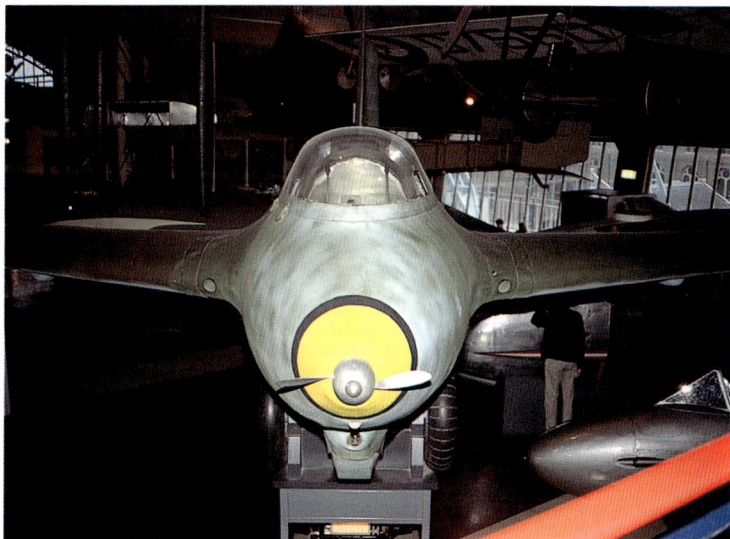

本機は、RAEの管轄下に調査、テストを受けた後、しばらく放置されていたが、1960～61年にかけてハールトン基地の訓練学校の生徒によってオーバーホールされ、その後ロンドン市内の科学博物館に寄贈された。

照準器、武装などは取り外されたままで、コクピット内部部品の欠落もあると思われるが、機体のコ

ンディションそのものは悪くない。

1960～61年のオーバーホールの際、塗装も手直しされたようだが、インクスポットの状態、W.Nr、機番号〝6〟の書体、サイズ、記入位置などは極力オリジナルに近くされ、違和感はない。エンブレムの類がないので当時の所属中隊は断定できないが、第7中隊（JG400）の可能性が高い。

This Komet was warehoused for a few years after its testing by the RAE, but from 1960 to 61 was overhauled by a group of students at the Hallton Air Base Flight School, and thereafter donated to the Science Museum in London, where it is still displayed.

The gunsight and armaments have been removed, and the cockpit is thought to be missing some equipment, but overall, the aircraft's condition is not too bad.

During its overhaul in 1960-'61, the plane seems to have been repainted, but the ink-spot design, W. Nr., aircraft number ("6"), and the size and location of the markings are all very close to the original, giving a quite natural impression. While no emblems remain on the plane, making absolute determination of its assignment impossible, it is likely that it was used by 7./JG 400.

Me163B-1a W.Nr 191060

写真／塩飽昌嗣
Photos by Masatsugu Shiwaku

インペリアル戦争博物館ダックスフォード

IMPERIAL WAR MUSEUM-DUXFORD

住所 Address：Duxford Airfield, Duxford, Cambrigeshire CB2 4QR, U.K.
TEL：0223-833963
開館時間 Admission hours：11:00〜17:30 (daily) Closed on Good Friday and May 2

本機は、イギリス到着後VF241の登録記号を附与され、RAEの管轄下にヴィッカース飛行場において、スピットファイアMkIXを曳航機にして何回かの滑空による飛行テストを受けた。1947年11月には、高度7,500mからの急降下により、720km/hの速度を記録した。

しかし、11月5日のテストにおいて着陸に失敗して機体を損傷し、テストは終わりを告げた。その後クランウエルの空軍大学内に教材として保管されていたが、1962年7月インペリアル戦争博物館に引き取られた。

機体は損傷したままだったため、博物館はとくに痛みの激しい前部胴体、コクピット周辺を修復し、同様に左主翼はW.Nr191400、垂直尾翼は同191660のそれを流用するなどして"合体"させたため、身元の証明に混乱を生じている。

当然、現在の塗装・マーキングは、オリジナルではなく、推定で施されたもの。テスト中の状態は、39ページの掲載写真で確認できるが、すでにこの時点でも相当のリタッチが加えられている。

This Komet was assigned identification number "VF241" by the RAE after its transfer to England. It was tested in unpowered flight several times at Vickers airfield, being towed into the air by a Spitfire Mk. IX. In November of 1947, it was clocked at 720 km/h in a dive from 7,500 meters.

However, testing was halted on November 5th of the same year when the plane was damaged in a landing mishap. Thereafter, it was kept as research material at Cromwell Air Force University, and eventually donated to the Imperial War Museum in July of 1962.

As the plane was still in its damaged condition, the museum staff undertook a restoration effort. The nose and cockpit area, most heavily damaged in the accident, were rebuilt. The left wing and vertical stabilizer, also damaged, were swapped with those from other Komets (W.Nr 191400 and W.Nr 191660, respectively) in order to complete the plane's "rebirth."

Naturally, the plane's markings are not original. It has been painted in a scheme typical of the period. Photos of this Komet during test flights can be found on page 39 of this book, but the plane's markings appear to have already been retouched at that point.

Me163B-1a W.Nr 191614

写真／野原 茂
Photos by Shigeru Nohara

イギリス空軍コスフォード航空宇宙博物館

RAF COSFORD AEROSPACE MUSEUM

住所 Address：RAF Cosford, Wolverhampton, West Midlands, WV7 3EX, U.K.
TEL：090-722-4872
開館時間 Admission hours：4月〜10月 10:00〜16:00、11月〜3月 土・日のみ 10:00〜16:00
From April to October (daily) 10:00〜16:00, From November to March (Sat./Sun.) 10:00〜16:00

本機も、RAEの管轄下に置かれたうちの1機で、調査終了後の経緯は不明だが、1976年以来コスフォード基地に保管され、現在は同基地内にオープンしている航空宇宙博物館にて一般展示中。

1990年11月の取材時点では、機体コンディションはまずまずで、コクピット内部も照準器、座席など一部々品が欠落しているものの、ほぼオリジナル状態を保っている。ただし、外面塗装はすっかり塗り直され、迷彩パターン、色調ともにオリジナルとは全く異なる。

本機のものではないが、傍らには副燃焼室をもつMe163C用のHWK109-509Cロケット・モーターが展示してあり、必見の価値がある。

What happened to this Komet following its acquisition by the RAE is unclear, but since 1976 it has been in the possession of the RAF's Cosford air base, and in public display at the RAF Cosford Aerospace Museum on the base. At the time these photos were taken in November of 1990, the plane was in near-original condition, with the gunsight, seat and a few other items missing, but otherwise in reasonable shape. Nevertheless, the aircraft has been repainted, and both the pattern and color of the markings shown here differ significantly from the original.

While not from this particular aircraft, a very rare HWK 109/509C rocket engine, the double-combustion chamber model developed for the Me163C, and planned for use in the Me263, is displayed alongside.

Me163B-1a W.Nr 191301

写真／野原 茂
Photos by Shigeru Nohara

アメリカ国立航空宇宙博物館　ポール・ガーバー保管施設

NATIONAL AIR AND SPACE MUSEUM
PAUL. E. GAHBAR PRESERVATION FACILITY

住所　Address：Suitland MD 20746, U.S.A
TEL：202-357-1552
開館日時　Admission：見学は予約確認が必要　By appointment only.

　正確な数はわからないが、アメリカもかなりの数のMe163を捕獲し、本国に運んでいる。その中の1機、W.Nr191301は、"FE-500"（のちにT2-500に変更）の登録記号を附与され、エドワーズ基地においてB-29を曳航機にして滑空による飛行テストを受けた。

　調査、テスト終了後は、NASMに移管され、主翼を取り外した状態で倉庫内に保管されていたが、1980年代に入り、シルバー・ヒルの同ポール・ガーバー施設内に限定展示されるようになり、現在に至っている。

　コクピット内部の状態は確認できなかったが、1987年の取材時点では、コンディションはそう悪くなかった。オリジナルの塗装を維持しているのも貴重だが、機首、胴体上面、主翼下面の剥離が著るしく、いずれは修復が必要となるだろう。

Although exact numbers are unknown, American forces also acquired and shipped back to the U.S. a large number of Komets. One of those, W.Nr 191301 (relabeled "FE–500" and later "T2–500") was tested in unpowered flight at Edwards Air Force Base after the war, towed up by a B–29.

Following testing, the aircraft was donated to the Smithsonian, where it was disassembled and stored for nearly three decades. However, in the 1980s, it was reassembled and put on limited display at the Paul E. Gahbar Preservation Facility in Silver Hill, Maryland, an arm of the National Air and Space Museum.

While the condition of the cockpit's interior could not be confirmed, the overall condition of the plane at the time photos were taken in 1987 was not too bad. This Komet is a particularly precious example of a bird which is still in its original colors. However, the nose, upperside of the fuselage, and lower side of the wings are peeling quite severely and restoration will be necessary at some point.

Me163B-1a

写真／紅谷 彰
Photos by Akira Beniya

プレーンズ・オブ・フェイム

PLANES OF FAME

住所　Address：Chino Airport, 7000 Merrill Ave. Chino, CA 91710, U.S.A
TEL：714-597-3722
開館時間　Admission hours：9：00〜17：00（daily）

　本機もアメリカ軍に捕獲された後、アメリカ本国に運ばれた多数のMe163B-1のうちの1機（W.Nr不明）である。アメリカ軍による飛行テスト、機体構造等の調査などが行われた後、民間に放出された本機は、カリフォルニア州チノに在るエド・マロニー氏に買い取られレストアされた。現在、同氏の私設航空博物館プレーンズ・オブ・フェイムに展示されている。

　コクピット内の一部のパーツや主翼付け根の機関砲が取り外されている他は、機体の状態は極めて良い。塗装はRLM74／75／76カラーに近い塗料でリペイントされ、機首に2./JG400の部隊章、胴体後部に11（白）の機番号が書き込まれている。また本機の傍にはヴァルターHWK109-509Aロケット・モーターも展示されておりMe163ともども一見の価値がある。

This Me163, a B–1 (W.Nr unknown), is also one of the many Komets seized by American forces and shipped to the United States. Following extensive flight testing, which included experiments involving modification of the plane's body, it was sold to Mr. Ed Maloney of Chino, California, and it presently displayed at his *Planes of Fame* museum.

With the exception of some parts missing from the cockpit, and the lack of armament, the aircraft is in excellent condition. It has been painted in colors very close to the original RLM 74/75/76, with the unit emblem of 2./JG 400 painted on the nose, and aircraft number "11" (in white) painted on the fuselage. An HWK 109–509A rocket engine is displayed next to the aircraft at the museum, allowing visitors to study its unique propulsion system.

写真1〜3：Me163Bは、動力にロケット・モーターを使用していたことに加え、実用機として初めて無尾翼形式を採用したことも特筆に値する。

写真4：Me163Bの機首左側。

写真5〜7：機首先端には、発電機駆動用の小プロペラが付いている。2枚のプロペラ・ブレードの取り付け位置がずれているのに注目。

Photo 1-3: The Me163B Komet, in addition to being powered by a rocket motor, was the world's first operational aircraft which employed a tailless design.

Photo 4: A view of the port side of the nose of the Me163B.

Photo 5-7: A small propeller, used to drive the plane's generator, is attached to the nose of the aircraft. Note that the two blades of the propeller are mounted offset of center on the spinner (see photo 6).

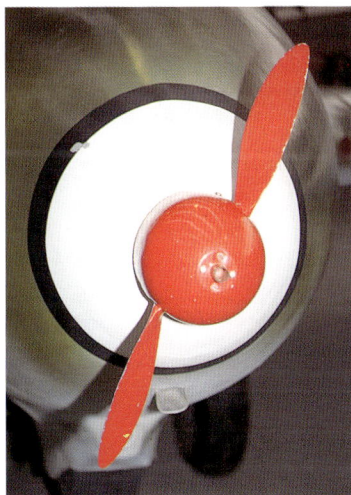

6

7

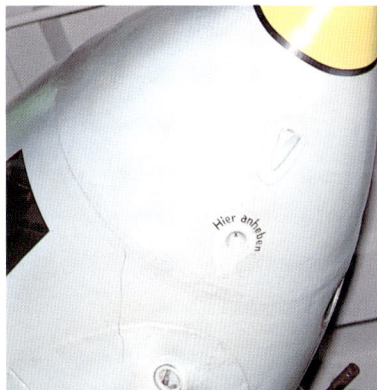

8

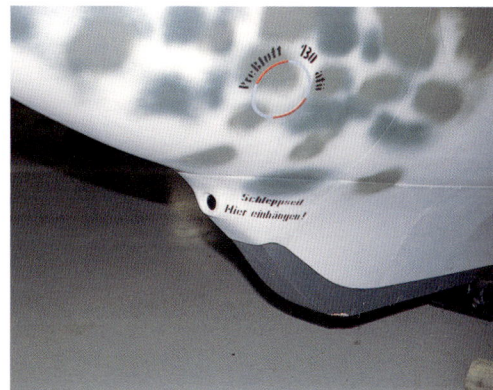

9

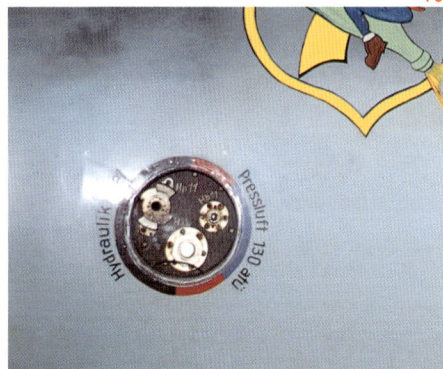

10

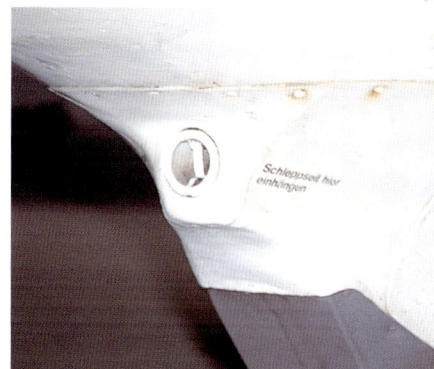

11

写真8：機首下面。前方の突起物は発電機冷却用のエア・スクープ、その後方の円形凹部は、ジャッキの取り付け部。

写真9：機首側面下方の円形パネルは圧搾空気供給口ハッチ。その下方、スキッドの上部に見える円孔は、曳航索の連結部である。

写真10：圧搾空気供給口のハッチを外した状態。内部には形状の異なる3つの接続部が設けられている。

写真11：曳航索連結部のクローズ・アップ。

写真12：胴体中央部左側。

写真13〜14：胴体中央部右側。

Photo 8: The underside of the nose. The small triangular object towards the front is an air intake scoop. The recessed area just behind it is a jack mounting point.

Photo 9: The lower port side of the front of the plane. The circular hatch on the side of the fuselage covers the compressed air supply port. The small circular opening below that on the front of the skid is the mount for a tow cable.

Photo 10: A view with the compressed air supply port hatch removed. Note that three different connectors for supply hoses were installed.

Photo 11: A close-up of the tow cable mount.

Photo 12: The central fuselage, viewed from the left side.

Photo 13-14: The central fuselage, viewed from the right side.

12

13

14

15

写真15：ドイツ博物館に展示されている Me163Bは、胴体後方右側面のパネルが一部切り取られているため、内部に搭載されているヴァルターHWK109-509Aロケット・モーター艤装状態がよくわかる。

写真16：胴体中央の背部（写真は左側）。三角形の後方視認窓の直後に見える止め具が付いたパネルは、主翼付け根に搭載された機関砲の弾倉に装弾する際に取り外せるようになっている。

写真17〜18：弾倉装塡用ハッチの後方にある、同じく止め具が付いたパネルは、C液燃料補給およびHWK109-509Aロケット・モーターの点検用ハッチ。その下方に見える小判形の小パネルもロケット・モーターの点検用ハッチである。

写真19：胴体上面、キャノピー直後には、FuG16ZE無線器用のアンテナを装着。アンテナの後ろに見える円形パネルはT液燃料の注入口ハッチ。

Photo 15: Sections have been cut out of the starboard rear portion of the fuselage of the Me163B at the Deutsches Museum, providing an excellent view of the structure of the aircraft's Walter HWK 109-509A rocket motor.

Photo 16: The top portion of the central fuselage (photo taken from the left side). The panel with the two silver latches visible just behind the triangular observation window is removed when reloading the two MK108 30mm cannon mounted in the wing roots.

Photo 17-18: The panel behind the ammunition loading panel with the same type of latches opens for refueling with *C-Stoff* fuel (a mixture of hydrazine hydrate, methyl alcohol and water), as well as for inspection of the Walter HWK 109-509A rocket motor.

Photo 19: The top of the fuselage. The antenna for the FuG16ZE radio is installed immediately aft of the cockpit. The round panel visible right behind the antenna is the fuel hatch for *T-Stoff* (80% hydrogen peroxide, 20% water).

16

17

18

19

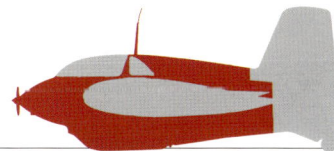

写真20：胴体中央部上面。
写真21：主翼下の胴体中央部（写真は左側）。
写真22：胴体下面の降着装置。通常の引き込み式主脚ではなく、着陸用のスキッド、離陸用の切り離し式ドリーを採用しているところが、いかにも大戦末期の急造機らしい。

写真23〜26：胴体下面の着陸用スキッド。スキッドの上下駆動は油圧式で、ドリー装着／離陸時は下げた状態、着陸時は上げた状態にセットされる。

Photo 20: A view of the top of the fuselage.
Photo 21: A view of the central fuselage, below the wing (photo taken from left side).
Photo 22: The Komet's "landing gear." The use of a primitive skid for landings, and a jettisonable dolly for takeoff speaks volumes about the rushed development environment in Germany towards the end of the war.
Photo 23-26: Close-ups of the landing skid. The skid moved up and down by a hydraulic mechanism, lowered (as in the photos) for takeoff when the dolly was attached, and raised for landings.

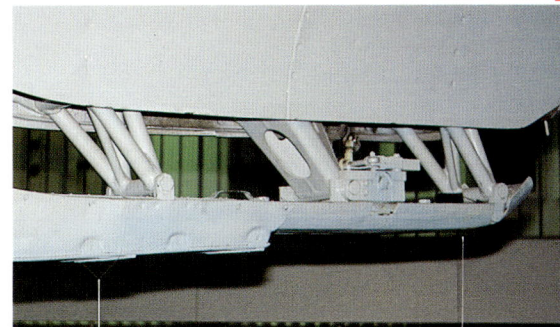

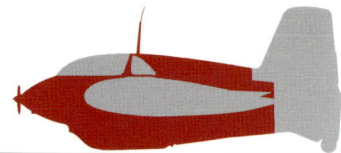

写真27〜28：胴体下面のスキッド後方にはT液、C液の排出口が設けられている。表示マークからも解るように前方がT液、後方がC液の排出口である。

写真29〜31：離陸時に使用するドリー。写真29〜30は前方より、写真31は後方より見たところ。

写真32：ドリーに装着された700mm×175mmサイズの低圧タイヤ。

Photo 27-28: Immediately behind the landing skid were fuel dump ports for *C-Stoff* and *T-Stoff*. As the plane's markings make clear, the forward port was for *T-Stoff*, and the rear one for *C-Stoff*.

Photo 29-31: Views of a takeoff dolly. Photos 29 and 30 are taken from the front, while Photo 31 is from the rear.

Photo 32: A close-up of the 700mm × 175mm low-pressure tires used on the dolly.

Photo 1〜4, 10, 12, 15〜20, 22, 25〜27, 29, 30／S.Nohara
Photo 5, 9, 14／A.Beniya
Photo 6〜8, 11, 13, 23, 24, 28, 31, 32／M.Shiwaku
Photo 21／N.Okazaki

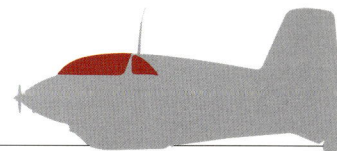

写真33〜34：Me163Bのキャノピー。写真33は左側。写真34は右側。

写真35〜36：開閉式キャノピーの後方に設けられた三角形状の後方視認用窓。写真35は左側、写真36は右側の窓である。

写真37〜38：キャノピーの開状態。Me262などと同様、キャノピーは右開き式である。

Photo 33-34: The canopy of the Me163. Photo 33 is from the left side, photo 34 from the right.

Photo 35-36: Two views of the triangular observation window just behind the canopy (open in these photos). Photo 35 is from the left side, photo 36 from the right.

Photo 37-38: The canopy in the open position. As in the Me262, it is hinged on the right side.

キャノピー＆コクピット CANOPY & COCKPIT

写真39〜40：Me163は、米陸軍4発重爆撃機の迎撃用に開発されたため、コクピット前面には、厚さ90mmの防弾ガラスが装着されている。写真の機体、RAFコスフォード航空宇宙博物館展示機は、防弾ガラス下部に付くRevi16B射撃照準器が取り外されている。

写真41：主計器板。Revi16B、コンパスをはじめ計器類の一部が紛失しており、さらに中央の水平儀、速度計、昇降計、回転計などもRAF規格のものに取り替えられているようだ。

写真42：主計器板と左サイド付近。左上方の赤いレバーは緊急時に使用するキャノピー投棄レバー、同位置に設置された円形グリップが付いたレバーはキャノピーの開閉レバー、また下方に見える球状グリップが付いたレバーはスロットル・レバーである。

写真43：主計器板下。方向舵ペダルと操縦桿の一部が見える。

Photo 39-40: The Me163, having been developed as an interceptor to defend against U.S. heavy bombers, had a 90mm thick sheet of bulletproof glass installed in the front part of the cockpit. The aircraft in the photo, the Me163 on display at the RAF Cosford Aerospace Museum, is missing its Revi 16B gunsight, which should be installed just below this glass.

Photo 41: The main instrument panel. Several instruments, including the compass and Revi 16B gunsight have been lost. In addition, a number of instruments visible in the center of the panel, including the artificial horizon, airspeed indicator, vertical speed indicator and turn coordinator appear to have been replaced with RAF-type units.

Photo 42: The main instrument panel and port side of the cockpit. The red-colored, rectangular lever visible in the upper left-hand side of the cockpit is for emergency jettison of the canopy. The lever in front of it with a disk-shaped grip is the latch for opening and closing the canopy. The lever with the spherical knob visible below the canopy levers is the throttle.

Photo 43: The area below the instrument panel. The rudder pedals and control stick are visible.

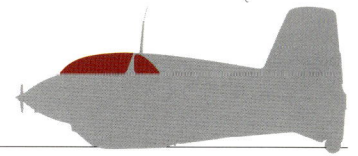

Photo 33〜35, 37〜48／S.Nohara
Photo 36／M.Shiwaku

写真44〜45：コクピット内左右壁面には、シートを挟むような形でT液タンク（長方形の黒いタンク）が設置されている。写真44は右サイド、写真45は左サイド。右サイドのT液タンク上の箱状のものは無線器、電気装置のスイッチボックス。
写真46：KG12E操縦桿。
写真47〜48：コクピット内後方。残念ながら、写真の機体はシートが取り外されているが、Me163Bでは、パイロットが12Gまで耐えれるように特製のシートが採用されていた。

Photo 44-45: On either side of the cockpit, tanks for *T-Stoff* fuel (the long, black box-shaped objects), sandwich the pilot's seat. Photo 44 is the starboard side, photo 45 is the port. The object on top of the *T-Stoff* tank on the right side is the radio and switch box for the plane's electrical system.
Photo 46: The KG12E control stick.
Photo 47-48: The rear section of the cockpit. Unfortunately, the pilot's seat has been removed from the plane in the photos. The Me163B featured a special seat which allowed the pilot to withstand up to 12 g's.

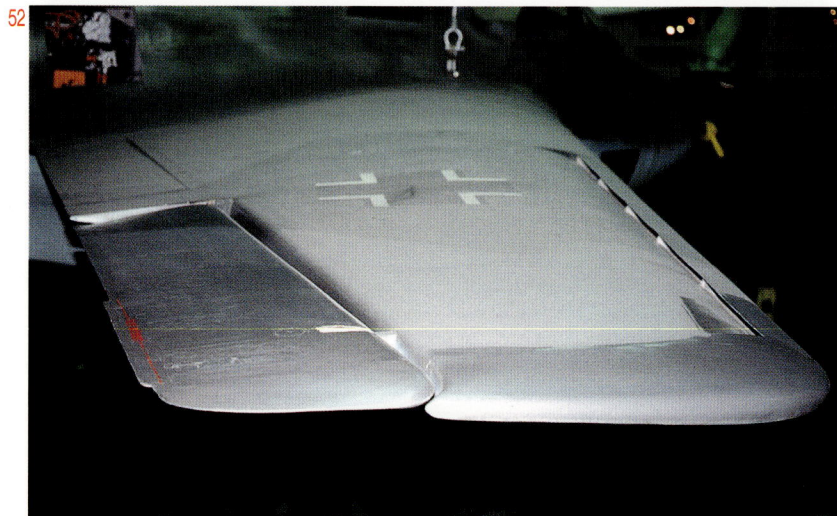

写真49〜53：Me163Bの主翼は23°の後退角
（主桁位置）を持つ全木製構造である。

Photo 49-53: The Me163B's wings were
swept back 23° (at the location of the main
spars), and constructed entirely of wood.

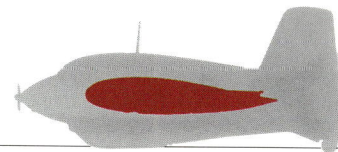

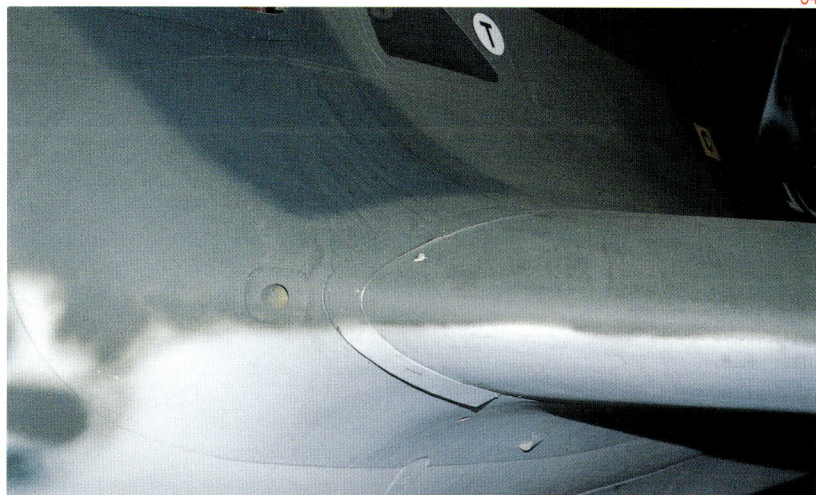

54

55

56

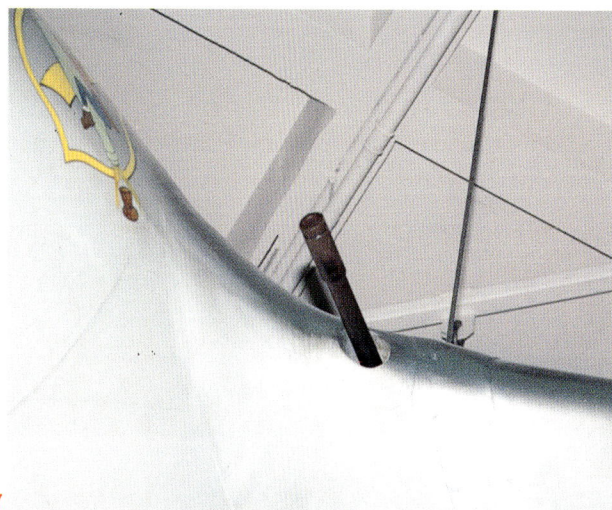

57

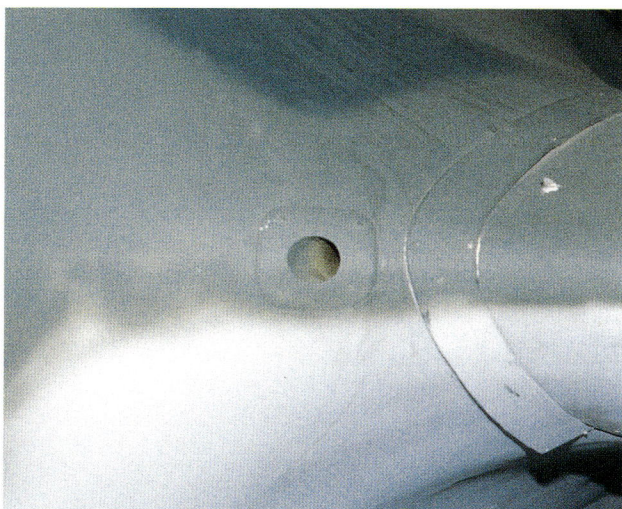

58

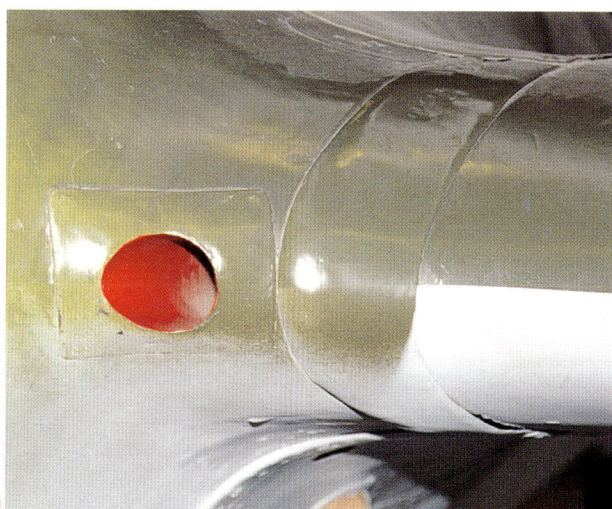

59

写真54〜55：主翼付け根付近。写真54は前縁部、写真55は翼上面の付け根。

写真56〜57：Me163Bは主翼付け根に機関砲を搭載。当初、MG151／20 20mm機関砲を搭載していたものの、Me163B-0の47号機以降からはより強力なMK108 30mm機関砲に変更された。写真のMe163Bに搭載されているのはMG151／20 20mm機関砲。

写真58〜59：主翼付け根の機関砲発射口。写真58はMG151／20の砲口（プレーンズ・オブ・フェイム展示機、機関砲は取り外されている）、写真59はMK108の砲口（インペリアル戦争博物館ダックスフォードの展示機）。両者の砲口の大きさの違いに注目。

Photo 54-55: A close-up of the wing roots. Photo 54 shows the leading edge. Photo 55 provides a top view of the wing root.

Photo 56-57: Cannons were installed in the Me163B's wing roots. Originally, the plane was built with the MG151/20 20mm cannon installed, but beginning with aircraft #47 of the Me163B-0 series, the more powerful MK108 30mm cannon became standard armament. The photograph shows the MG151/20 20mm cannon.

Photo 58-59: Close-ups of the holes in the wing roots for the cannon (the cannons have been removed from these aircraft). Photo 58 is the Me163 displayed at the Planes of Fame museum, with holes for a 20mm cannon. Photo 59 is the Komet at the Imperial War Museum, with holes for a 30mm cannon. Note the vast difference in the size of the openings.

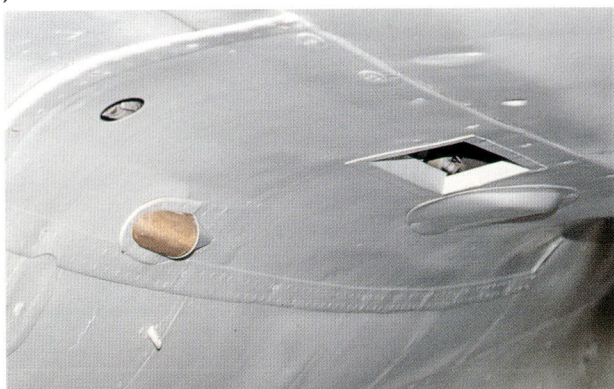

写真60：主翼下面付け根に設けられた開口部は、機関砲弾の空薬莢排出口。その直後の膨らみを持つ円形パネルは機関砲の点検パネルである。

写真61〜64：主翼前縁には、固定式のスラットが設置されている。写真61、62は下方より、写真63、64は上方より見たところ。

Photo 60: The rectangular opening on the underside of the wing root is the ejection port for spent cannon cartridges. The circular panel immediately aft of it is an inspection port for the cannon.

Photo 61-64: The leading edge of the wing had fixed-position slats. Photos 61 and 62 show the underside of the wing. Photos 63 and 64 are taken from the top.

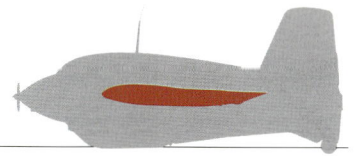

65

66

67

68

69

70

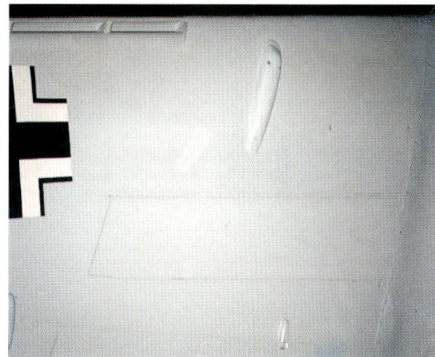

71

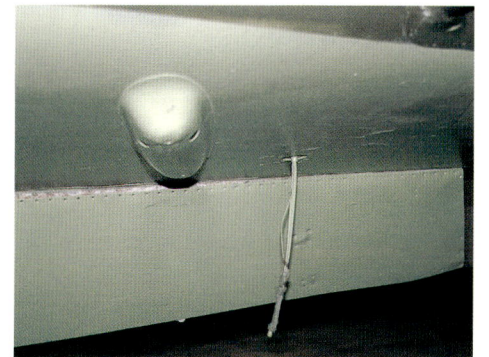

72

写真65〜68：主翼後縁外側の補助翼。補助翼は昇降舵の働きも兼ねており、上方22°、下方27°の範囲で作動する。

写真69〜70：主翼上面のフラップ位置表示棒。写真は、フラップを下げた状態を示す。

写真71〜72：主翼下面の突起物は、C液燃料パイプのカバー。その後方に着陸フラップが見える。写真71は右主翼下面、写真72は左主翼下面（フラップ下げ状態）。

Photo 65-68: Close-ups of the ailerons on the outer edges of the wings. In the tailless Komet, the ailerons also performed the function of the elevator, being able to move in a range from 22° up to 27° down.

Photo 69-70: In the Komet, a rod would protrude from the upper surface of the wing to indicate the position of the flaps. The photos show the rod indicating that the flaps are down.

Photo 71-72: The small protruding object on the bottom of the wing is a cover for a *C-Stoff* fuel pipe. The flaps are visible behind the cover. Photo 71 is the bottom of the starboard wing. Photo 72 is the port wing (with the flaps in the down position).

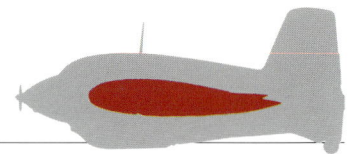

73

74

75

77

76

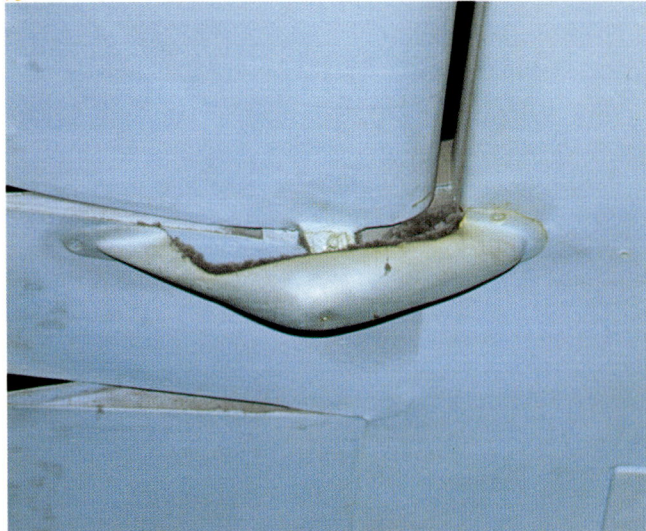

78

79

写真73～74：C液燃料パイプ・カバーのクロー
ズ・アップ。写真73は右主翼、写真74は左主翼。
写真75～76：左主翼前縁中央部に設置された
ピトー管。写真76は、ピトー管の先端のクロー
ズ・アップ。
写真77：左主翼下面のFuG25a　IFF用ロッ
ド・アンテナ。
写真78～79：主翼下面の補助翼操作桿のフェ
アリング。写真78は右主翼、写真79は左主翼下
面のフェアリングである。

Photo 73-74: Close-ups of the *C-Stoff* fuel
pipe cover. Photo 73 is the starboard wing,
photo 74 is the port.
Photo 75-76: Shots of the pitot tube attached
to the mid-section of the port wing's leading
edge. Photo 76 is a close-up of the tube's tip.
Photo 77: The FuG25a IFF rod antenna on
the bottom of the port wing.
Photo 78-79: Close-ups of the aileron control
rod fairings on the bottom of the wings. Photo
78 is the starboard wing, photo 79 is the port.

Photo 49, 50, 53, 56, 61, 63, 64, 68, 72,
75, 77／S.Nohara
Photo 51, 52, 57, 59, 60, 62, 66, 69～71,
73, 74, 76, 78／M.Shiwaku
Photo 79／N.Okazaki
Photo 54, 55, 58, 65, 67／A.Beniya

＞ エンジン ENGINE

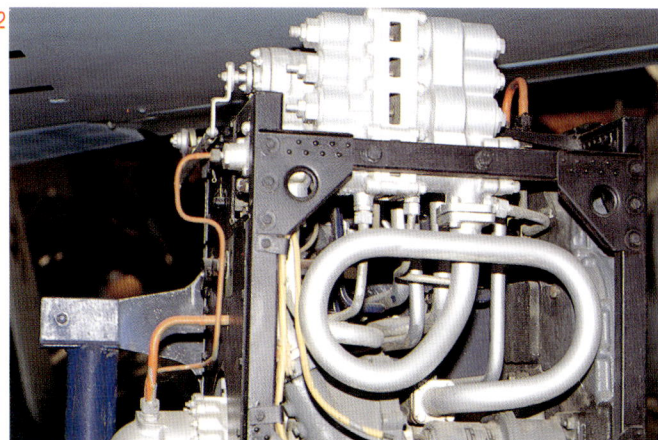

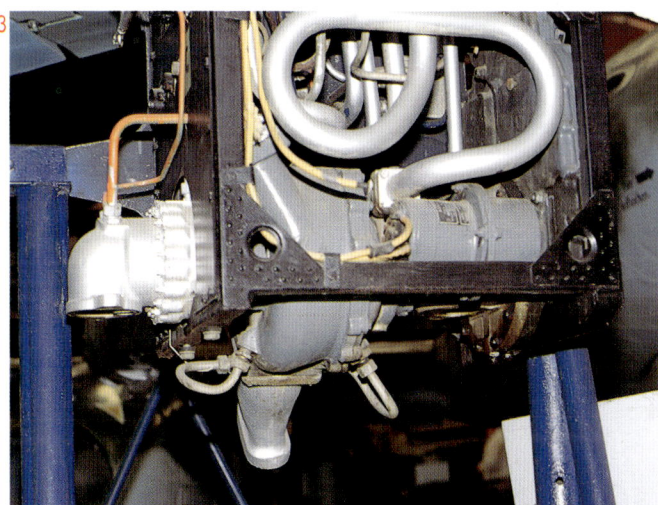

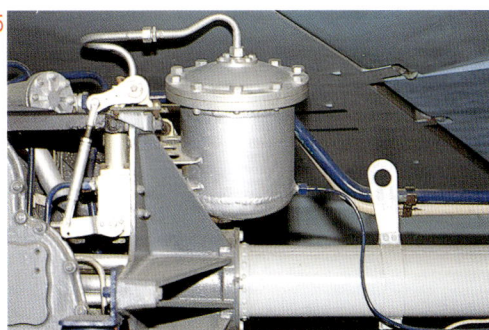

写真80：Me163Bの動力となったヴァルター－HWK109-509Aロケット・モーター。重量369kg、シンプルな構造ながら、最大推力1,700kgの性能を有する。
写真81～82：ロケット・モーター前部の制御室。
写真83：ロケット・モーター制御室の下部には、タービン・ポンプとスターターモーターが設置されている。

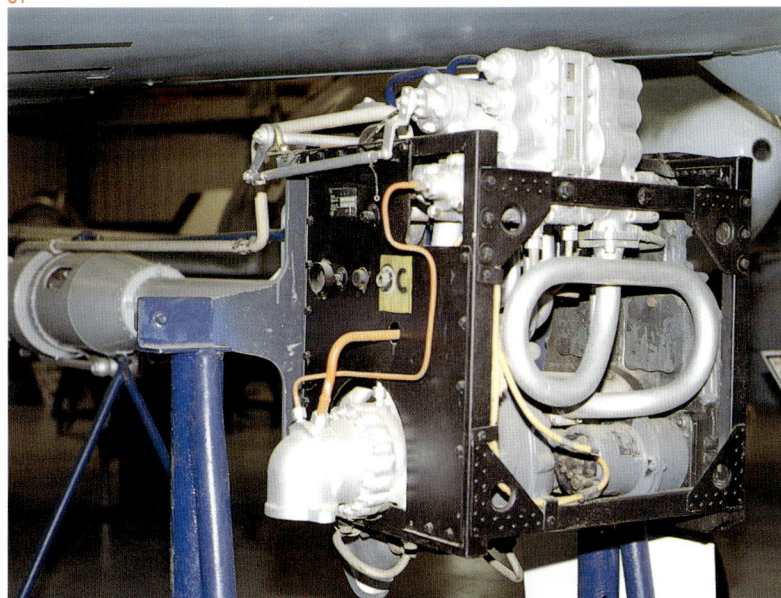

写真84：制御室左側の伝動ギアハウジング（グレーの部分）。下方に４個見える円形部分は、ギアの軸受け。
写真85：制御室後部上方に取り付けられている銀色の円筒状パーツは、Ｔ液の気化フィルター。

Photo 80: The powerplant of the Me163B, the Walters HWK109-509A rocket motor. Despite its simple design, this 369kg motor could produce 1,700kg of thrust.
Photo 81-82: Close-ups of the mechanism at the front of the motor.
Photo 83: The turbine pump and starter motor were installed on the bottom of the motor.
Photo 84: The gearbox on the left side of the motor (the gray assembly). The four circular protrusions at the bottom are mounts for the gear shafts leading into the turbine pump.
Photo 85: The silver cylinder visible in this photo of the upper-rear portion of the motor mechanism is the carburetor filter for *T-Stoff* fuel.

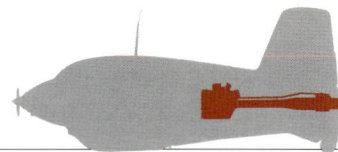

写真86〜87：制御室を後方より見たところ。HWK109-509Aロケット・モーターは制御室後部の推力板（グレーのパネル）から左右に伸びた取り付け基部によって機体に固定されている。制御室の下方に見える楕円状のパイプは、T液の排出管。

写真88〜90：ロケット・モーター後端の燃焼室。上方に付いた細いパイプは、冷却用C液リターンパイプ（青色のパイプ）と冷却用C液送液パイプ（白色のパイプ）。また下方のパイプは、C液の投棄用パイプである。

写真91〜92：Me163Bの性能向上型Me163C、Me263の動力となったヴァルター109-509Cロケット・モーター。HWK109-509Aで問題となったロケット・モーターの作動時間の短さを少しでも改善するため109-509Cでは、巡航用の副燃焼室を追加し作動時間の延長が図られた。写真92を見ればわかるように副燃焼室が、燃焼室の下に取り付けられている。

Photo 86-87: Views of the HWK109-509A from the rear. The motor was mounted to the Komet's fuselage by the two spars projecting off the left and right sides of the gray thrust plate. The rounded silver pipe visible below the motor is the exhaust for *T-Stoff* fuel.

Photo 88-90: Close-ups of the combustion chamber at the rear of the motor. The white pipe leading from the motor carried *C-Stoff* coolant to the chamber, while the blue pipe carried it back. The small pipe on the bottom of the chamber is for dumping *C-Stoff*.

Photo 91-92: The Walters 109-509C rocket motor, a more powerful unit which was used in the Me163C and Me263A. In order to extend the motor's running time, a major problem with the 109-509A, an additional combustion chamber was added. The second, smaller chamber (visible below the main chamber in photo 92) produced a fixed thrust of about 200kg and was used for cruising and level flight. The larger, main chamber, used for take-off and climb, was step-controlled and could produce up to 2,000kg of thrust. This arrangement allowed much more efficient use of fuel, and greatly extend the motor's running time.

86

Photo 80／A.Beniya
Photo 81〜90／T.Shiwaku
Photo 91, 92／S.Nohara

87

90

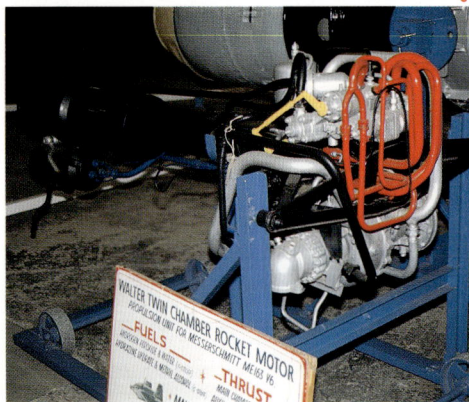

91

92

88

89

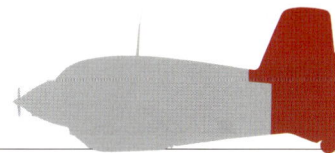

写真93〜96：Me163Bの尾部。写真94は右側、写真93、95、96は左側。
写真97：垂直尾翼左側。方向舵中央の凸部は方向舵ホーン・バランス。下方の水滴状のバルジは、方向舵操作桿のフェアリング。

Photo 93-96: The tail section of the Me163. Photo 94 is from the right side. Photos 93, 95 and 96 are from the left.
Photo 97: A close-up of the vertical stabilizer and rudder. The connection in the middle of the rudder can be clearly seen. The bulge at the bottom of the vertical stabilizer is the fairing covering the rudder control rod.

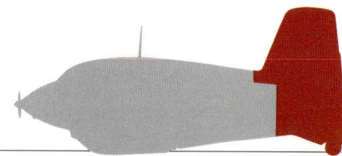

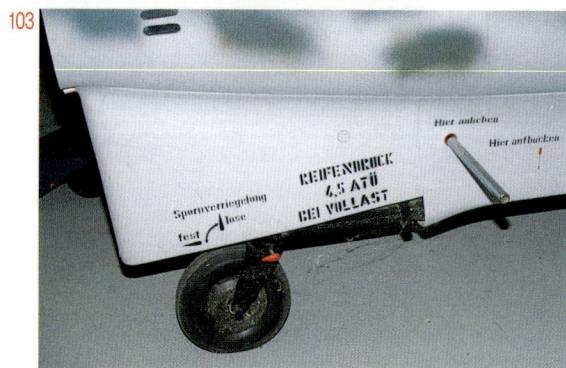

写真98〜100：ノズル部付近。ドイツ博物館のMe163B（写真99）は、一部パネルが切り取られており、尾部内のロケット・モーター燃焼管が見えるようになっている。

写真101〜104：Me163Bの尾脚。先行量産型B-0の後期生産機からは、点検整備、尾輪交換などを考慮し、タイヤが露出するようにフェアリングの一部を切り欠いたり（写真101、102）、フェアリングそのものを取り外した機体（写真103、104）が多い。

Photo 98-100: Close-ups of the engine nozzle area. Sections have been cut out of the starboard rear portion of the fuselage of the Me163B at the Deutshes Museum (photo 99), providing an excellent view of the structure of the aircraft's Walter HWK 109-509A rocket motor as installed.

Photo 101-104: The Komet's tail wheel. In order to simplify inspection, maintenance and tire changes, many planes beginning with the latter part of the B-0 series had the fairings cut back to expose the tail wheel (as in photos 101 and 102) or had the fairings removed altogether (photos 103 & 104).

Photo 93／M.Shiwaku
Photo 94〜102／S.Nohara
Photo 103／A.Beniya
Photo 104／N.Okazaki

Me163の迷彩塗装&マーキング

Camouflage & Markings of Me163
作図・解説／野原　茂 Illustrations & Commentary by Shigeru Nohara

■Me163B RLM81／82／76グリーン迷彩
Me163B RLM81／82／76 Green Camouflage

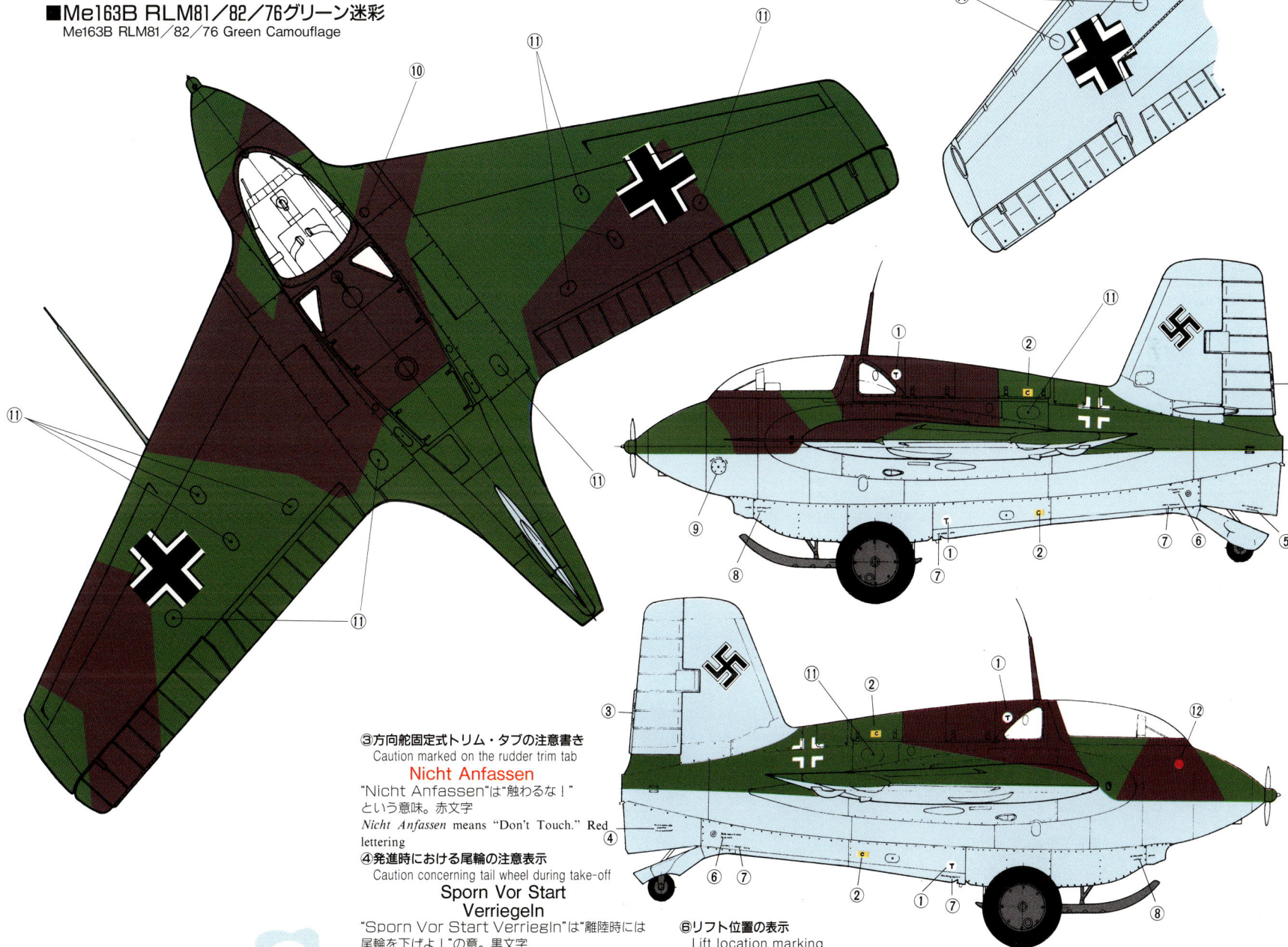

RLM74
RLM75
RLM76
RLM81
RLM82
RLM02

③方向舵固定式トリム・タブの注意書き
Caution marked on the rudder trim tab

Nicht Anfassen

"Nicht Anfassen"は"触わるな！"
という意味。赤文字
Nicht Anfassen means "Don't Touch." Red lettering.

④発進時における尾輪の注意表示
Caution concerning tail wheel during take-off

**Sporn Vor Start
Verriegeln**

"Sporn Vor Start Verriegln"は"離陸時には尾輪を下げよ！"の意。黒文字
Sporn Vor Start Verriegeln means "Lower tail wheel during take-off." Black lettering.

⑤タイヤの空気圧表示
Tire pressure marking

**Reifendruck 4.5 atü
Bei Vollast**

"Reifendruck 4.5 atü Bei Vollast"は"全負荷状態でのタイヤ圧は4.5気圧"という意味。黒文字
Reifendruck 4.5 atü Bei Vollast means "Tire pressure when fully loaded: 4.5 atmospheres." Black lettering.

①T液注入口表示マーク
T-Stoff fuel fill marking
白円に黒の"T"が入る
A Black "T" in a white circle.

②C液注入口表示マーク
C-Stoff fuel fill marking
黄色の四角形内に黒の"C"が入る
A Black "C" in a yellow rectangle.

⑥リフト位置の表示
Lift location marking

Hier anheben

"Hier anheben"は"ここを吊り上げよ！"の意。黒文字
Hier anheben means "Lift (sling) here." Black lettering.

⑦ジャッキ位置表示
Jack location marking

Hier aufboken

"Hier aufboken"は"ここを持ち上げよ！"の意。黒文字

Hier aufboken means "Lift (jack) here." Black lettering.

⑧曳航時の注意書き
Caution related to towing the aircraft

**Schleppseil
Hier einhängen！**

"Schleppseil Hier einhängen！"は"ここを接続して牽引せよ！"の意。黒文字
Schleppseil Hier einhängen means "Connect tow cable here." Black lettering.

23

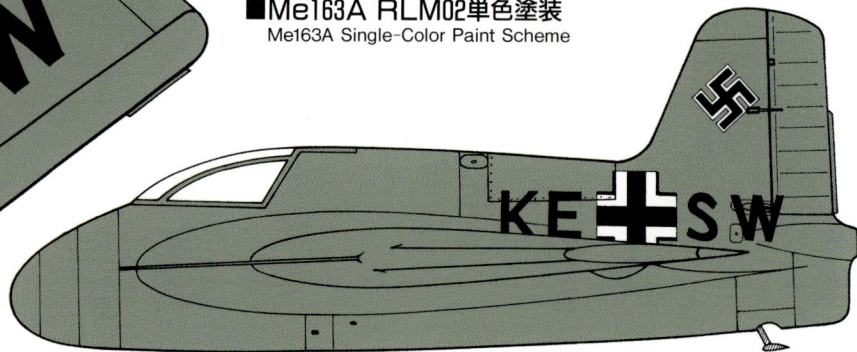

■Me163A RLM02単色塗装
Me163A Single-Color Paint Scheme

■Me163B RLM74／75／76
グレー迷彩
Me163B RLM74／75／76
Gray Camouflage

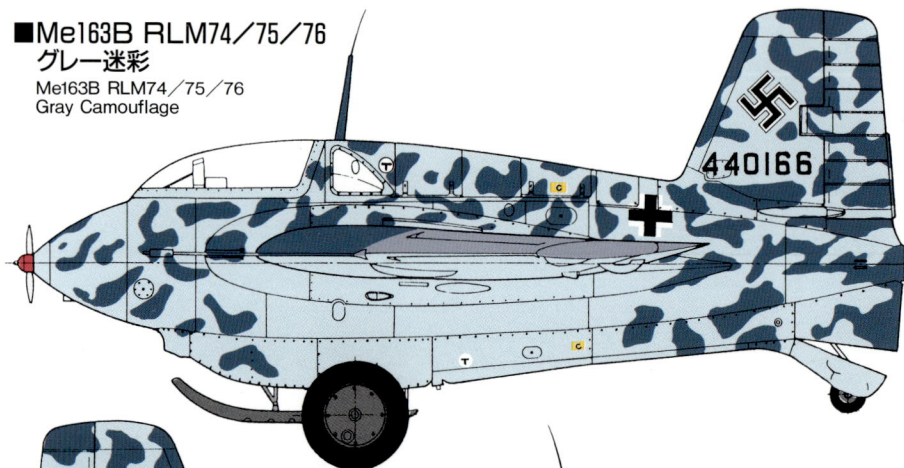

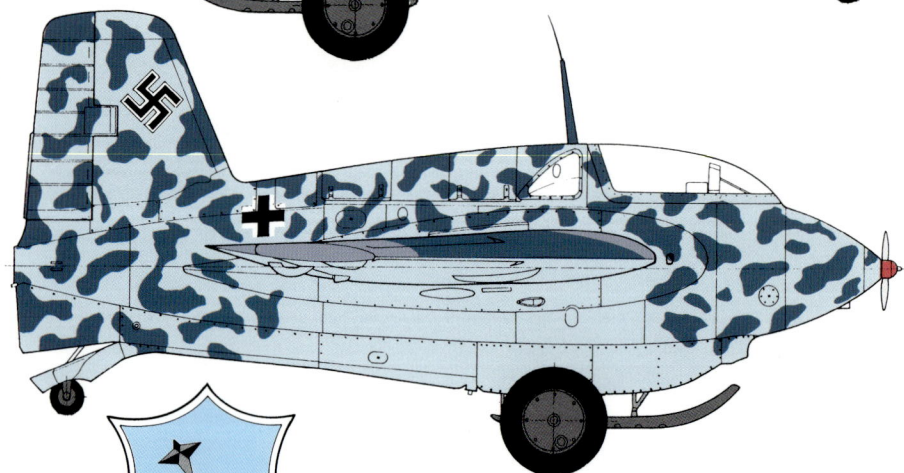

JG400飛行中隊章
JG400 Staffel Emblem

1.／JG400

1.／JG400

2.／JG400

7.／JG400

13.／JG400

14.／JG400

⑨圧搾空気供給口表示マーク
Compressed air supply
port marking

青と赤の円に黒文字。"Preßluft 130 atü"は
"圧搾空気130気圧"の意
Black lettering in a blue and red circle. *Preßluft 130 atü* means "Fill to 130 atmospheres."

⑩酸素供給口表示マーク
Oxygen fill port marking

青の円内に2本の白線と白文字が入る
White lettering and two white stripes in a blue circle.

⑪点検ハッチ表示マーク（主翼下面も同じ）
Inspection hatch marking

ネジ位置を示す"Auf"(開)と"Zu"(閉)は黒文字
The *Auf* (open) and *Zu* (closed) markings indicating screw position are in black lettering.

⑫外部電源接続口表示マーク
External power attachment socket marking

赤円形に塗られた接続口と電圧(24v)を示す黒文字
Socket and black lettering indicating voltage (24v) in a red circle.

Me163B-0 V33 "BH+IN" 第16実験隊 1943年 バト・ツヴィッシェナーン／ドイツ
Me163B-0 V33 "BH+IN" Erprobungs Kommando 16 1943 Bad Zwischenahn／Germany

全面RLM02、ラジオ・コード"BH＋I
N"は黒で主翼下面にも記入。方向舵は赤も
しくは迷彩色（RLM74?）。垂直安定板下方
に"V33"（黒）の文字あり。アンテナ支柱直
前にFuG16ZY用のD/Fループ・アンテナ
をオプション装備している。

Painted entirely in RLM 02. Radio Code
"BH+IN" is in black, and also appears on
underside of wings. Rudder is red or camouflage (RLM 74?). "V33" painted in black
near bottom of vertical stabilizer. D/F loop
antenna for FuG16ZY radio installed immediately in front of main antenna post.

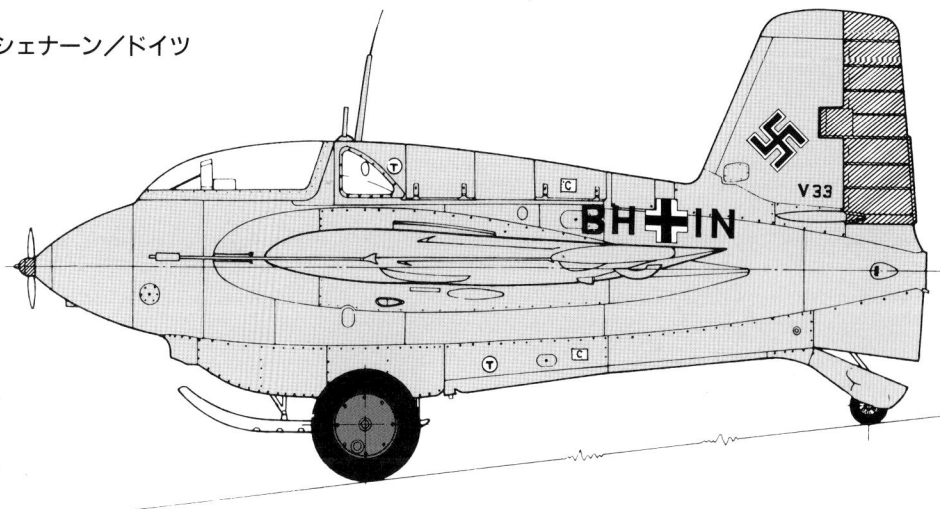

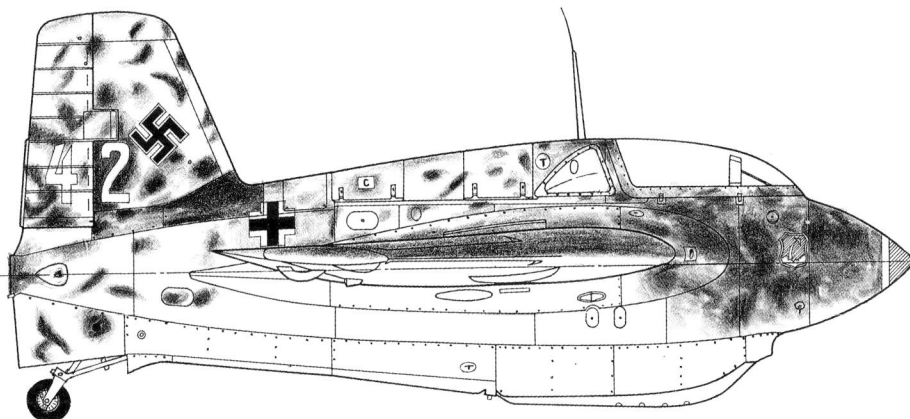

Me163B-0 第400戦闘航空団第14飛行中隊 1945年 ドイツ
Me163B-0 14./JG400 1945 Germany

上面RLM81／82、下面RLM76、胴体、
垂直尾翼はRLM76地にRLM81／82のモッ
トリング。機首先端は白フチ付き赤（発電機
駆動用小プロペラなし）、機首両側に14./JG
400の中隊章あり。機番号"42"は白、主翼上
面の国籍標識は黒十字に白／黒のフチが付い
た初期タイプ。

Upper surfaces are RLM 81/82, underside
is RLM 76. Fuselage and vertical stabilizer
in RLM 76 with mottling in RLM 81/82.
Nose is red with white stripe (no small propeller for generator). Emblem of 14./JG 400 on
both sides of nose. Aircraft number "42" is
in white. National insignia on upperside of
wings is early-type black cross with white/
black edge.

◀第16実験隊に配備されたMe163B-0の主翼上面の国
籍標識バリエーション
A different version of the national insignia found on the
upper surface of the wings of Komets assigned to EK16.

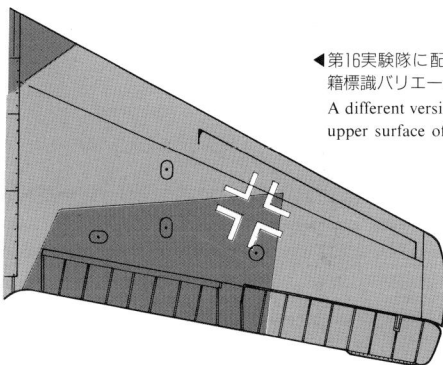

Me163B-0 第16実験隊 1944年 バト・ツヴィッシェナーン／ドイツ
Me163B-0 Erprobungs Kommando 16 1944 Bad Zwischenahn／Germany

上面はRLM81／82、下面RLM76、垂直尾翼はR
LM81／82のモットリング。機番号"05"は白。
Upper surfaces are RLM 81/82, underside is RLM 76.
Vertical stabilizer is mottled with RLM 81/82. Aircraft
number "05" is in white.

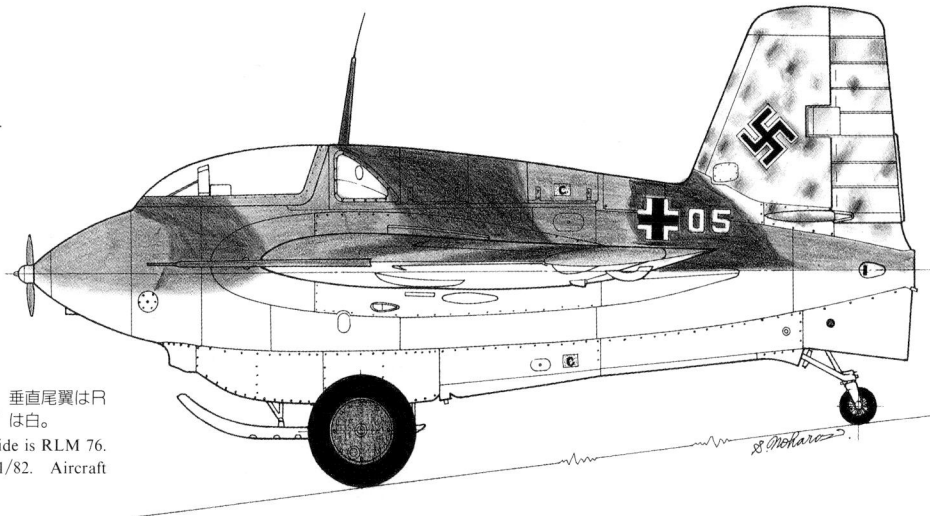

Me163B-0 第400戦闘航空団第14飛行中隊 1945年 ドイツ
Me163B-0 14./JG400 1945 Germany

上面RLM81／82、下面RLM76、胴体、垂直尾翼はRLM76地にRLM81／82のモットリング、機首先端は白フチ付き赤、ドリーのホイール・ハブも白と赤の塗り分け。機首両側に14./JG400の中隊章あり。垂直尾翼下方の機番号"54"は白。

Upper surfaces are RLM 81/82, underside is RLM 76. Fuselage and vertical stabilizer in RLM 76 with mottling in RLM 81/82. Nose is red with white stripe. Wheel hubs of take-off dolly painted red and white in quarters. Emblem of 14./JG 400 on both sides of nose. Aircraft number "54" is in white.

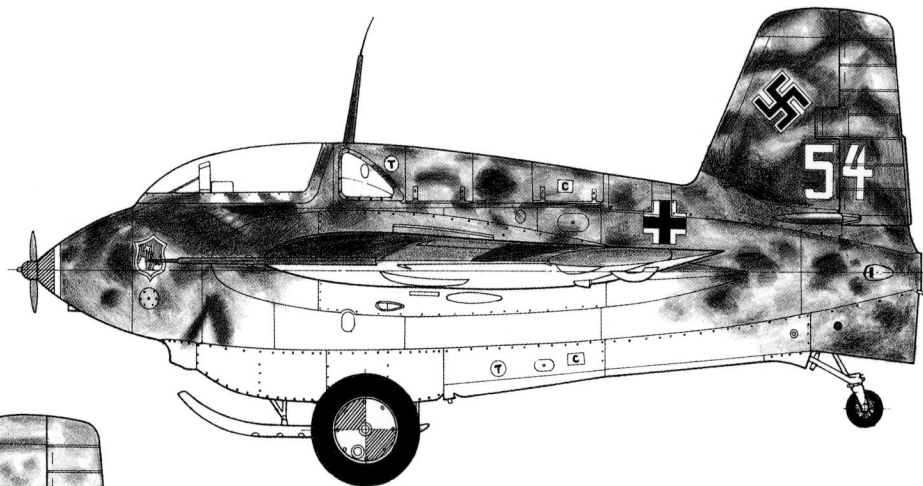

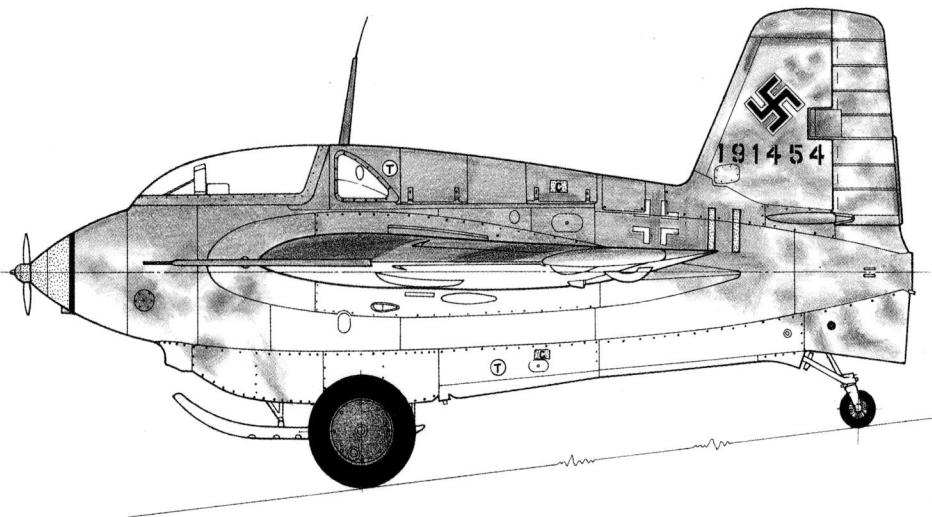

Me163B-1a W.Nr191454 第400戦闘航空団第6飛行中隊 1945年5月 シュレスヴィヒ・ホルシュタイン州フズム／ドイツ
Me163B-1a W.Nr191454 6./JG400 May 1945 Husum (Schleswig-Holstein)/Germany

主翼上面RLM81／82、下面RLM76、胴体、垂直尾翼はRLM76地にグレー2色（RLM74/75?）のモットリング。機首先端は黒フチ付き黄、機番号"11"はグレーのフチ付き黄。W.Nr191454は黒（左側のみ）。

Upper surfaces are RLM 81/82, underside is RLM 76. Fuselage and vertical stabilizer in RLM 76 with mottling in two other shades of gray (RLM 74/75?). Nose is yellow with black stripe. Aircraft number "11" is yellow with gray stripe. W.Nr 191454 is in black (appears on port side only).

Me163B-1a W.Nr191659 第400戦闘航空団第6飛行中隊 1945年5月 シュレスヴィヒ・ホルシュタイン州フズム／ドイツ
Me163B-1a W.Nr191659 6./JG400 May 1945 Husum (Schleswig-Holstein)/Germany

上面RLM81／82、下面RLM76、垂直尾翼はRLM76地にRLM81／82のモットリング。機首先端は黒フチ付き黄、機番号"15"も黒フチ付き黄。胴体、垂直尾翼の国籍標識は白フチのみの末期タイプだが、主翼上下面の国籍標識は黒十字に白／黒のフチが付いた初期タイプ。

Upper surfaces are RLM 81/82, underside is RLM 76. Vertical stabilizer in RLM 76 with mottling in RLM 81/82. Nose is yellow with black stripe. Aircraft number "11" is also yellow with black stripe. National insignia on fuselage and vertical stabilizer are late-type white outlines only, but those on the upper and lower surfaces of the wings are early-type black crosses with white/black edges.

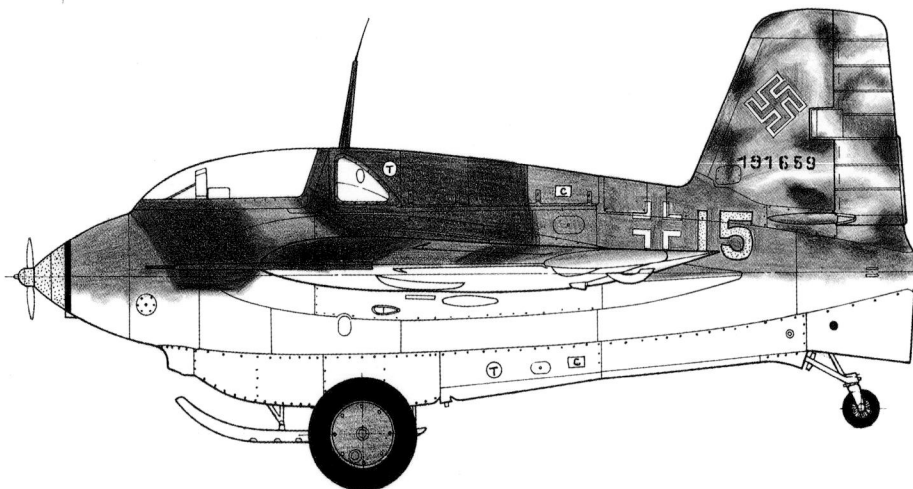

Me163B-1a 第400戦闘航空団第2飛行中隊 1944年6月 ブランディス／ドイツ
Me163B-1a 2./JG400 Jun 1944 Brandis/Germany

上面RLM81／82、下面RLM76、胴体、垂直尾翼もRLM81／82の折線分割パターン。機首先端は黒フチ付きの白、発電機駆動用の小プロペラ（スピンナー、プロペラ・ブレードともに）は赤。機番号"10"は白、機首左側のみ2./JG400の中隊章あり。胴体背部にD/Fループ・アンテナをオプション装備している。主翼上面の国籍標識は初期タイプ。

Upper surfaces are RLM 81/82, underside is RLM 76. Fuselage and vertical stabilizer are also RLM 81/82 in diagonal strip pattern. Nose is white with black stripe. Small generator propeller and spinner on nose is red. Aircraft number "10" is white. Emblem of 2./JG 400 appears on port side of nose only. D/F loop antenna installed on top of midsection. National insignia on upper surface of wings is early type.

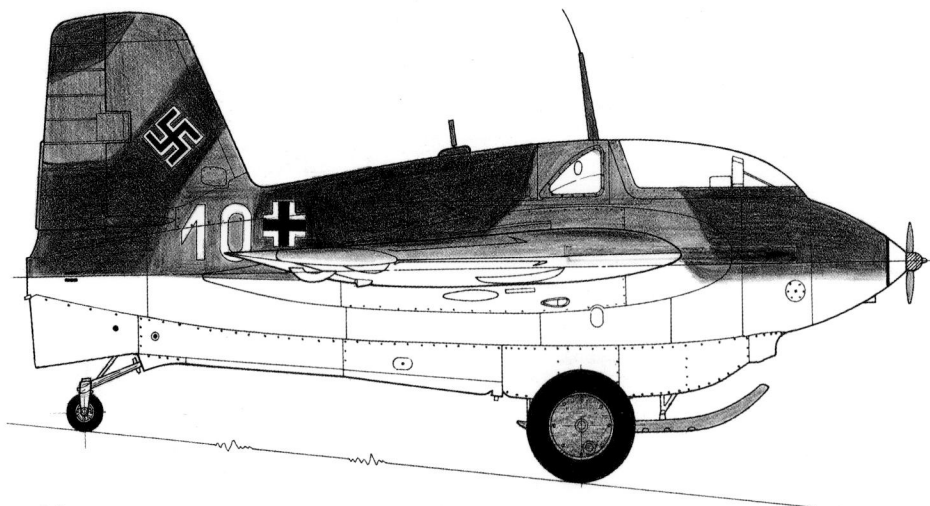

Me163 ディテール・イラスト
DETAIL ILLUSTRATION

作図・解説／野原 茂

Illustrations and Commentary by Shigeru Nohara

機首 NOSE

Me163Bの発電機 駆動用プロペラ
Generator propeller on nose of Me163B

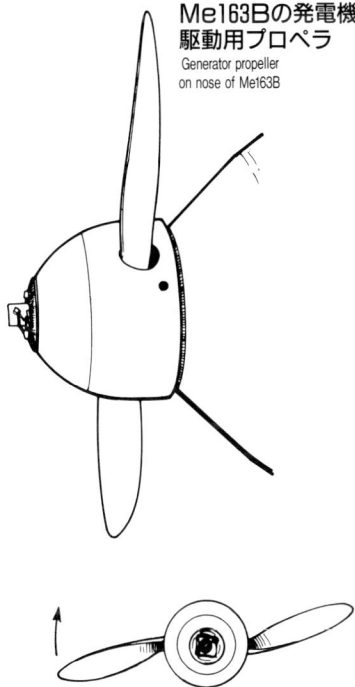

Me163B機首および コクピット内装甲板配置
Location of armor plate and bulletproof glass in cockpit of Me163B

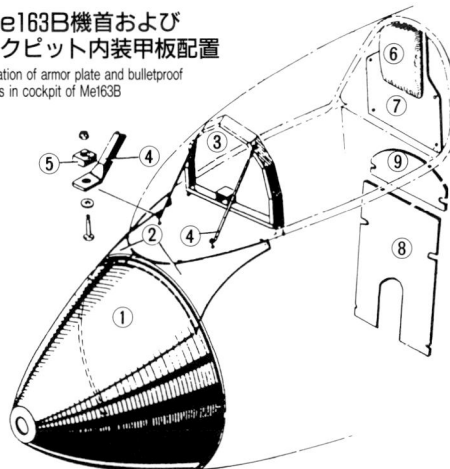

① 装甲ノーズキャップ（15mm厚）
　Armored nose cap（15mm thick）
② 前上方装甲板
　Forward armor plate
③ 防弾ガラス（90mm厚）
　Bulletproof glass（90mm thick）
④ 防弾ガラス取り付け支柱
　Support braces for bulletproof glass

⑤ ナット
　Nut
⑥ ヘッドレスト
　Headrest
⑦ 頭部防弾板
　Armor plate（head）
⑧ 背部防弾板
　Armor plate（back）
⑨ 肩部防弾板
　Armor plate（shoulders）

武装 ARMAMENT

Me163B-0　武装配置
Location of armament in Me163B-0

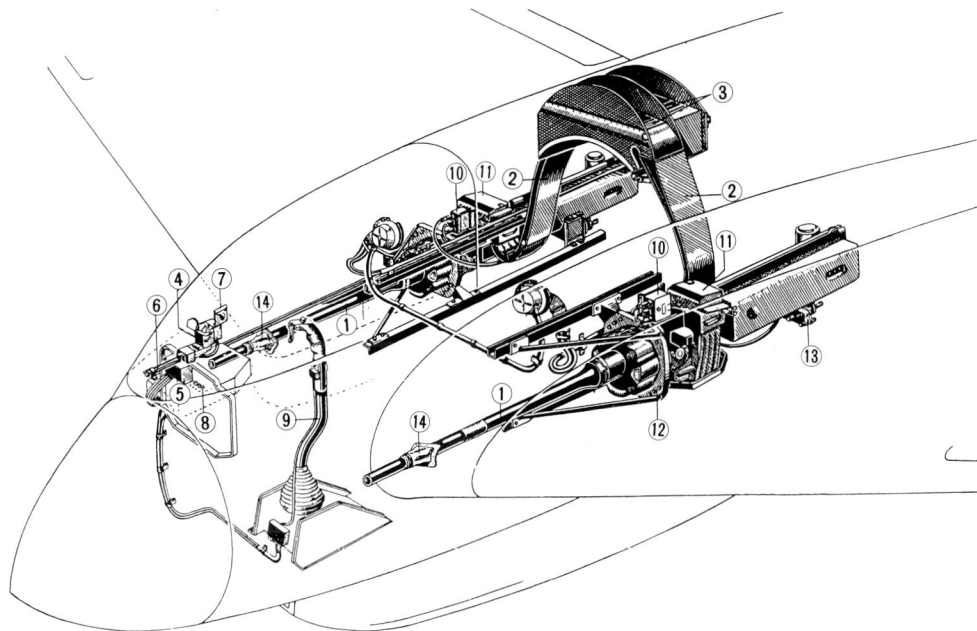

Me163B-1a　武装配置
Location of armament in Me163B-1a

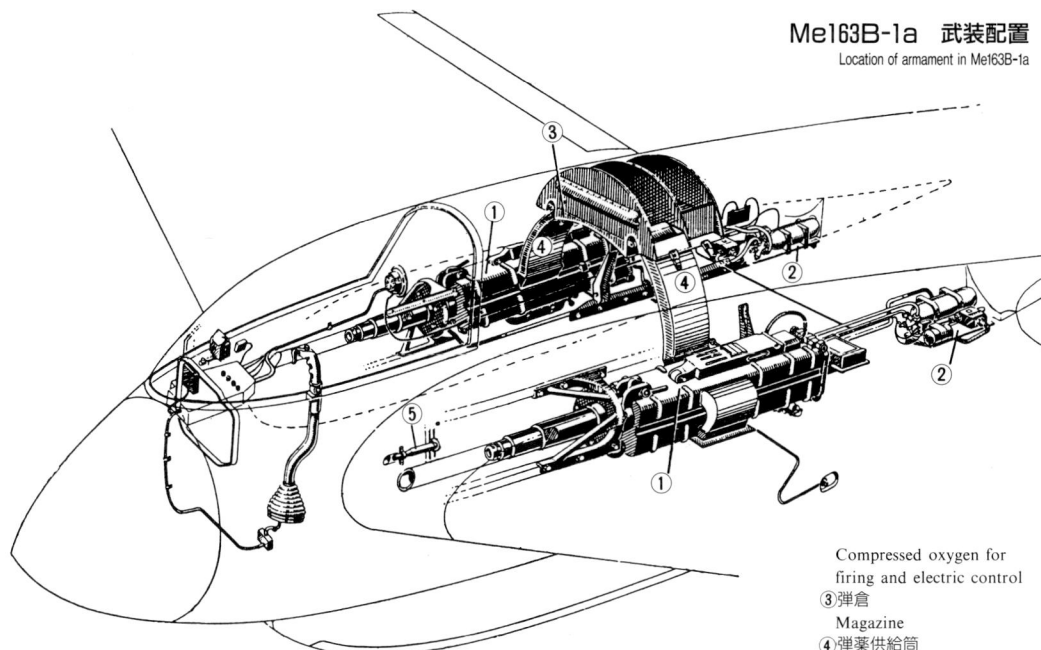

① MG151／20　20mm機関砲
　MG151／20 20mm machine cannon
② 弾薬供給筒
　Shell supply chute
③ 弾倉
　Magazine
④ Revi16B射撃照準器
　Revi16B gunsight
⑤ SZKK 4残弾表示器
　SZKK4 ammunition supply indicator
⑥ 弾道検査器
　Trajectory tester
⑦ フィルター
　Filter
⑧ 自動回路遮断器
　Automatic circuit breaker
⑨ KG12E操縦桿
　KG12E Control stick
⑩ EDKS-B1電気装置
　EDKS-B1 Electric control
⑪ SVK1-151装填装置
　SVK1-151 Feed mechanism
⑫ 機関砲前方取り付け金具
　Forward mounting bracket for machine cannon
⑬ 機関砲後方取り付け金具
　Rear mounting bracket for machine cannon
⑭ 防塵カバー
　Dust cover

① MK108　30mm機関砲
　MK108 30mm machine cannon
② 射撃用圧搾酸素および電気装置
　Compressed oxygen for firing and electric control
③ 弾倉
　Magazine
④ 弾薬供給筒
　Shell supply chute
⑤ 弾道検査器
　Trajectory tester

27

胴体構造 FUSELAGE STRUCTURE

Me163B-0 胴体内部配置
Schematic of Me163B-0

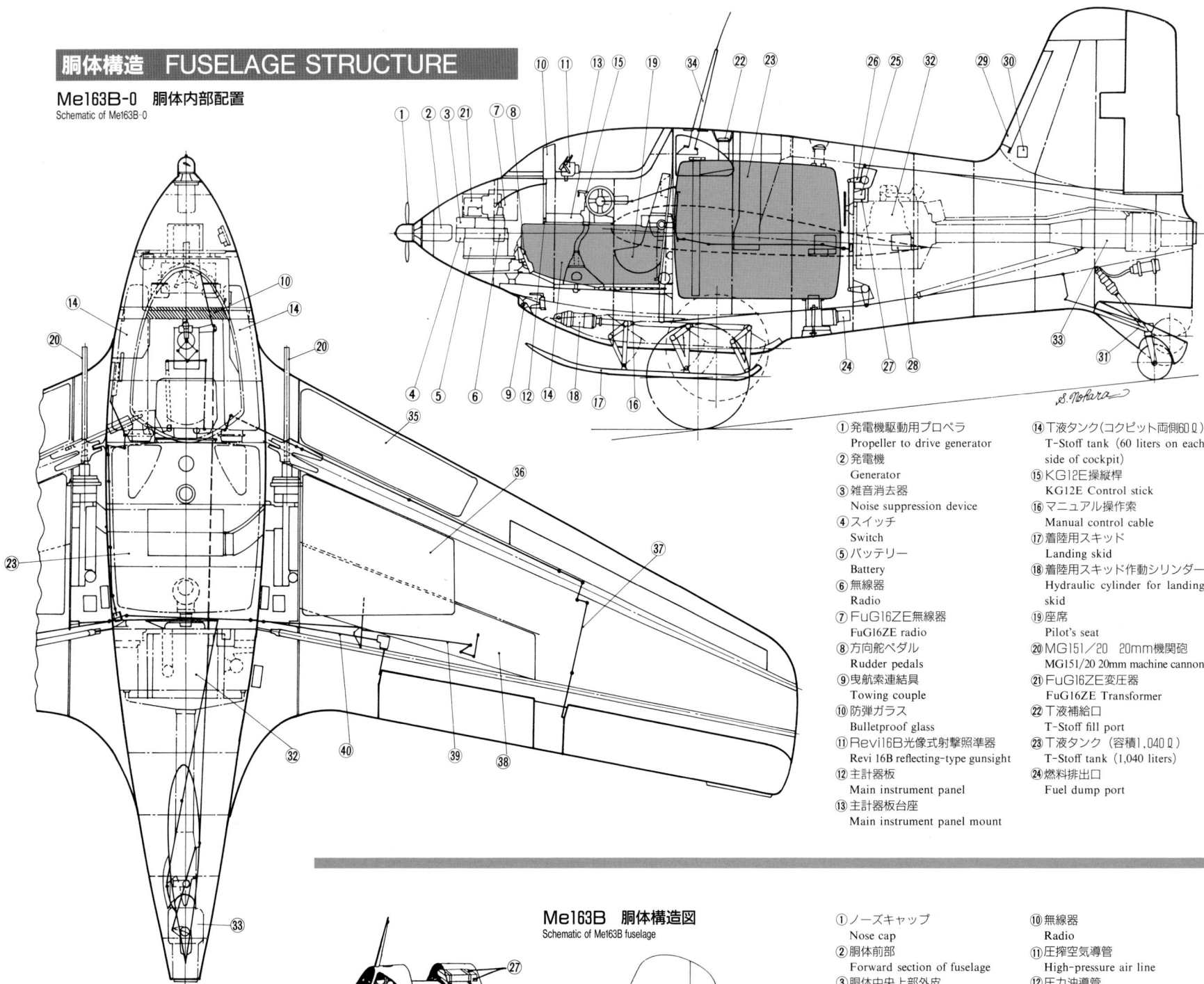

① 発電機駆動用プロペラ
　Propeller to drive generator
② 発電機
　Generator
③ 雑音消去器
　Noise suppression device
④ スイッチ
　Switch
⑤ バッテリー
　Battery
⑥ 無線器
　Radio
⑦ FuG16ZE無線器
　FuG16ZE radio
⑧ 方向舵ペダル
　Rudder pedals
⑨ 曳航索連結具
　Towing couple
⑩ 防弾ガラス
　Bulletproof glass
⑪ Revi16B光像式射撃照準器
　Revi 16B reflecting-type gunsight
⑫ 主計器板
　Main instrument panel
⑬ 主計器板台座
　Main instrument panel mount

⑭ T液タンク(コクピット両側60ℓ)
　T-Stoff tank (60 liters on each side of cockpit)
⑮ KG12E操縦桿
　KG12E Control stick
⑯ マニュアル操作索
　Manual control cable
⑰ 着陸用スキッド
　Landing skid
⑱ 着陸用スキッド作動シリンダー
　Hydraulic cylinder for landing skid
⑲ 座席
　Pilot's seat
⑳ MG151/20 20mm機関砲
　MG151/20 20mm machine cannon
㉑ FuG16ZE変圧器
　FuG16ZE Transformer
㉒ T液補給口
　T-Stoff fill port
㉓ T液タンク(容積1,040ℓ)
　T-Stoff tank (1,040 liters)
㉔ 燃料排出口
　Fuel dump port

Me163B 胴体構造図
Schematic of Me163B fuselage

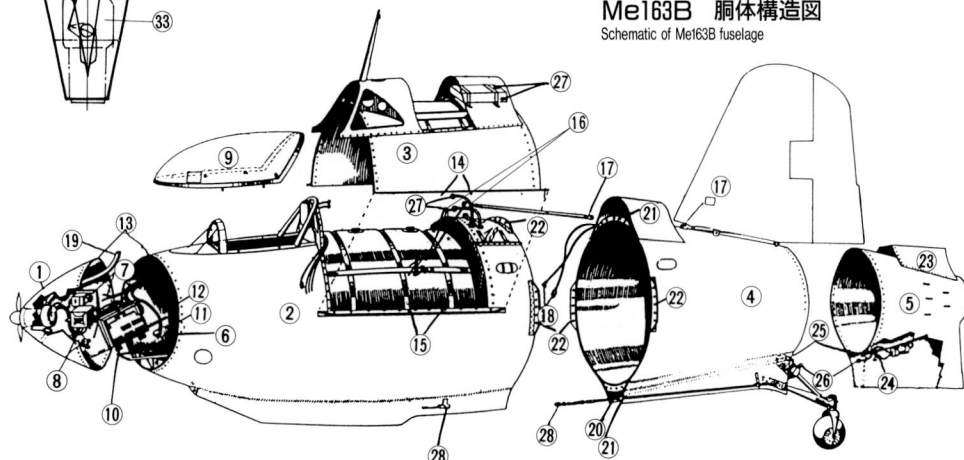

① ノーズキャップ
　Nose cap
② 胴体前部
　Forward section of fuselage
③ 胴体中央上部外皮
　Fuselage mid-section upper panel
④ 胴体後部
　Aft section of fuselage
⑤ 胴体尾部
　Tail section of fuselage
⑥ バッテリーコード差し込み部
　Battery cord attachment
⑦ 雑音消去器用電気コード
　Noise suppression device electric cord
⑧ レギュレーター用電気コード
　Electric cord for regulator
⑨ キャノピー
　Canopy

⑩ 無線器
　Radio
⑪ 圧搾空気導管
　High-pressure air line
⑫ 圧力油導管
　High-pressure oil line
⑬ ネジ差し込み部
　Screw socket
⑭ 固定ピン差し込み部
　Fixed pin socket
⑮ 固定ピン・ガイド
　Fixed pin guide
⑯ プッシュロッド前方連結部
　Push-rod front-end connector
⑰ 方向舵操作用プッシュロッド後方連結部
　Rudder push-rod connector
⑱ 電気コード接続部
　Electric cord connector
⑲ 電気配線

Me163S-1　胴体内部配置
Schematic of Me163S-1 fuselage interior

① 操縦桿
Control stick
② 訓練生
Trainee
③ 操縦桿
Control stick
④ 教官
Instructor

⑤ 方向舵ペダル
Rudder pedals
⑥ 方向舵ペダル
Rudder pedals
⑦ 水バラストタンク
Water ballast tank

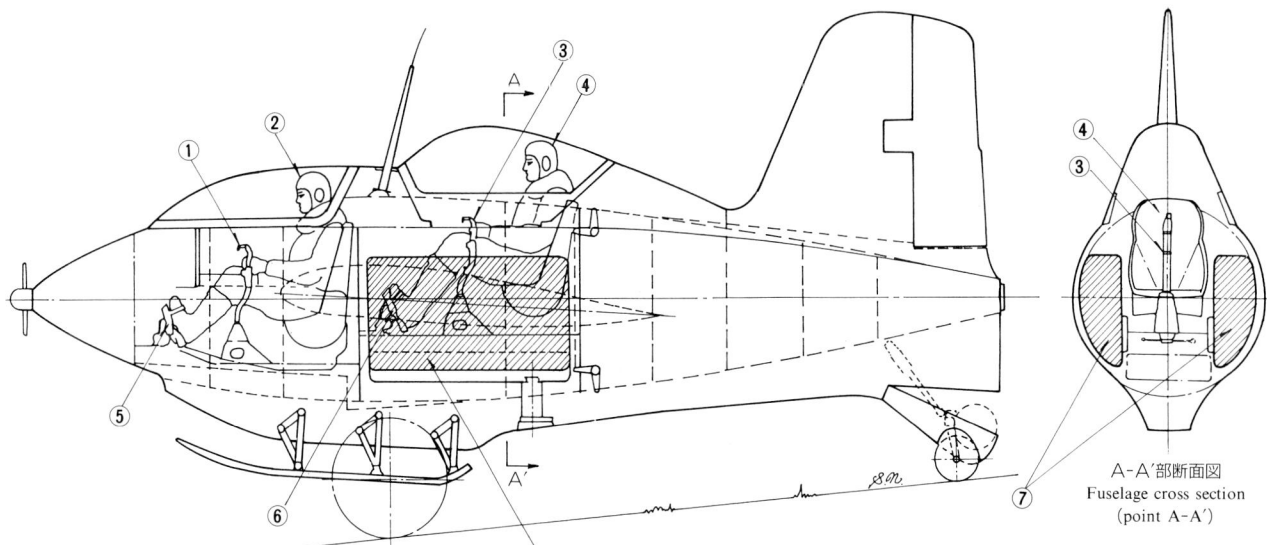

㉕ 大雑音消去器
Large noise suppression device
㉖ 小雑音消去器
Small noise suppression device
㉗ 調節器
Regulator
㉘ 配電ボックス
Wire box
㉙ FuG16ZE励磁曳裾
FuG16ZE plate antenna
㉚ FuG16ZE用アンテナ調整器
FuG16ZE antenna adjuster
㉛ 尾脚
Tail wheel
㉜ ヴァルターHWK109-509A
ロケット・モーター
Walter HWK 109-509A
rocket motor
㉝ 燃焼管
Combustion chamber
㉞ FuG16ZE無線器用アンテナ支柱
FuG16ZE radio antenna rod
㉟ 主翼前縁C液タンク（容量78ℓ）
Leading edge C-Stoff tank
(78 liters)
㊱ 主翼中央C液タンク（容積177ℓ）
Mid-wing C-Stoff tank (177 liters)
㊲ 補助翼操作ロッド
Elevon control rod
㊳ 着陸フラップ（下面）
Landing flaps (underside)
㊴ 着陸フラップ操作ロッド
Landing flap control rod
㊵ トリムフラップ操作ロッド
Trim flap control rod

Electric cables
⑳ 圧力油導管
High-pressure oil line
㉑ 圧搾空気導管
High-pressure air line
㉒ 前、後胴体接続部
Fore and aft fuselage
connection points
㉓ 方向舵下部フェアリング
Fairing for lower
portion of rudder
㉔ 圧力油導管
High-pressure oil line
㉕ 圧搾空気導管
High-pressure air line
㉖ 圧力油導管
High-pressure oil line
㉗ T液導管
T-Stoff fuel line
㉘ 尾脚操作桿
Tail wheel control rod

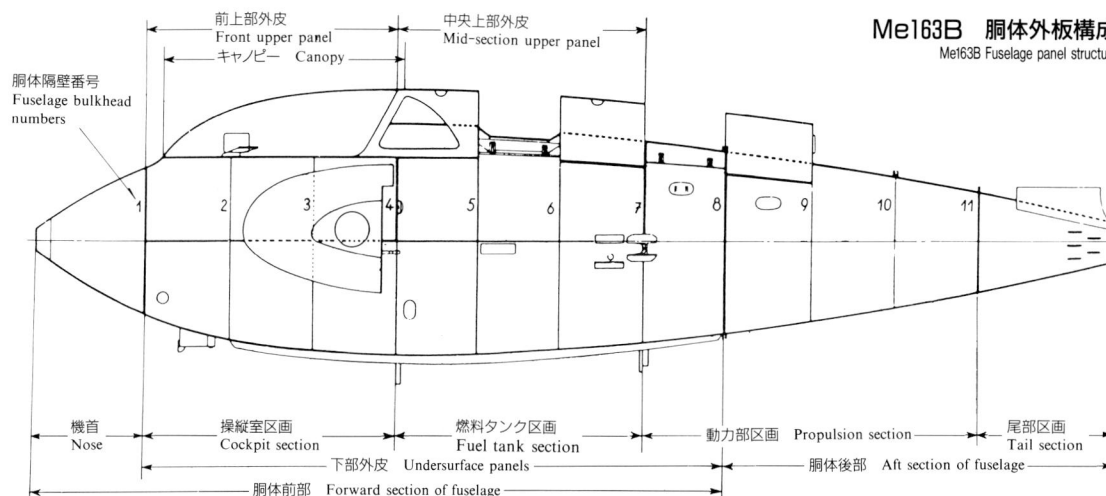

A-A'部断面図
Fuselage cross section
（point A-A'）

Me163C　胴体内部配置
Schematic of Me163C fuselage interior

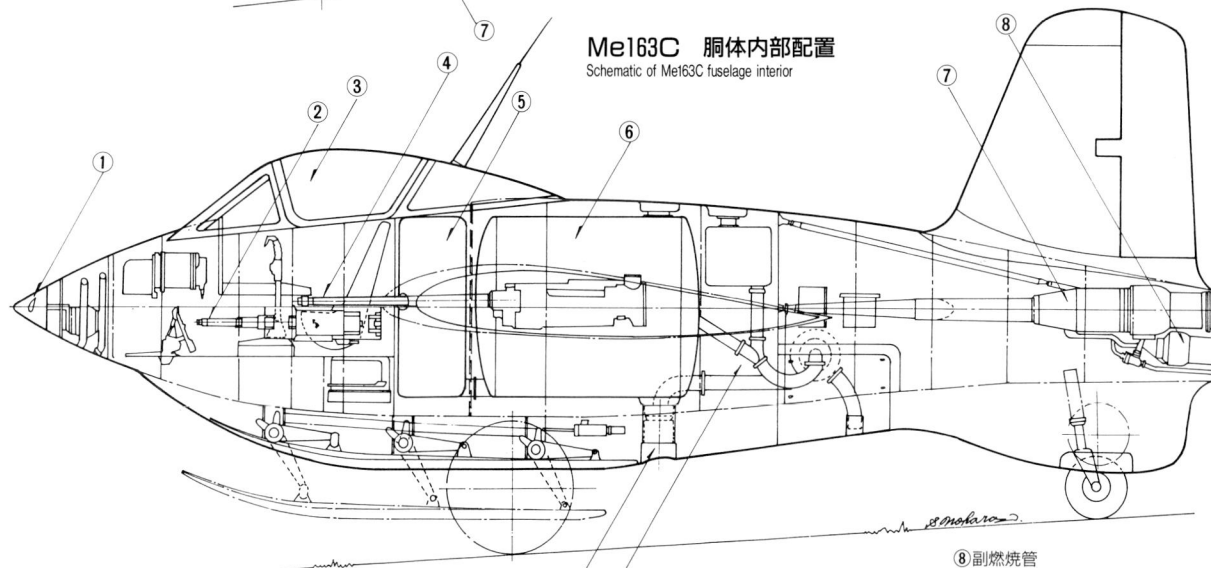

① 発電機駆動用プロペラ
Propeller to drive generator
② 機首武装MK108　30mm機関砲
Nose-mounted　MK108　30mm
machine cannon
③ 与圧式キャビン
Pressurized cockpit
④ 主翼付け根武装MK108
30mm機関砲
Wing-root mounted MK108
30mm machine cannon
⑤ C液タンク
C-Stoff tank
⑥ T液タンク
T-Stoff tank
⑦ 主燃焼管
Main combustion chamber
⑧ 副燃焼管
Auxiliary combustion chamber
⑨ 非常時燃料排出口
Emergency fuel dump port
⑩ ヴァルターHWK109-509C
ロケット・モーター
Walter HWK 109-509C rocket motor

Me163B　胴体外板構成
Me163B Fuselage panel structure

前上部外皮
Front upper panel
中央上部外皮
Mid-section upper panel
キャノピー　Canopy
胴体隔壁番号
Fuselage bulkhead
numbers

機首
Nose
操縦室区画
Cockpit section
燃料タンク区画
Fuel tank section
動力部区画　Propulsion section
尾部区画
Tail section
下部外皮　Undersurface panels
胴体後部　Aft section of fuselage
胴体前部　Forward section of fuselage

Me163B　曳航索連結部
Me163B Towing couple

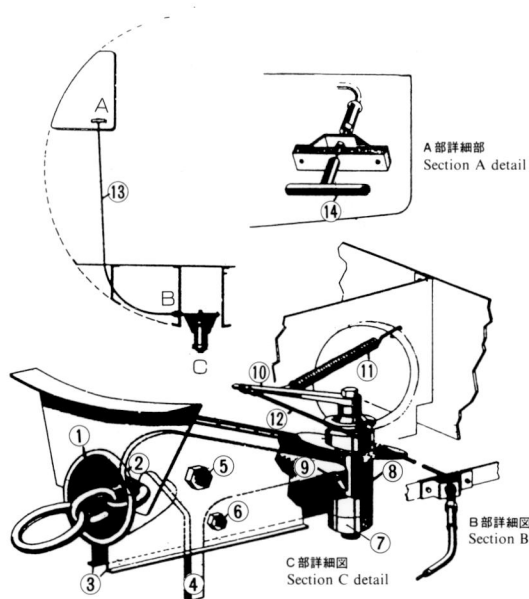

Me163B　機体部品構成
Me163B Parts diagram

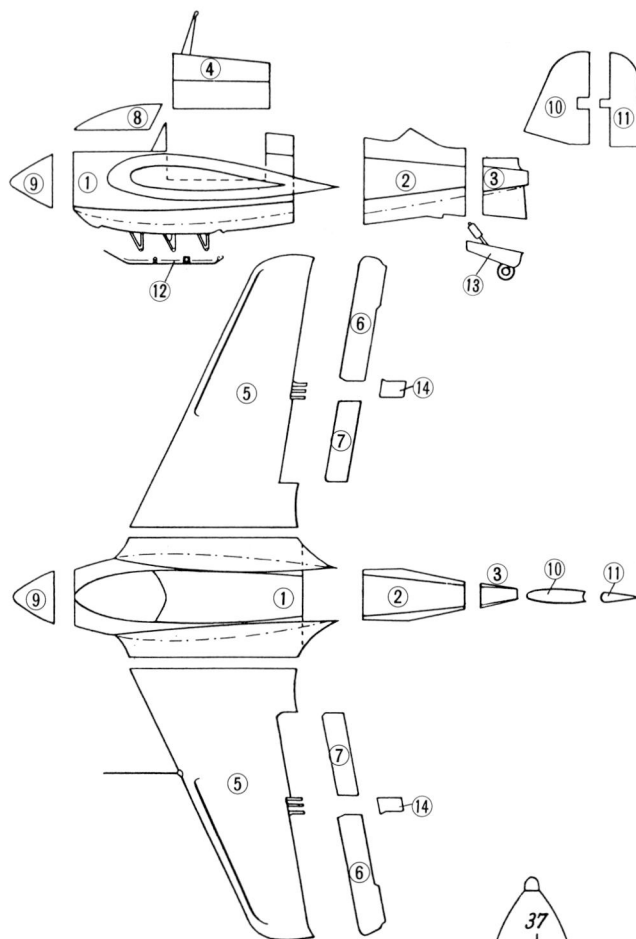

① ガイドリング
   Guide ring
② 前部壁
   Forward bulkhead
③ 側壁
   Side bulkhead
④ 連結レバー
   Connecting lever
⑤ ボルト
   Bolt
⑥ ストップネジ
   Stop screw
⑦ ガイド軸
   Guide axle
⑧ ロッキングバー
   Locking bar
⑨ ロッキングカム
   Locking cam
⑩ レバー
   Lever
⑪ ロッキング
   スプリング
   Locking spring
⑫ レリーズ
   Release
⑬ ボーデン索
   Borden line
⑭ レリーズ
   ハンドル
   Release handle

A部詳細部
Section A detail

B部詳細図
Section B detail

C部詳細図
Section C detail

① 前部胴体
   Forward section of fuselage
② 動力部胴体
   Propulsion section of fuselage
③ 胴体尾部
   Tail section of fuselage
④ 胴体上部
   Upper section of fuselage
⑤ 主翼本体
   Wings
⑥ 補助翼
   Elevons
⑦ トリム・フラップ
   Trim flaps
⑧ キャノピー
   Canopy
⑨ ノーズ・キャップ
   Nose cap
⑩ 垂直安定板
   Vertical stabilzer
⑪ 方向舵
   Rudder
⑫ 着陸用スキッド
   Landing skid
⑬ 尾脚
   Tail wheel
⑭ 取り外し式主翼後縁外板
   Removable trailing edge panels

Me163B　外板パネル構成
Me163B exterior panel structure

左側面
Port elevation

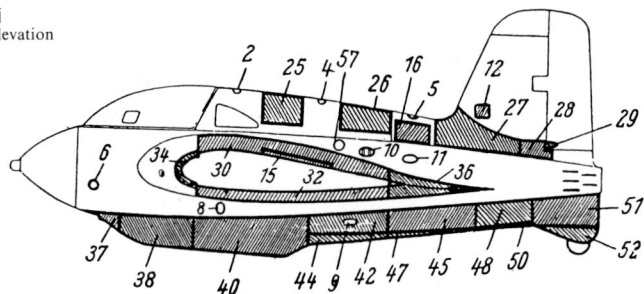

上面
Top view

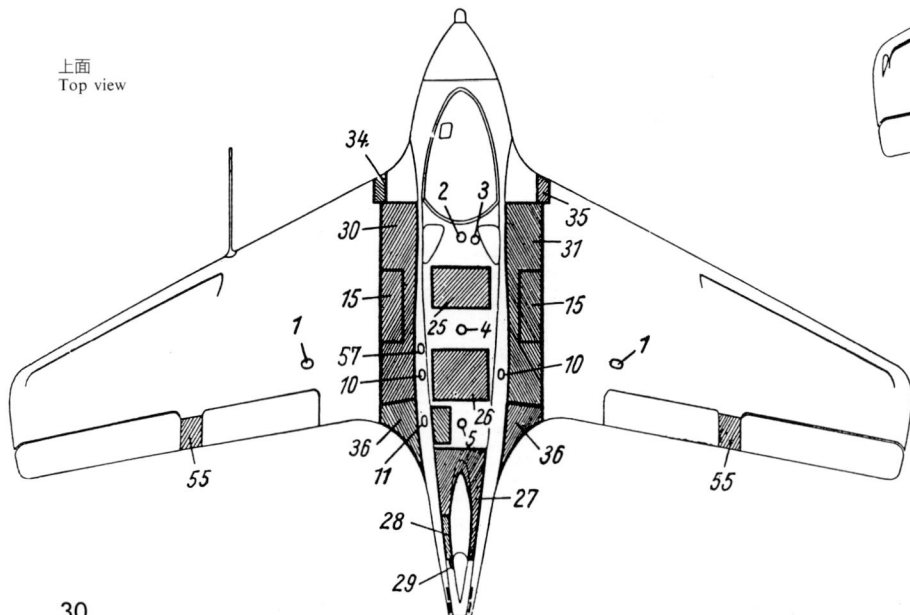

下面
Bottom view

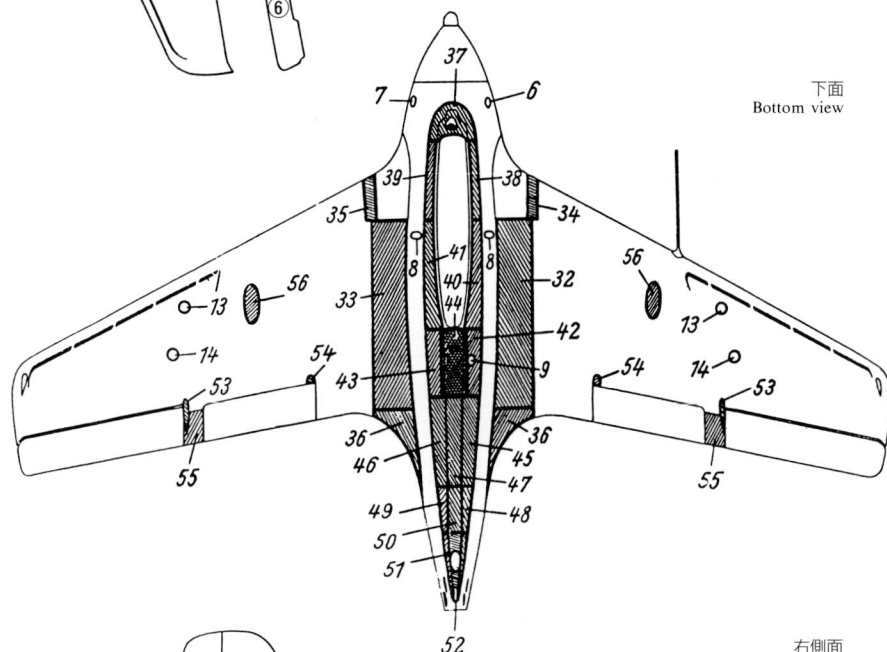

右側面
Starboard elevation

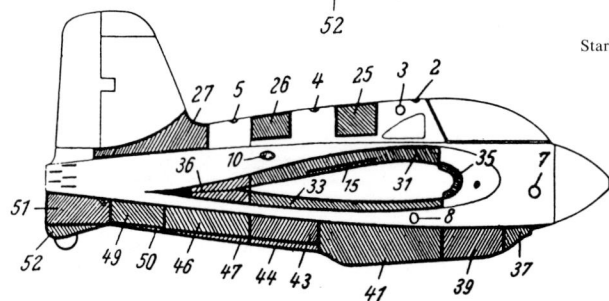

ヴァルターHWK109-509Aロケット・モーター
Walter HWK109-509A rocket motor

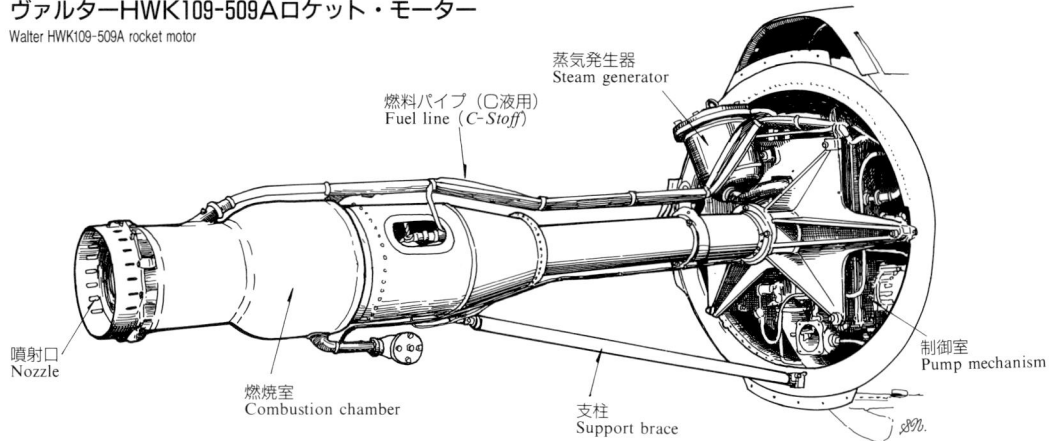

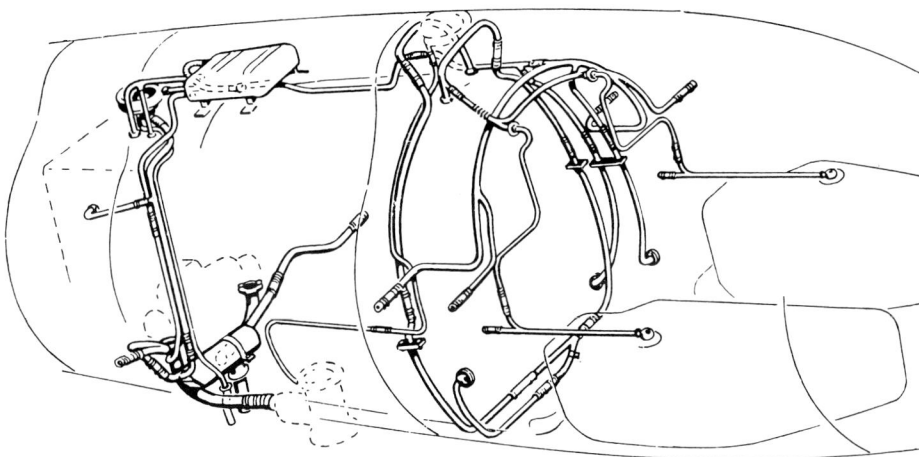

蒸気発生器
Steam generator

燃料パイプ（C液用）
Fuel line (C-Stoff)

噴射口
Nozzle

燃焼室
Combustion chamber

支柱
Support brace

制御室
Pump mechanism

Me163B 各燃料タンクへの配管図
Me163B fuel line diagram

Me163B 燃料タンク配置
Me163B
Fuel tank location

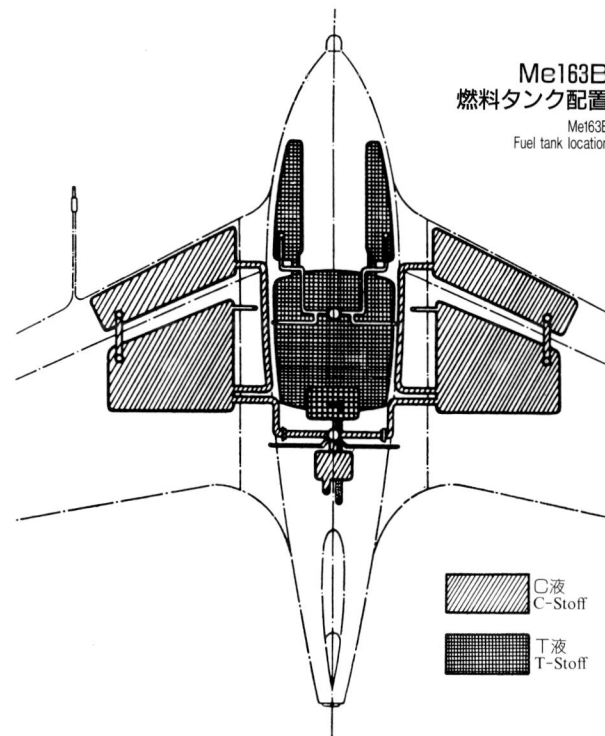

C液
C-Stoff

T液
T-Stoff

Me163B-0のノズル周囲
Nozzle area of Me163B-0

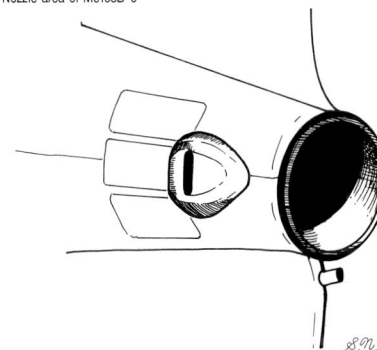

▼▶Me163B-1aのノズル付近。ロケット・モーターのノズルの下に見える細いパイプはC液投棄用のパイプ。（写真／野原　茂）

Nozzle area of Me163B-1a. The small pipe visible under the engine nozzle is for dumping C-Stoff (Photo by S. Nohara)

Me263のノズル周囲
Nozzle area of Me263

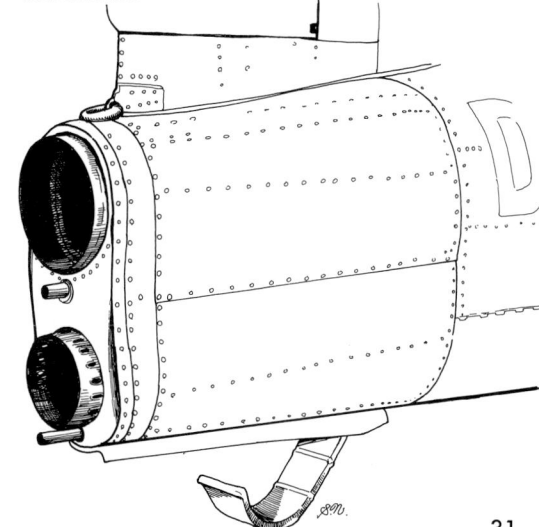

31

キャノピー＆コクピット　CANOPY & COCKPIT

Me163Bのキャノピー周囲
Canopy area of the Me163B

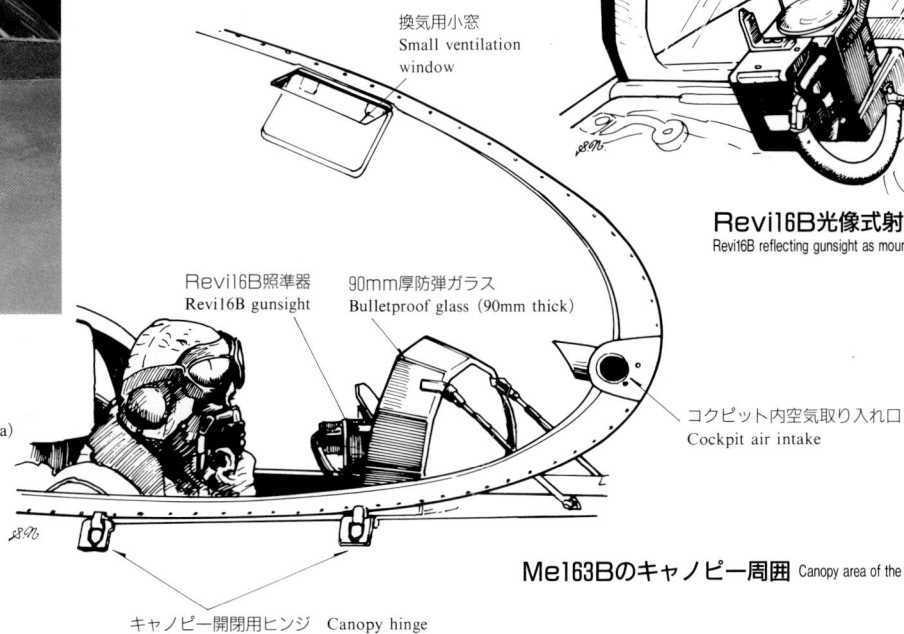

換気用小窓
Small ventilation window

Revi16B光像式射撃照準器取り付け状態
Revi16B reflecting gunsight as mounted

Revi16B照準器
Revi16B gunsight

90mm厚防弾ガラス
Bulletproof glass (90mm thick)

コクピット内空気取り入れ口
Cockpit air intake

▲▼Me163B-1aのキャノピー。高速機には不釣り合いなキャノピー・ヒンジがいかにも急造機らしい。(写真/野原　茂)
The canopy of the Me163B-1a. The very unaerodynamic canopy hinge, despite the fact that the Komet was to be a high-speed interceptor, testifies to the rapid construction of the aircraft. (Photo by S.Nohara)

キャノピー開閉用ヒンジ　Canopy hinge

Me163Bのキャノピー周囲　Canopy area of the Me163B

方向舵ペダル
Rudder pedals

（前上方より見る　Front view）

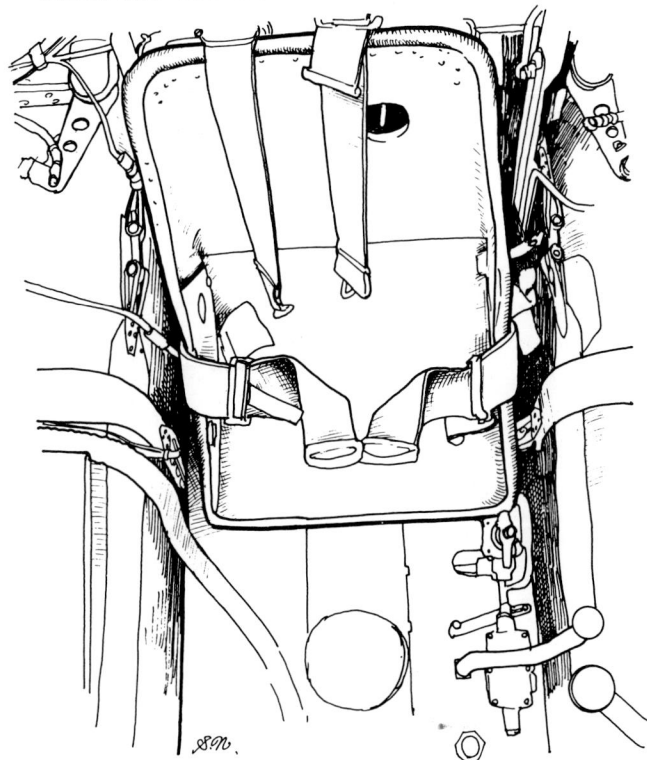

（背面より見る　Rear view）

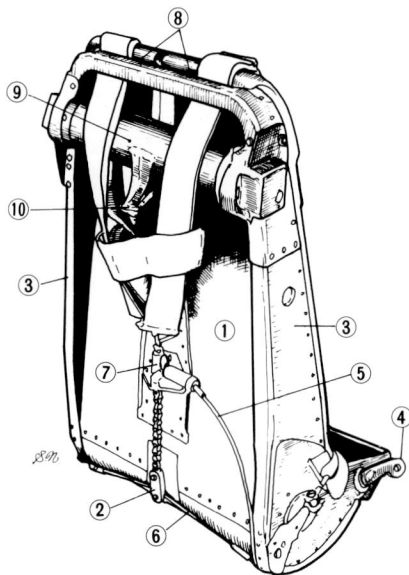

Me163Bパイロット・シート
Me163B pilot seat

①シート
　Seat
②ガイドローラー
　Guide roller
③シートフランジ
　Seat flange
④ベルト調節レバー
　Belt adjustment lever
⑤ボーデン索
　Borden cable
⑥ゴム索
　Rubber line
⑦チェーンガイド
　Chain guide
⑧背部ベルト通し
　Rear belt guides
⑨スプリング
　Spring
⑩サスペンション・フック
　Suspension hook

Me163Aのコクピット内
Cockpit Interior of the Me163A

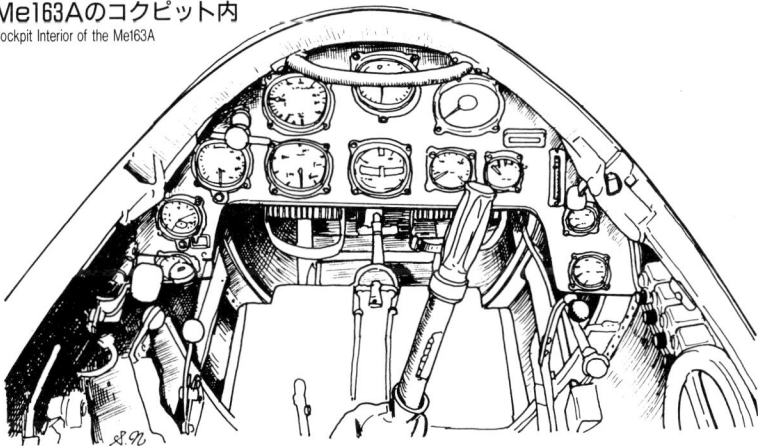

▶Me163Bのコクピット。Revi16B照準器や航空時計、エンジン推力計などの一部の計器類が欠落しているものの、Me163Bのコクピット内の配置はよくわかる。
The cockpit of the Me163B. Although the Revi16B gunsight, flight clock, engine power meter and some other instruments are missing, this photo provides an excellent view of the cockpit's layout.

Me163B-1のコクピット内配置
Cockpit interior of the Me163B-1

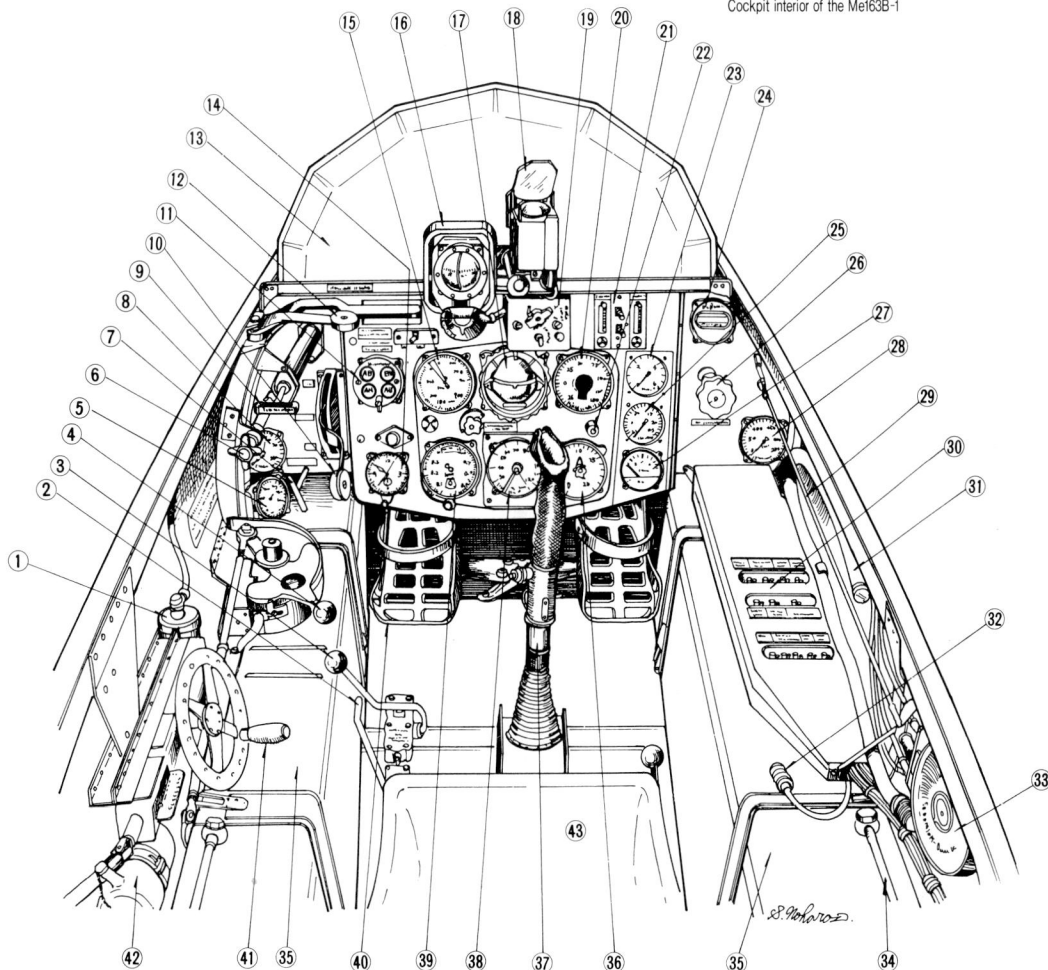

① 油圧作動タンク
Hydraulic oil pressure reservoir

② 着陸フラップ操作レバー
Landing flap control lever

③ 着陸フラップ手動ポンプレバー
Landing flap manual pump lever

④ スロットルレバー
Throttle

⑤ 降着装置非常操作用圧力計
Pressure gauge for emergency landing skid operation

⑥ 非常時燃料投棄レバー
Emergency fuel dump lever

⑦ 牽引索切り離しレバー
Tow cable release lever

⑧ 降着装置非常投棄用圧搾空気圧力計
Pressure gauge for emergency take-off dolly jettison apparants

⑨ 降着装置非常投棄コック
Emergency take-off dolly jettison cock

⑩ 降着装置下げレバー
Landing skid deployment lever

⑪ 降着装置位置表示計
Take-off dolly/landing skid position indicator

⑫ キャノピー・ロックハンドル
Canopy lock handle

⑬ 防弾ガラス（90mm厚）
Bulletproof glass (90mm)

⑭ 航空時計
Flight clock

⑮ 速度計
Airspeed indicator

⑯ コンパス
Compass

⑰ 人工水平儀
Artifical horizon

⑱ Revi16B光像式射撃照準器
Revi16B reflecting gunsight

⑲ FuG25a無線器操作盤
FuG25a radio control panel

⑳ 昇降計
Vertical speed indicator

㉑ 機関砲弾残量ゲージ
Ammunition supply gauge

㉒ 燃料切れ警告灯
No fuel warning light

㉓ エンジン圧力計
Engine pressure gauge

㉔ 酸素流量計
Oxygen flow gauge

㉕ エンジン推力計
Engine thrust gauge

㉖ 酸素バルブ
Oxygen valve

㉗ 温度計
Temperature gauge

㉘ 酸素圧力計
Oxygen pressure gauge

㉙ キャノピー非常時投棄索
Emergency canopy release handle

㉚ 無線器、電気装置関係スイッチ盤
Radio & electrical control box

㉛ 酸素供給ホース
Oxygen supply hose

㉜ ヘルメット接続部（無線器用）
Radio connection cable for pilot's helmet

㉝ 酸素供給装置
Oxygen supply mechanism

㉞ 燃料（T液）パイプ
Fuel line (T-Stoff)

㉟ T液タンク（容量60ℓ）
T-Stoff tank (60 liters)

㊱ 燃料計
Fuel gauge

㊲ 操縦桿
Control stick

㊳ 回転計
Tachometer

㊴ 高度計
Altimeter

㊵ 方向舵ペダル
Rudder pedals

㊶ トリムフラップ操作ハンドル
Trim flap control handle

㊷ 着陸フラップ作動油タンク
Hydraulic reservoir for landing flaps

㊸ 座席
Pilot's seat

33

主翼構成（右翼下面）
Structure of wings (starboard wing underside)

① 主桁
　Main spar
② 補助桁
　Auxiliary spar
③ 前縁リブ
　Leading edge ribs
④ 中央リブ
　Central ribs
⑤ 後縁リブ
　Trailing edge ribs
⑥ スラット
　Slats
⑦ 翼端キャップ
　Wingtip cap
⑧ 主桁連結部
　Main spar connection
⑨ 補助桁連結部
　Auxiliary spar connection
⑩ 補助翼
　Elevon
⑪ トリム・フラップ
　Trim flap

⑫ 着陸フラップ
　Landing flap
⑬ トリム・フラップ軸受け
　Trim flap pivot mount
⑭ 補助翼軸受け
　Elevon pivot mount
⑮ 補助翼操作桿フェアリング
　Elevon control rod fairing
⑯ 取り外し式後縁パネル
　Removable trailing edge panel
⑰ 前部C液タンクカバー
　Front section C-Stoff tank cover
⑱ 後部C液タンクカバー
　Rear section C-Stoff tank cover
⑲ 燃料パイプ・フェアリング
　Fuel line fairing

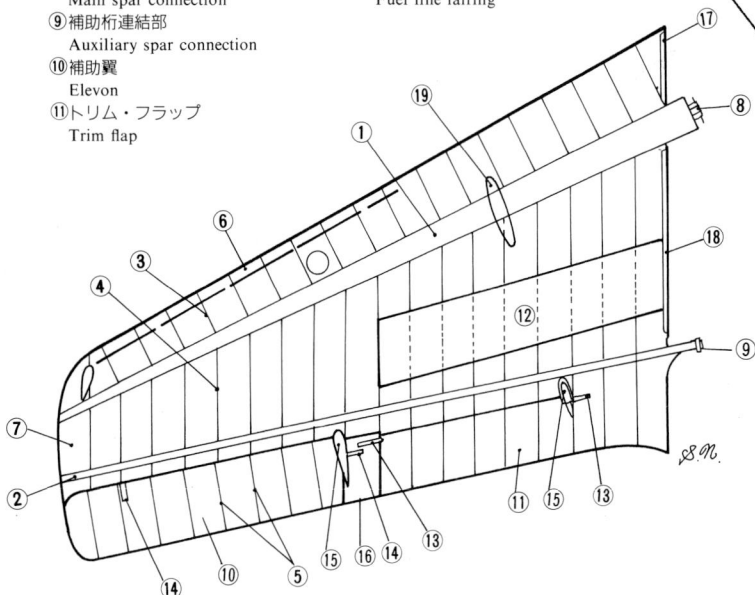

補助翼、トリム・フラップ構成図（左主翼上面）Elevon & trim flap structure (Port wing upper side)

A部詳細
Section A Detail

① 左主翼
　Port wing
② 補助翼
　Elevon
③ トリム・フラップ
　Trim flap
④ 後縁外皮
　Trailing edge panel
⑤ カバーキャップ
　Cover cap
⑥ 補助翼操作レバー
　Elevon control lever
⑦ 補助翼操作桿
　Elevon control rod

⑧ 六角ボルト
　Hexagonal bolt
⑨ 補助翼取り付け軸
　Elevon pivot
⑩ 補助翼外側取り付け軸
　Outboard elevon pivot
⑪ 取り付け軸基部
　Outboard elevon pivot mount
⑫ 取り付け軸フランジ
　Elevon pivot flange
⑬ キャップカバー・リング
　Cap cover ring
⑭ トリム・フラップ取り付け部
　Trim flap mount

⑮ トリム・フラップ操作桿
　Trim flap control rod
⑯ 六角ボルト
　Hexagonal bolt
⑰ トリム・フラップ外側取り付け軸
　Outboard trim flap pivot mount
⑱ トリム・フラップ内側取り付け軸
　Inboard trim flap pivot mount
⑲ 取り付け軸フランジ
　Trim flap pivot flange

主翼前縁固定式スラット（左主翼下面）
Fixed leading edge slats (Port wing underside)

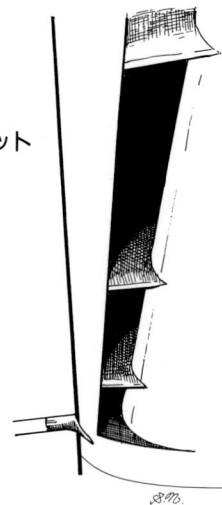

垂直尾翼部品構成
Vertical stabilizer parts diagram

① 垂直安定板前部フィン
　Forward fin
② 垂直安定板後部フィン
　Rear fin
③ 無線器アンテナ用配線
　Radio antenna
④ 垂直安定板
　Vertical stabilizer
⑤ 方向舵
　Rudder
⑥ 方向舵操作桿フェアリング
　Rudder control rod fairing
⑦ 方向舵取り付け軸
　Rudder mounts
⑧ 方向舵ホーンバランス
　Rudder horn balance

⑨ 方向舵取り付け軸点検窓
　Rudder mount inspection hatches
⑩ 方向舵操作桿
　Rudder control rod
⑪ 方向舵操作用ロッカー・レバー
　Rudder control rod locking lever
⑫ 方向舵操作桿連結部
　Rudder control rod connection
⑬ 垂直安定板前部取り付けヒンジ
　Vertical stabilizer forward mount hinge
⑭ 垂直安定板後部取り付けヒンジ
　Vertical stabilizer rear mount hinge
⑮ 点検パネル
　Inspection panel

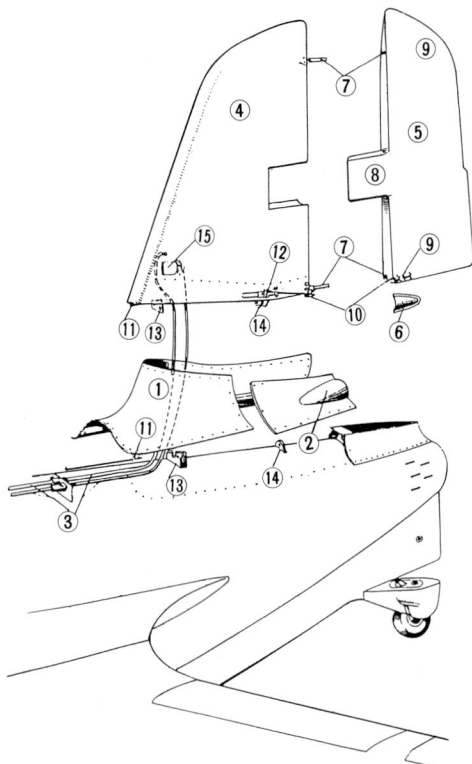

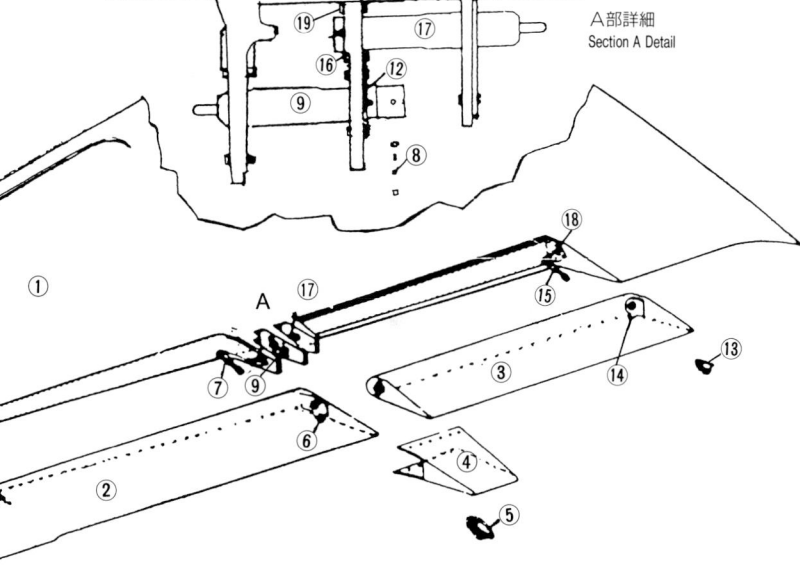

補助翼操作桿フェアリング
Elevon control rod fairing

降着装置 LANDING GEAR

離陸用ドリー装着状態
Attachment of take-off dolly

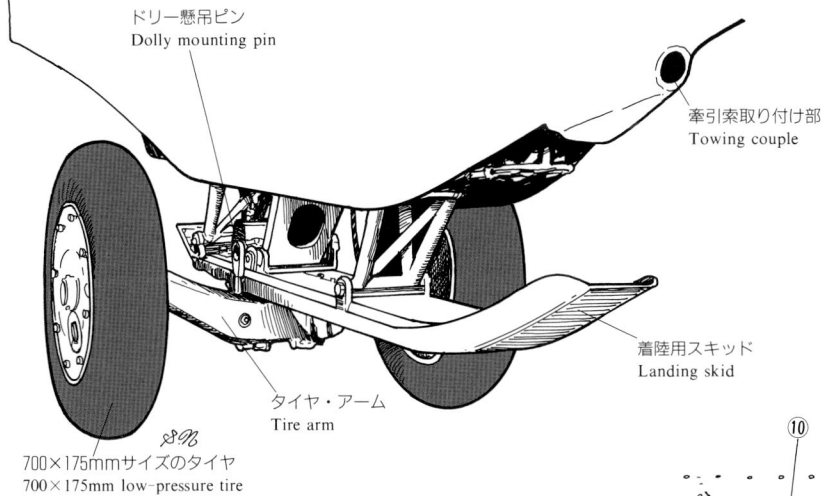

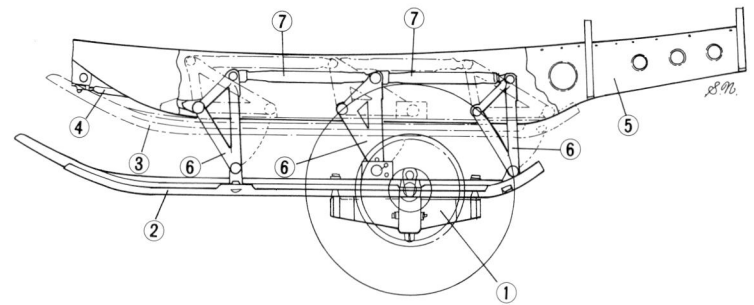

ドリー懸吊ピン
Dolly mounting pin

牽引索取り付け部
Towing couple

着陸用スキッド
Landing skid

タイヤ・アーム
Tire arm

700×175mmサイズのタイヤ
700×175mm low-pressure tire

尾脚フェアリングの変化 Changes in the Komet's tail wheel cover

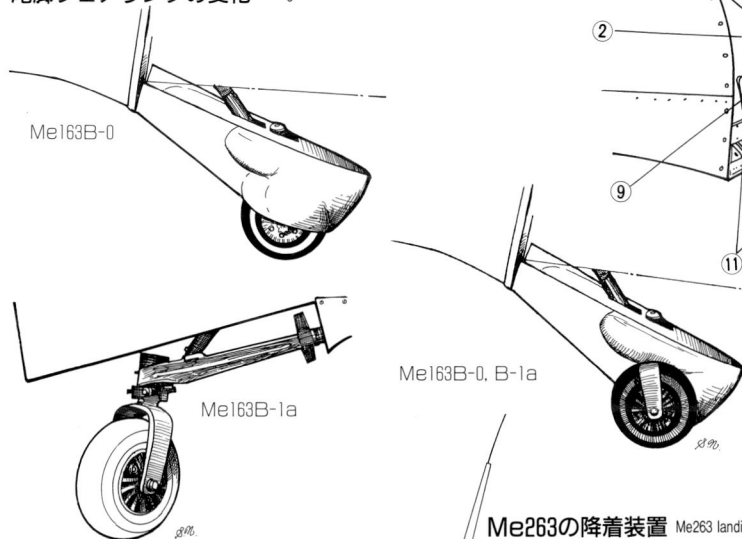

Me163B-0

Me163B-1a

Me163B-0, B-1a

着陸用スキッド構造図 Landing skid structure

① ドリー
Take-off dolly
② スキッド（展開位置）
Skid (deployed position)
③ スキッド（収納位置）
Skid (raised position)
④ 支柱
Support brace
⑤ スキッド支持架
Skid support frame
⑥ スキッド取り付け／作動アーム
Skid attachment & operation arms
⑦ 取り付け／作動アーム連結桿
Attachment arm linkage rods

尾脚構造 Tail wheel structure

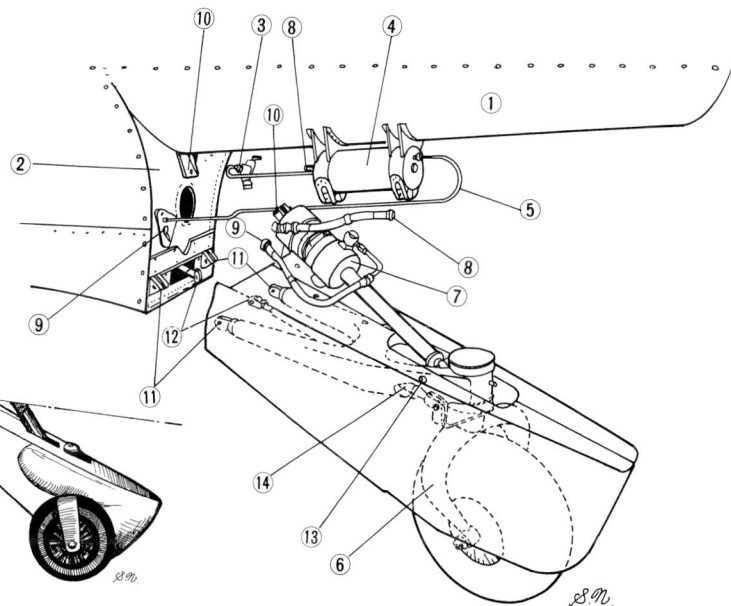

① 胴体尾部
Tail section of fuselage
② 胴体第11隔壁
Fuselage bulkhead #11
③ 圧力油導管連結部
Hydraulic oil line connection
④ シリンダー
Hydraulic cylinder
⑤ 圧搾空気導管
Compressed air line
⑥ 尾輪フォーク
Tail wheel fork
⑦ 油圧シリンダー
Hydraulic oil cylinder
⑧ 圧力油導管連結部
Hydraulic line connection
⑨ 圧力油導管連結部
Hydraulic line connection
⑩ 油圧シリンダー連結部
Hydraulic cylinder connection
⑪ 尾脚取り付け部
Tail wheel assembly mount
⑫ 尾脚支柱取り付け部
Tail wheel support brace connection
⑬ ピストン槓桿取り付けボルト
Piston rod attachment bolt
⑭ 尾輪操作槓桿
Tail wheel control rod

Me263の降着装置 Me263 landing gear

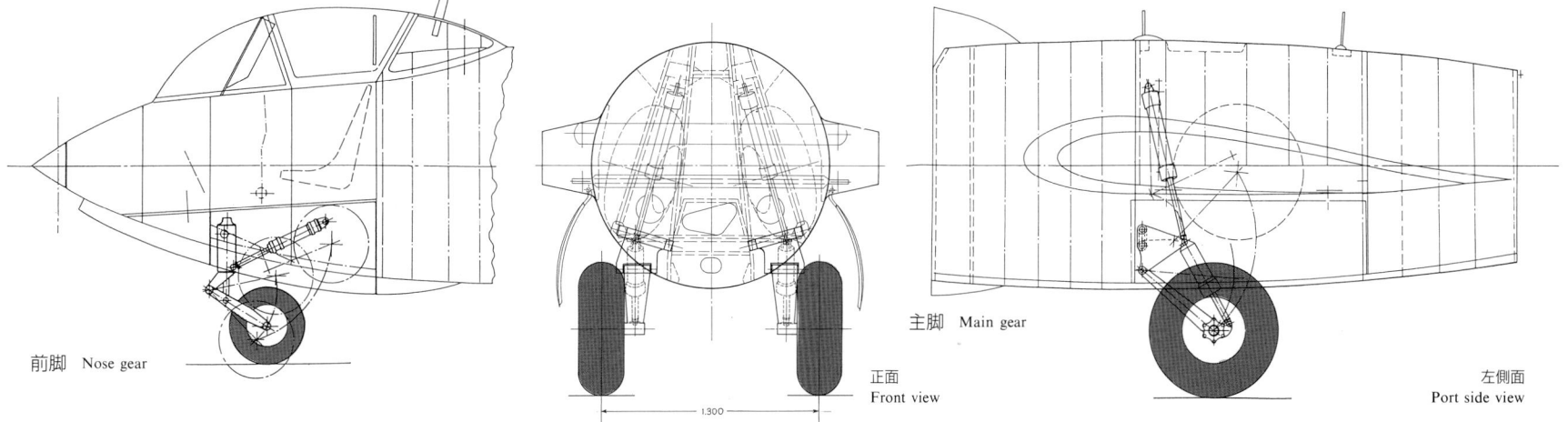

前脚 Nose gear

1.300

正面
Front view

主脚 Main gear

左側面
Port side view

35

写真 1：HWK-RⅠロケット・モーターを噴かして、離陸しようとするDFS194。のちのMe163Bとはまったく異なる胴体形状がよくわかる。主翼を押さえている地上員と比較すれば、その機体サイズが把握できよう。

Photo 1: Its HWK-RI rocket motor ignited, a DFS 194 gets ready to attempt a take-off. The differences between the shape of its fuselage and that of the Me163B are clear. The size of the plane can be determined by comparing it with the size of the figure holding on to the plane's wing.

写真 2：1940年末に機体のみは完成していたMe163A V1、ラジオ・コード "KE＋SW"。DFS194に比較すると、アウトラインは相当に洗練されており、胴体と主翼の接点は、のちのブレンデッド・ウィングボディなみに滑らかである。方向舵の下方にみえる膨らみがロケット・ノズルで、頼りないほどに小さい。

Photo 2: A prototype body (no engine) of a Me163A-V1 completed in late 1940, with the radio code "KE+SW." When compared to the DFS 194 in the previous photo, the smoothing of the plane's lines is clear. The joint between the fuselage and wing has also been smoothed into the Komet's characteristic "blended-wing body." The rocket nozzle of the engine is visible below the vertical stabilizer, seemingly too small to do any good.

写真 3：Me163乗員の訓練を担当したⅢ.／JG400の指揮官、アドルフ・ニューマイヤー少尉の発案により、両主翼下面に１基ずつ計24発のR4M55mm空対空ロケット弾を懸吊するテスト機に充てられた、EK16所属のMe163A V5、ラジオ・コード "CD＋IO"。しかし、この兵装は正式に導入されることなく終った。1945年２月、ウーデットフェルトにて撮影。

Photo 3: An Me163A-V5 of EK16 (radio code "CD+ IO") with 24 (12 on each side) R4M 55mm air-to-air rockets installed under the wings for testing. The idea for the rockets was developed by the *Kommandeur* of Ⅲ./JG 400, Adolf Numayer. Nevertheless, the idea was never officially adopted. This plane was photographed at Udetfeld in February of 1945.

写真 4：真上に近いアングルからみたMe163B-0の2号機、ラジオ・コード "VD＋EL"。平面形の把握に最適の写真で、主翼前縁スラット、補助翼（エレボン）、トリム・フラップの位置、サイズがよくわかる。全面RLM02又は76カラーの単色塗装。

Photo 4: An Me163B-0 (aircraft number "2," radio code "VD＋EL") viewed from almost directly overhead. The photo provides and excellent view of the aircraft's shape, as well as allowing easy confirmation of the location and size of its leading edge slats, elevons and trim flaps. The aircraft appears to have been painted entirely in RLM 02 or perhaps RLM 76.

写真 5：左真横からみたMe163B-0の8号機、ラジオ・コード "VD＋ER"。クリアーな写真であり、ディテール、外板ラインがひと目でみてとれる。ピトー管に重なって、主翼付け根前縁からMGl51／20 20mm機関砲が突出しているのが確認できる。生産型B-1aではMK108に換装されたため、砲身は突出しない。ロケット・ノズル周囲の放熱孔のアレンジもB-1aとは異なっている。

Photo 5: A view of the port side of an Me163B-0, (aircraft number "8," radio code "VD＋ER"). This exceptionally clear photograph provides a good view of the aircraft's lines and the details of its structure. The pitot tube on the leading edge of the wing, as well as the protruding muzzle of the MG151/20 20mm cannon can be seen. In the production model B-1a, the armament was changed to the Mk108, which does not protrude. The fuselage arrangement around the nozzle of the B-1a also differed from this pre-production example.

写真 6：バトツヴィシェナーン基地の第16実験隊に配属され、実用テスト中のMe163B-0、機番号 "05"（白）。新しいグリーン系迷彩を施している。主翼付け根の機関砲はMG151／20を取り外しただけの状態か、MK108に換装したかどちらかであり、後者ならばB-0の第47号機以降の後期生産機である。尾脚カバーは、他の多くの機と同様に取り外している。

Photo 6: An Me163B-0 undergoing flight tests with *Erprobungs Kommando* 16 at the air base in Bad Zwischenahn. The plane sports the new green marking scheme, and aircraft number "05" in white. Whether the Mk151/20 cannons have been removed or replaced by Mk108s is impossible to determine, but if its the latter, it would make this aircraft the 47th or later of the B-0 pre-production series. Like many examples of the Komet, the tail wheel cover has been removed.

写真 7：これもバトツヴィシェナーン基地の第16実験隊におけるMe163B-0、機番号 "04"（白）の実用テスト中のスナップで、隊員たちが "シャープ発進" と呼んだ、緊張の離陸シーン。ロケット・ノズルから噴出するトラ縞模様の衝撃波は、スロットル全開状態を示している。わずかの操作ミス、何らかの衝撃が加わると、恐ろしいロケット燃料はたちまち爆発し、人機もろとも四散させてしまう。

Photo 7: This photo also shows an Me163B-0 undergoing tests with EK 16 at Bad Zwischenahn. This shot shows the tension-filled moment of the aircraft beginning its take-off roll following the ground attendants' cries of "Sharp start!" The striped pattern of the exhaust puffs coming out of the nozzle testify that the pilot has applied full throttle. Even a tiny operational error or shock to the aircraft could cause the volatile rocket fuel to explode, annihilating plane and pilot.

写真8〜9：戦後、アメリカに運ばれたMe163B-0の1
機、機番号 "54"（白）。機首左側に描かれたエンブレム
からもわかるように、訓練中隊の14./JG400で使われて
いた機体である。本機はグレー迷彩で引き渡されたのち、
グリーン迷彩に変更された。胴体のモットリングはきわ
めて濃密に施されている。機首先端は赤と白、ドリーの
車輪ホイール・ハブも赤／白に塗り分けていることに注
目。写真9では、胴体上、下面パネルが外され、T液タ
ンクや骨組みが見えている。

Photo 8-9: An Me163B-0 (aircraft number "54" in white)
that was shipped to the United States following the war.
As can be established by the emblem marked on the left
side of the plane's nose, it was used by the training unit
14./JG 400. Although this Komet was captured with a
gray paint scheme, it was soon repainted in a mottled
green. The red and white strip on the plane's nose, and the
red and white pattern on its take-off dolly are rather
unusual. In photo 9, the upper fuselage panel has been
removed, revealing the plane's *T-Stoff* tank and internal
structure.

写真10：穏やかな秋の陽射しを浴びて、Me163B-1aの主
翼上で仮眠をむさぼる2./JG400のパイロット。彼と比
較すれば、本機がいかに小さな機体であったかがわかる
だろう。機首先端は白く塗り、その後方に第2中隊章の
"シャープ発進"するノミを描いている。濃密な81カラー
のモットリングが目立つ。本機は、胴体上面にD／F
ループ・アンテナをオプション装備している。1944年秋、
ブランディス基地にて。

Photo 10: Under the mild autumn sun, a pilot of 2./JG
400 appears to be taking a nap on the wing of an Me163B
-1a. Comparing him with the plane reveals just how small
an aircraft the Komet actually was. The nose of the plane
is painted white, and just behind it, the emblem of the 2nd
Staffel of *Jagdgeschwader* 400, which depicted a "sharp
starting" flea, can be seen (In the Luftwaffe's organization
scheme, each *Jagdgeschwader*, or "JG," was usually made
up of 2 or 3 *Gruppe*, designated by Roman numerals, and
each *Gruppe* was usually made up of three 12-plane
Staffel, designated by Arabic numerals). The coloring
scheme, a very dense mottling in RLM 81, stands out. The
plane is equipped with an optional direction finder, as
evidenced by the loop antenna visible on top of the
fuselage. This photo was taken in the fall of 1944 at
Brandis Air Base.

12

写真11〜12：1946年、イギリスのヴィッカース飛行場にてテストされる、もとJG400のMe163B-1a W.Nr191060。オリジナルなコンディションを維持しているが、その後のテストにて事故をおこし、損傷した部分を他の機体部品で流用したのち、I.W.Mに移管され、現在もダックスフォード基地の博物館にて一般公開されている。

Photo 11-12: An Me163B-1a, W.Nr 191060, originally assigned to JG 400 being tested at Vickers Air Base in the U.K. in 1946. As seen in the photos, excluding markings, the plane is in close to original condition. Nevertheless, this plane was heavily damaged in a landing accident in November of 1947. Repaired by hand, and with parts from other Komets, it was transferred to the Imperial War Museum in Duxford, England, and is still on public display there today.

写真13：本機もイギリス軍に捕獲され、本国に送られたうちの1機Me163B-1a W.Nr191912。写真は、捕獲した他のドイツ機とともに、1945年10月〜11月にかけてRAEにて展示された際のもの。各パネルが外されて内部が見られるようにしてある。左奥はHe162A-2。本機はその後の消息がわからず、スクラップ処分されたと思われる。

Photo 13: The Komet in this picture, a Me163B-1a (W.Nr 191912) was one of several captured by the British and shipped to the U.K. It is depicted here being displayed by the RAE along with other captured German aircraft sometime in October or November of 1945. Several panels have been removed in order to provide views of the internal mechanism. An He162A-2 is visible to the left behind it. The fate of this aircraft is unknown, but it is believed to have been scrapped.

写真14〜15：戦後アメリカに運ばれたMe163B-1aの1機 W.Nr191301。主翼フィレットのみ、他機のものと交換しているが、ほぼオリジナル状態を保っている。本機は、このあと"FE-500"の登録記号を附与され、B-29に曳航されて滑空テストなどを受けたのち、分解して保管され、現在はNASMのポール・ガーバー施設内にて限定展示中。いずれ復元が行われるだろう。

Photo 14-15: An Me163B-1a (W.Nr 191301) captured by the Allies and shipped to the United States after the war. Except for the installation of wing fillets from another aircraft, it appears to be in near-original condition. This Komet was relabeled "FE-500" and tested in unpowered flight, being towed aloft by a B-29. Following testing, it was disassembled and stored in a warehouse for several decades until the late 1980s, when it was reassembled and put on limited display at the Paul E. Gahbar Preservation Facility in Silver Hill, Maryland, an arm of the National Air and Space Museum. The plane is expected to be fully restored at some point.

写真16：Me163の欠点を改良し、実用性を高めた発展型として開発されたMe263（Ju248）。写真は、1944年8月に完成した原型機、W.Nr380001、ラジオ・コード"DV＋PA"。真円断面の長い胴体、与圧キャビンを覆う水滴状キャノピー、油圧引き込み式の降着装置など、Me163のイメージをまったく感じさせないフォルムである。空軍は、本機に大きな期待をかけたが、敗戦までに量産型は完成しなかった。

Photo 16: The many shortcomings of the Me163 were addressed, and an advanced, higher-performance version of the rocket fighter, the Me263 (a.k.a. Ju248) was developed late in the war. The photo shows the prototype, W.Nr 380001, radio code "DV＋PA." With the addition of a pressurized cockpit, teardrop canopy, and retractable landing gear, the plane is a far cry from the Me163. Hopes for the design were high, but Germany's defeat prevented any further examples from being completed.

Me163各型変遷
Variations of the Me163

作図・解説／野原 茂
Illustrations and Commentary by Shigeru Nohara
図版はすべて1/48スケール
All diagrams are 1/48 scale

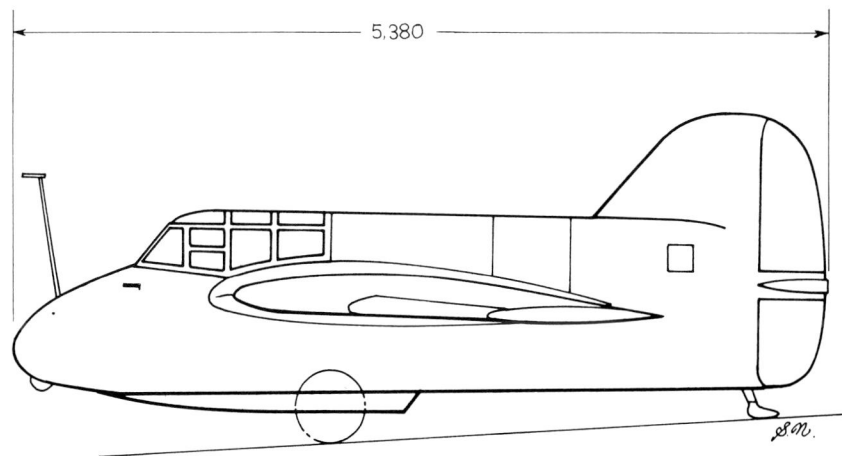

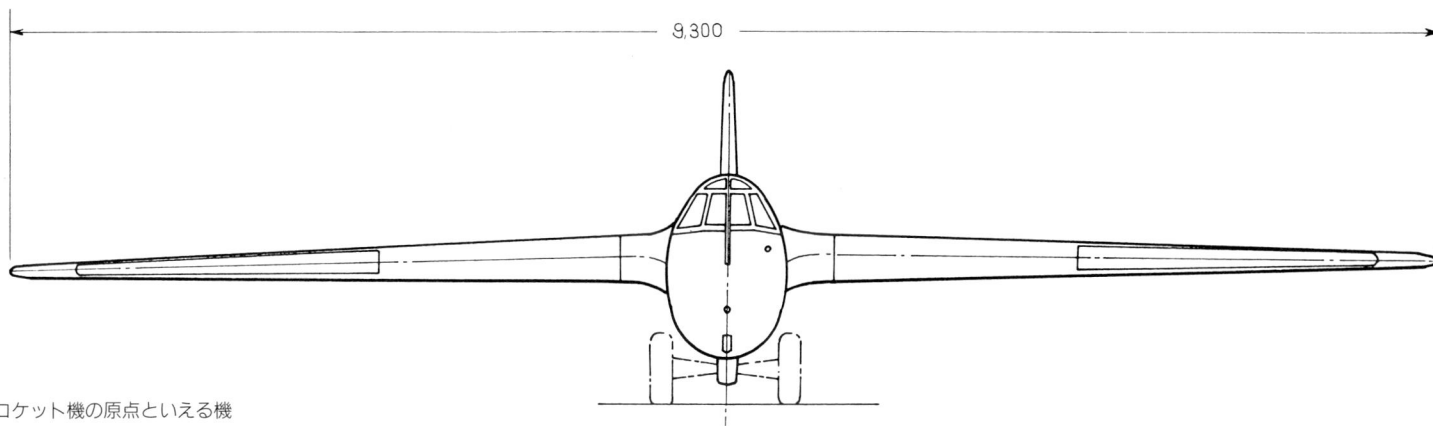

5,380

9,300

DFS194

リピッシュ博士の無尾翼ロケット機の原点といえる機体。ロケット・モーターはHWK-RⅠ〔推力400kg〕。胴体は金属製、主翼は木製で、主翼前縁に2段の後退角がついているものの、全体のフォルムはロケット機というより、無尾翼グライダーのような印象を与える。もちろん、離陸にはドリーを使い、着陸の際は胴体前部下面に付けられたスキッド（橇）を使って行う。

Perhaps the most basic of Dr. Alexander Lippisch's tailless designs, the DFS 194 was powered by the HWK-RI rocket motor, producing 400kg of thrust. The plane had a metal fuselage and wooden wings swept at two different angles. Rather than that of a rocket plane, the aircraft gives one the impression more of a tailless glider. Naturally, it used a dolly for take-off and the landing skid on the forward bottom of the fuselage for landing.

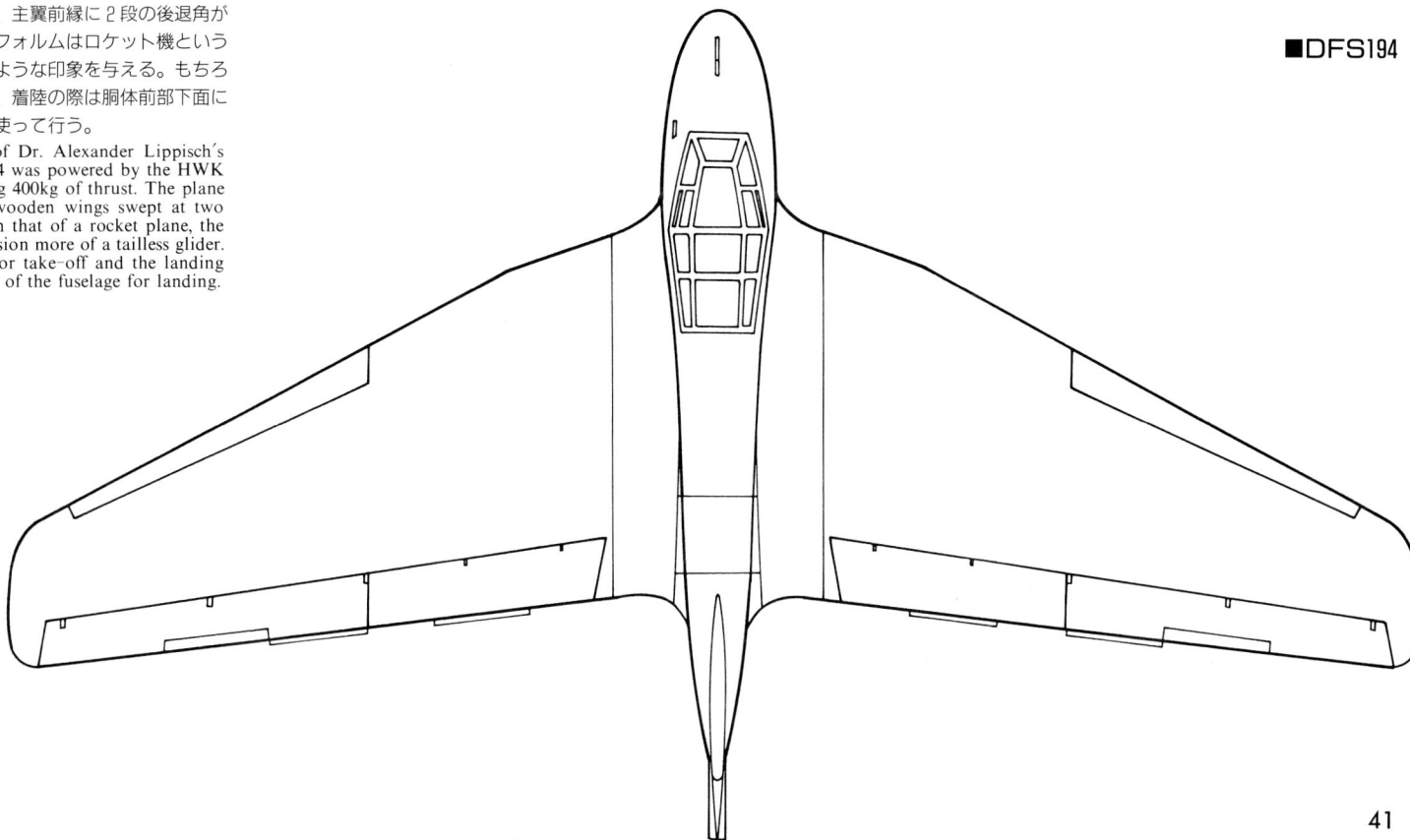

■DFS194

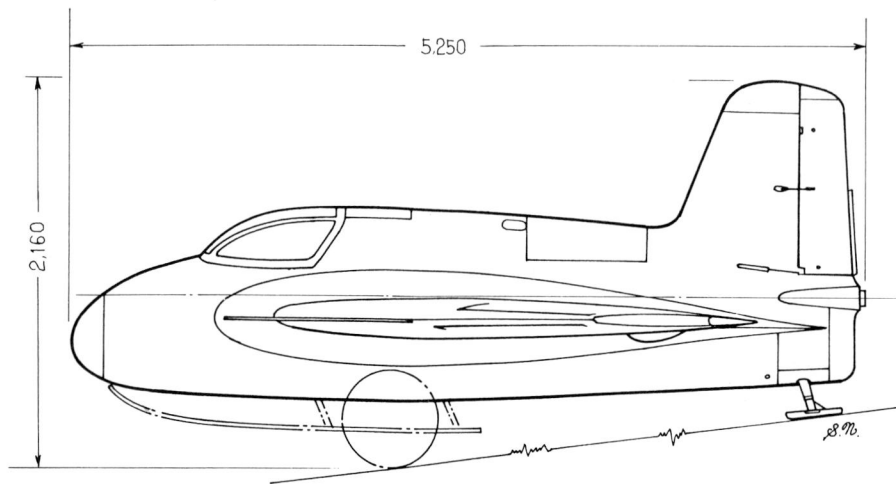

Me163A

　DFS194を、さらに洗練したフォルムに再設計しており、主翼の後退角度も少し強くなっている。ロケット・モーターはHWK-RII-203（推力750kg）。DFS194では外翼前縁にスラットを付けていたが、本機では固定スラットに変わっている。

　A more refined version of the DFS 194, the plane's lines were smoothed overall, and the sweep of the wings was increased. The plane was powered by a HWK-RII-203 rocket motor, producing 750kg of thrust. While the DFS 194 employed standard-type slats on the leading edges, the Me163A had fixed slats.

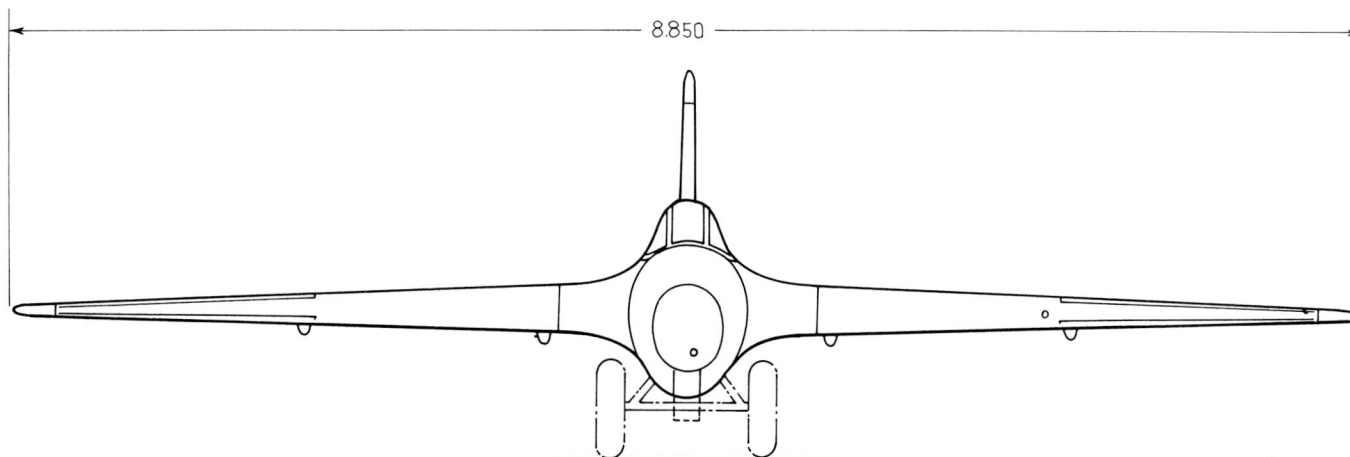

■Me163A

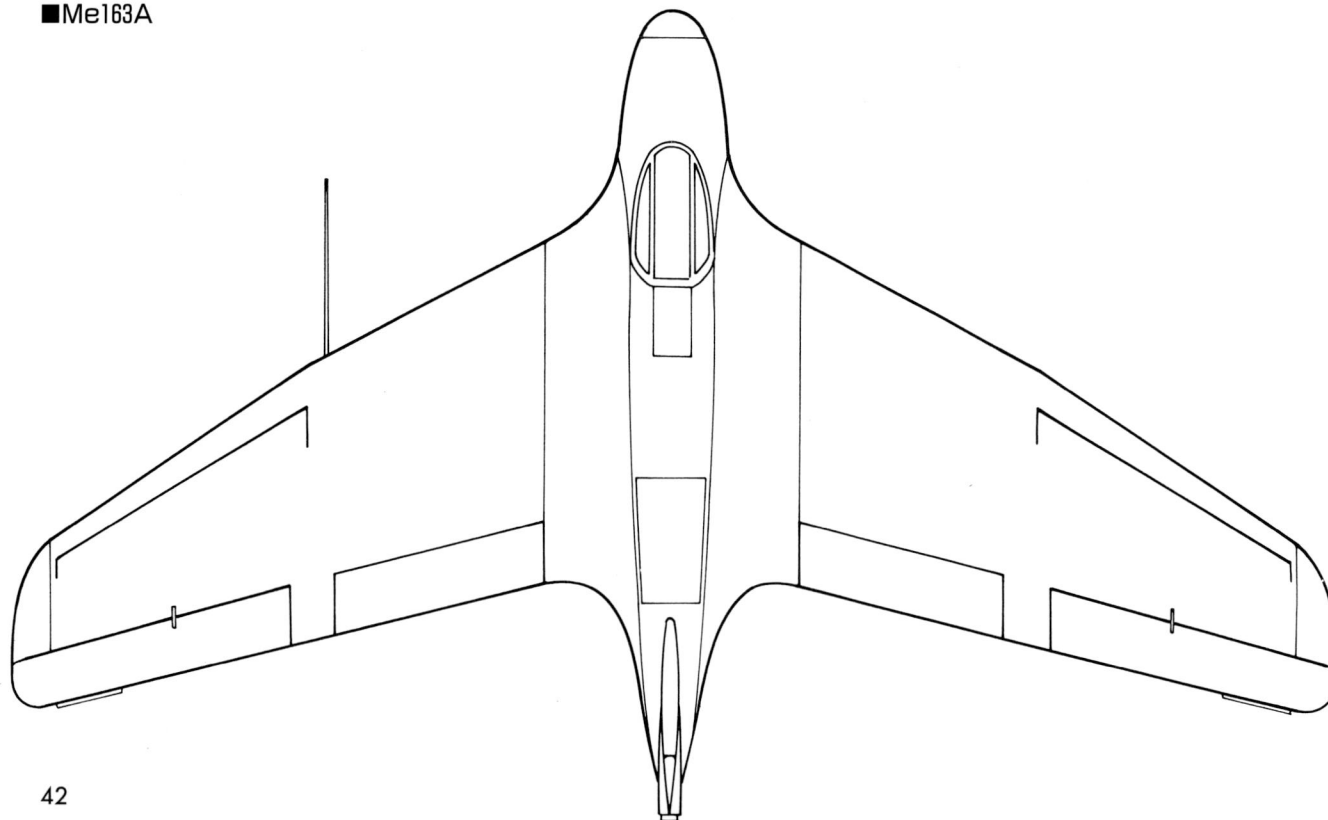

Me163B-0

B型は実用戦闘機としての諸装備を施すために、Me163Aとは事実上まったく異なり新設計となった。B-0はその先行量産型として計70機発注された。著しく太くなった胴体は、前半部は機首の無線器室、コクピット、機関砲用弾倉、燃料タンクで占められ、後半部がロケット・モーター収容部となっている。胴体下面の着陸用スキッド、および尾脚は引き込み式となり、離陸時は、"出"状態のスキッドに2車輪のドリーを取り付けて行った。武装は、両主翼付け根にMG151/20 20mm機関砲各1門（弾数各100発）。

主翼は骨組み、外皮とも木製で、前縁はスッキリした直線となり、失速防止用に翼端に向って5.7°の振り下げが付けられた点がMe163Aとの大きな相違。

B-0の1号機は機体そのものは1942年4月に完成したが、搭載予定のHWK109-509Aロケット・モーターが間に合わず、実際にB-0が本格的な動力飛行テストを開始したのは、実にそれから1年もあとのことであった。

The B-series of the Me163 was essentially redesigned from the ground up to make the aircraft practical for actual military use. At least 70 B-Os were ordered as the first production model. The front section of the plane's now fatter fuselage contained the radio equipment in the nose, cockpit, magazines for the machine cannons and fuel tanks, while the rear section contained the rocket motor. Both the landing skid on the bottom of the fuselage and the tail wheel were retractable, with a two-wheeled dolly being attached to the skid (in the extended position) for take-off. Armament consisted of one MG 151/20 20mm machine cannon in each wing root with 100 rounds apiece.

The wings, both the spars and the outer panels, were of wooden construction. Perhaps the biggest difference with the Me163A was the change of the wing leading edge to a smooth, straight-line design with a 5.7° downward tilt near the wingtips to help prevent speed loss.

The airframe of the first Me163B-O was completed in April of 1942, but development of the HKW 109-509A rocket motor to be employed in the plane was delayed, and actual powered flight tests didn't take place until a year later.

Me163S

B-1aのロケット・モーターを撤去し、従来のコクピットの後方に一段高く教官席を設けた練習機型。重心の変化を調節するために、教官席の左、右には水バラスト・タンクが追加された。1944年8月に1号機が造られ、ブランディス基地のJG400に配備されたが、戦況の悪化、Me163自体の活動の鈍りなどで、ほとんど使う機会のないまま、侵攻してきたソ連軍に捕獲された。終戦までに少なくとも7機のMe163Sが造られた。

A trainer version of the B-1a, with its rocket motor removed and an instructor's seat added immediately above and behind the existing cockpit. In order to compensate for the change in the plane's center of gravity, ballast tanks filled with water were installed on either side of the instructor's seat. The first example was completed near August 1944 and assigned to JG400 operating at Brandis. However, as the Germans' war situation deteriorated and use of the Komet itself dropped off, the plane was hardly used at all before its capture by advancing Russian forces. At least seven Me163Ss were completed before the end of the war.

■Me163B-0

①量産型B-1aと異なるピトー管
Pitot tube different from that on the production model B-1a
②MG151/20 20mm機関砲（弾数100発）
MG151/20 20mm machine cannon (100 rounds)
③タイヤ被覆部分の多い尾輪カバー
Rear wheel cover with large tire-covering area

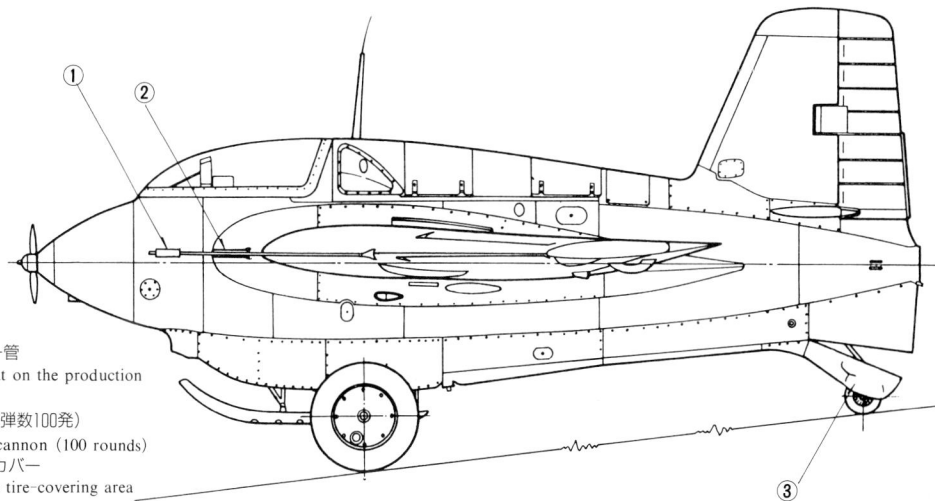

■Me163B-1a　練習機仕様
Me163B-1a　Trainer version

①発電機駆動用プロペラを撤去
Nose propeller to drive generator removed
②面積の大きい後方視界窓
Larger rear observation window

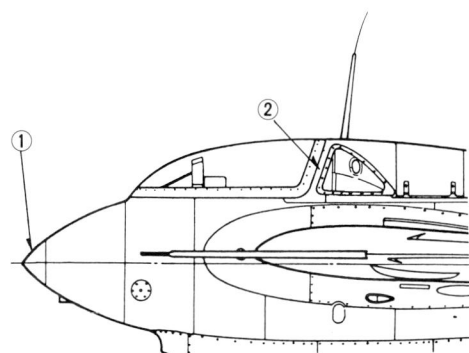

■Me163S-1　複座練習機
Me163S-1　Two-seat trainer version

①武装を撤去
Armament removed
②アンテナ支柱の取り付け位置を変更
Location of antenna mount changed
③後席を新設
Rear seat added
④ロケット・モーターを撤去
Rocket motor removed

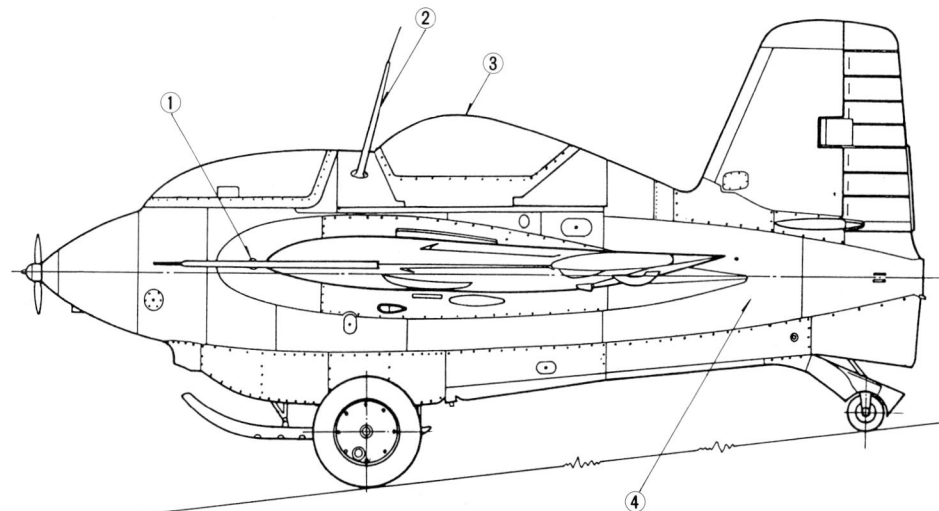

（左側面 Port elevation）

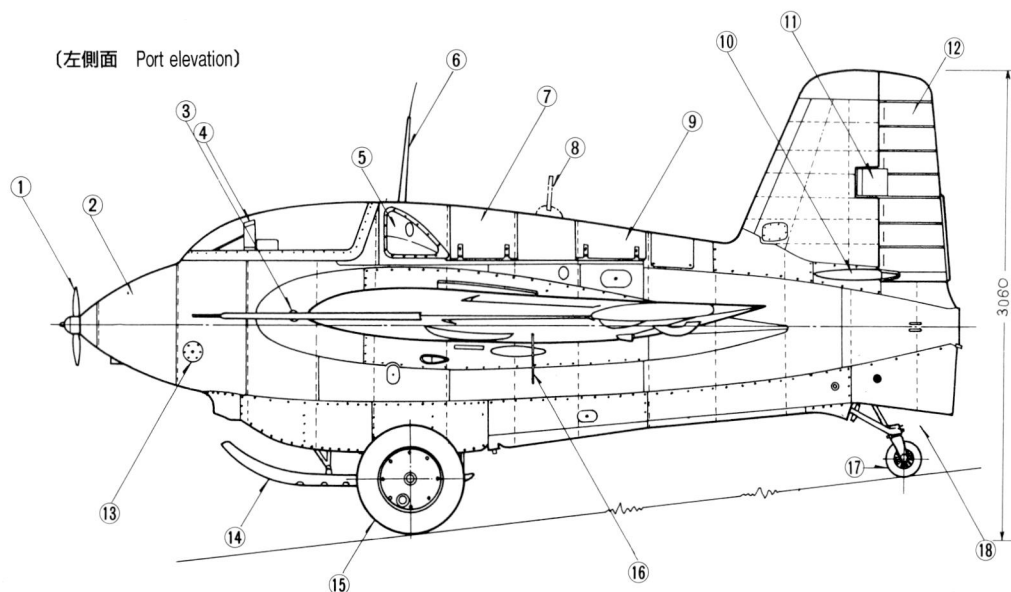

Me163B-1a

B-0に続いて発注された量産型。武装がMK108 30mm機関砲2門に変更された以外は、基本的にB-0と変わらない。ただし、ピトー管、尾脚カバーなどの細部には変更が加えられており、一部の機は胴体上面にD/Fループ・アンテナを追加するなどした。訓練中隊のJG400第13、14中隊で使用したB-1aの中には、機首先端の発電機用プロペラを撤去し、後方視界窓を大きくした機もあった。

B-1aは、1944年中に237機、1945年に42機、計279機造られた。

The second version to be produced in quantity, following the B-O. Except for the armament being changed to MK108 30mm machine cannons, the plane is essentially identical to the B-O. Some details were modified, however, such as the pitot tube and tail wheel cover, and some examples had D/F loop antennas installed on top of the fuselage. Among the B-1a Komets used by the 13th and 14th training *Staffel* of JG 400, some had the generator propellers removed from the nose of the plane, as well as enlarged rear observation windows.

During 1944, 237 B-1a Komets were produced, followed by 42 more in 1945 for a total production run of 279.

（右側面 Starboard elevation）

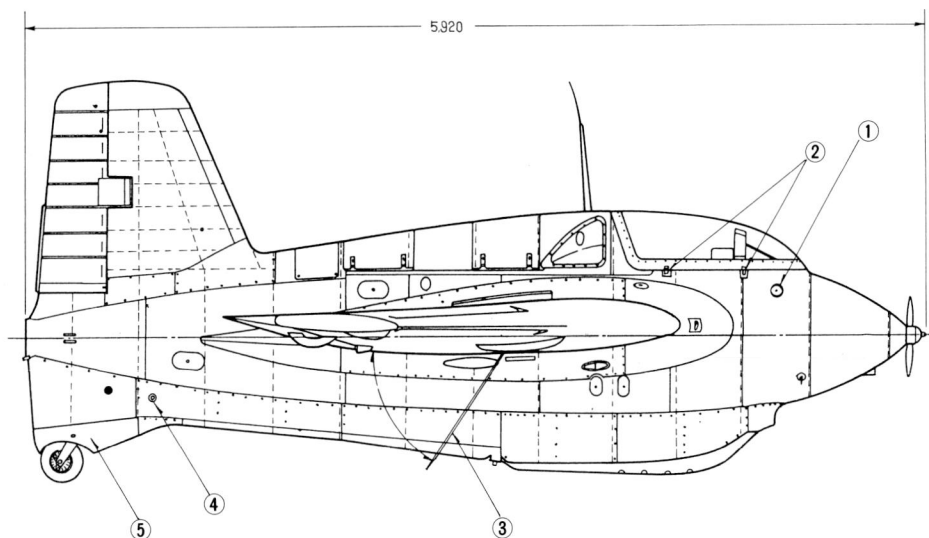

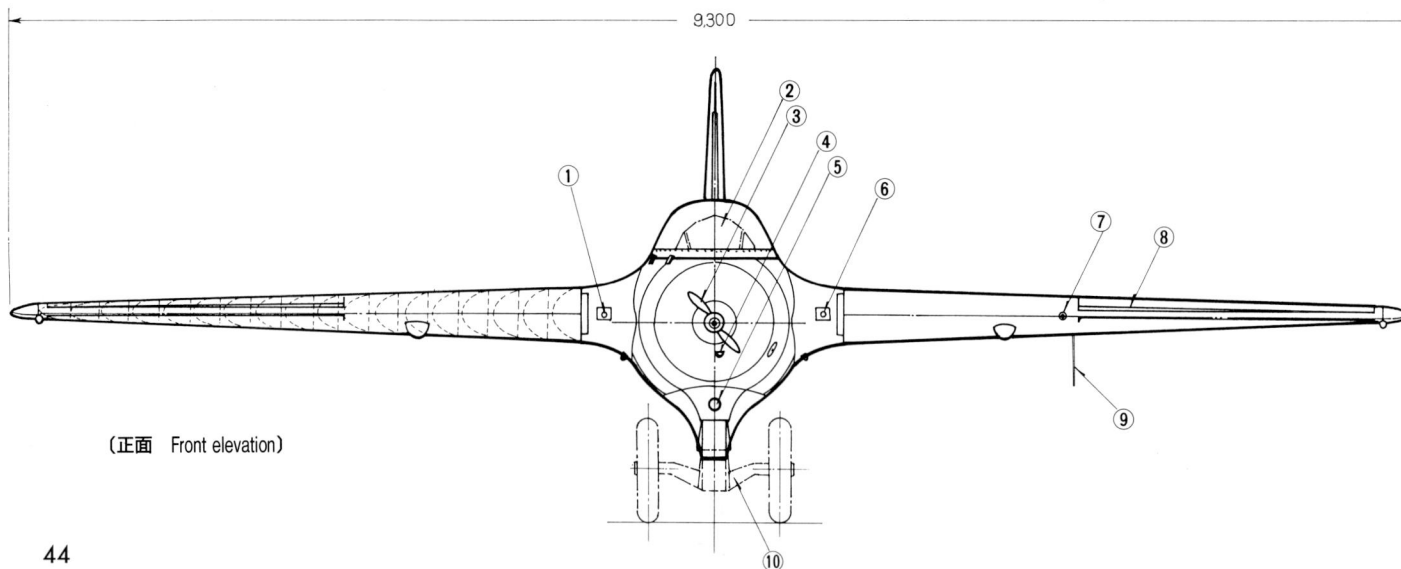

■Me163B-1a

（左側面 Port elevation）

① 発電機駆動用プロペラ
　Propeller to drive generator
② 15mm厚装甲ノーズキャップ
　Armored nose cap (15mm thick)
③ MK108 30mm機関砲（弾数60発）
　MK108 30mm machine cannon (60 rounds)
④ 90mm厚防弾ガラス
　90mm bulletproof glass
⑤ 後方視認窓
　Rear observation window
⑥ FuG16ZE無線器用アンテナ支柱
　FuG16ZE radio antenna mount
⑦ 弾倉ハッチ
　Magazine hatch
⑧ 一部の機体はD/Fループアンテナを追加装備
　Some examples had D/F loop antenna installed
⑨ C液補給、ロケット・モーター点検ハッチ
　C-Stoff fuel fill and rocket motor inspection hatch
⑩ 方向舵操作桿フェアリング
　Rudder control rod fairing
⑪ 方向舵ホーン・バランス
　Rudder horn balance
⑫ 羽布張り方向舵
　Fabric-covered rudder

⑬ 圧搾空気補給口
　Compressed air supply port
⑭ 着陸用スキッド
　Landing skid
⑮ 700×175mm低圧タイヤ
　700×175mm low-pressure tires
⑯ FuG25a IFF用ロッド・アンテナ
　Rod antenna for FuG 25a IFF
⑰ 260×85mmタイヤ
　260×85mm tire
⑱ 実用機の多くは尾輪カバーを撤去
　Many planes in actual service had rear wheel cover removed

（右側面 Starboard elevation）

① 外部電源接続口
　External power supply socket
② キャノピー開閉ヒンジ
　Canopy hinge
③ フラップ最大開度45°
　Maximum flap angle 45°
④ リフト・バー差し込み口
　Lift bar attachment opening
⑤ タイヤ被覆部を切り取った尾輪カバー
　Rear wheel cover with tire protection portion removed

（正面 Front elevation）

① MK108 30mm機関砲発射口
　MK108 30mm machine cannon muzzle port
② 90mm厚防弾ガラス
　90mm bulletproof glass
③ 発電機駆動用プロペラ
　Propeller to drive generator
④ エア・スクープ
　Air scoop
⑤ 曳航索連結部
　Towing couple
⑥ MK108 30mm機関砲発射口
　MK108 30mm machine cannon muzzle port
⑦ ピトー管
　Pitot tube
⑧ 前縁固定スラット
　Fixed leading edge slats
⑨ FuG25a IFF用ロッド・アンテナ
　FuG25a IFF rod antenna
⑩ 離着陸ドリー
　Take-off dolly

（正面 Front elevation）

（上面　Top view）

（上面　Top view）

①MK108機関砲用弾倉の搭載位置
　　Location of magazines for MK108 machine cannons
②MK108 30mm機関砲発射口
　　Muzzle port of MK108 machine cannon
③T液注入口ハッチ
　　T-Stoff fuel fill hatch
④コクピット内空気取り入れ口
　　Cockpit air intake
⑤FuG16ZE無線器用アンテナ支柱
　　Mount for FuG16ZE radio antenna
⑥MK108 30mm機関砲発射口
　　Muzzle port of MK108 machine cannon
⑦酸素補給口
　　Oxygen supply port
⑧MK108点検ハッチ
　　MK108 inspection hatch
⑨C液タンクの積載位置
　　Location of C-Stoff tank
⑩トリム・フラップ操作桿点検ハッチ
　　Trim flap control rod inspection hatch
⑪着陸フラップ操作桿点検ハッチ
　　Landing flap control rod inspection hatch
⑫補助翼操作桿点検ハッチ
　　Elevon control rod inspection hatch
⑬MK108用圧搾空気補給口ハッチ
　　Oxygen supply port for MK108s
⑭ロケット・モーター点検ハッチ
　　Rocket motor inspection hatch
⑮方向舵作動角
　　Range of motion of rudder
⑯始動用T液注入口ハッチ
　　Engine start-use T-Stoff fuel fill
⑰ロケット・モーター点検パネル
　　Rocket motor inspection hatch
⑱蒸気発生器点検パネル
　　Steam generator inspection hatch

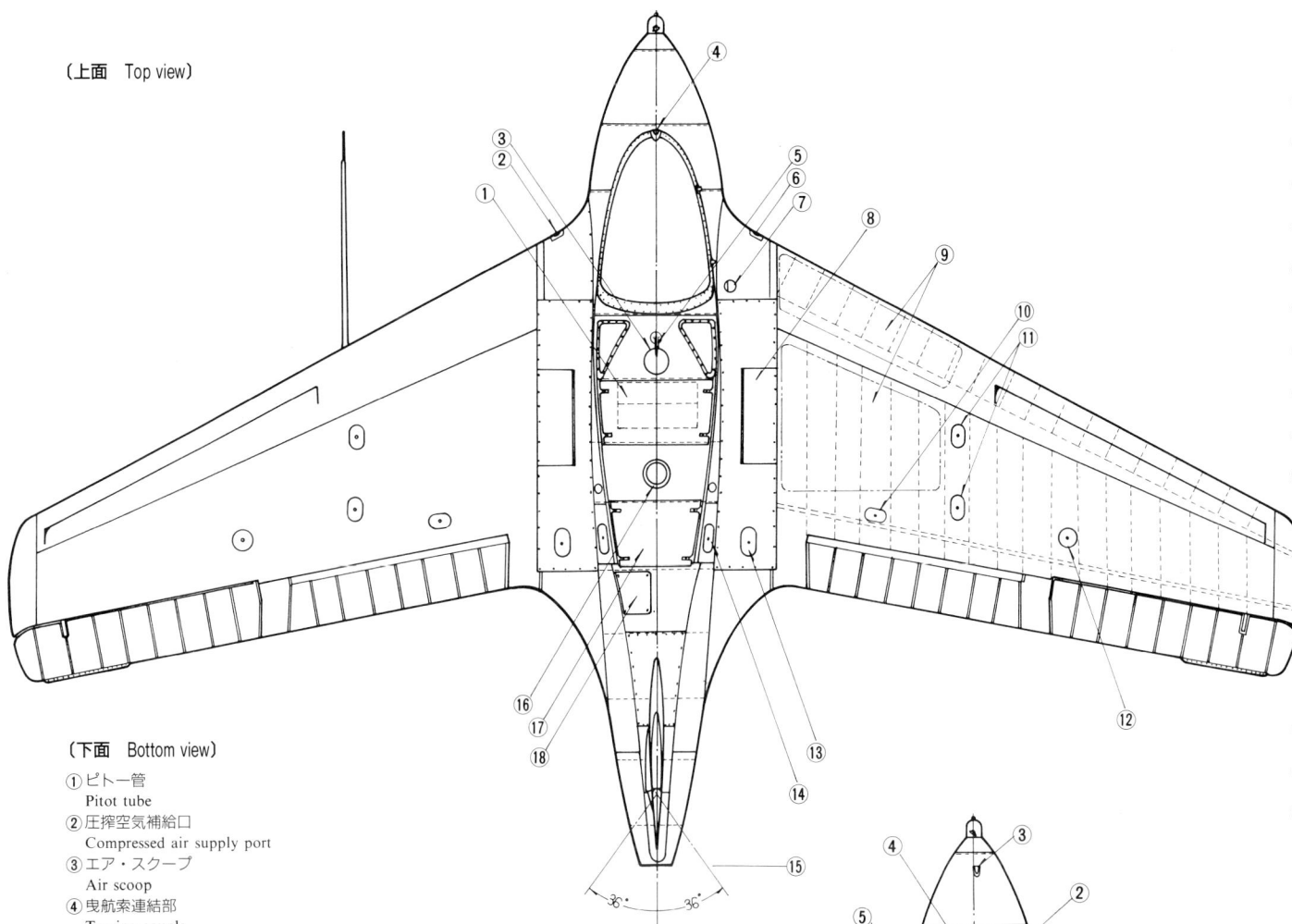

（下面　Bottom view）

①ピトー管
　　Pitot tube
②圧搾空気補給口
　　Compressed air supply port
③エア・スクープ
　　Air scoop
④曳航索連結部
　　Towing couple
⑤着陸用スキッド
　　Landing skid
⑥エア・スクープ
　　Air scoop
⑦MK108 30mm砲弾空薬莢排出口
　　Spent cartridge ejection port for
　　MK108 30mm machine cnnon
⑧MK108点検パネル
　　MK108 inspection panel
⑨主桁
　　Main spar
⑩C液用パイプ・カバー
　　C-Stoff pipe cover
⑪着陸フラップ
　　Landing Flaps
⑫補助翼操作桿点検ハッチ
　　Elevon control rod inspection
⑬前縁固定スラット
　　Fixed leading edge slats
⑭翼端保護用スキッド
　　Wingtip protection skids
⑮固定トリム・タブ
　　Fixed trim tabs
⑯補助桁
　　Support spar
⑰補助翼操作桿カバー
　　Elevon control rod cover
⑱トリム・フラップ
　　Trim flaps
⑲羽布張り内空気抜き用穴
　　Fabric-covered internal air release port
⑳トリム・フラップ操作桿カバー
　　Trim flap control rod cover

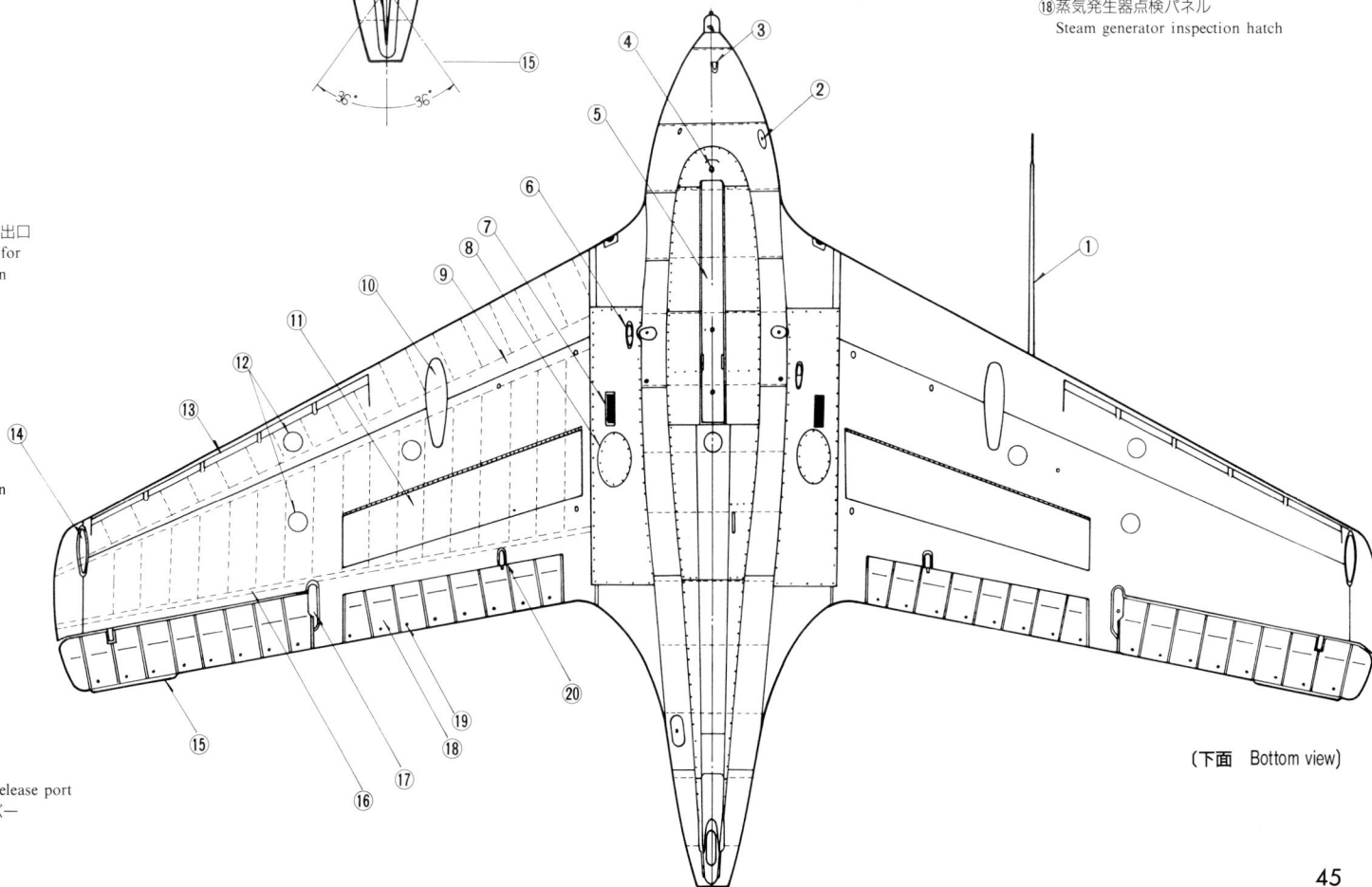

（下面　Bottom view）

36°　36°

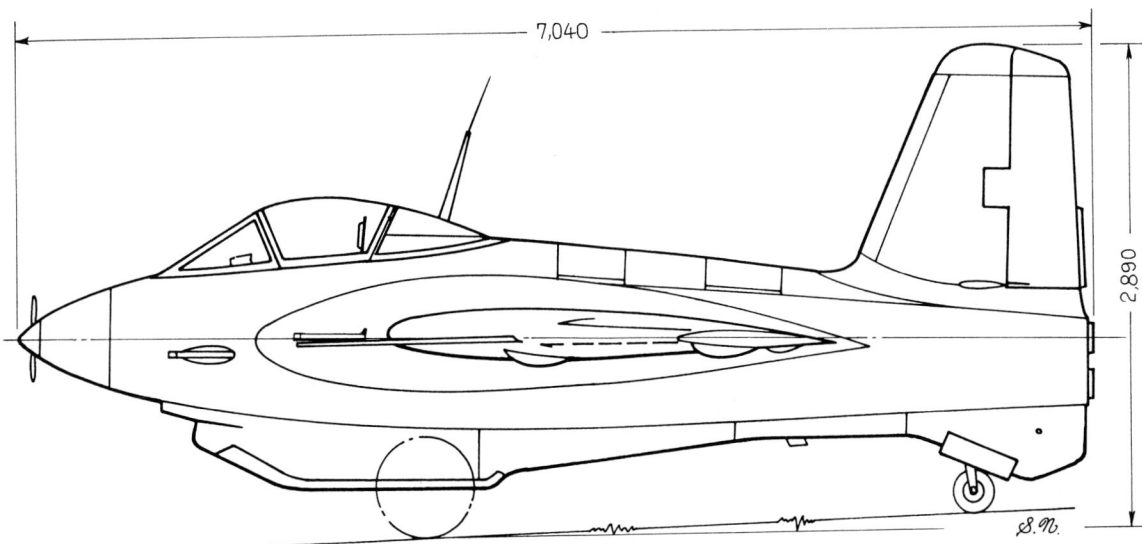

7,040

2,890

（左側面　Port elevation）

■Me163c

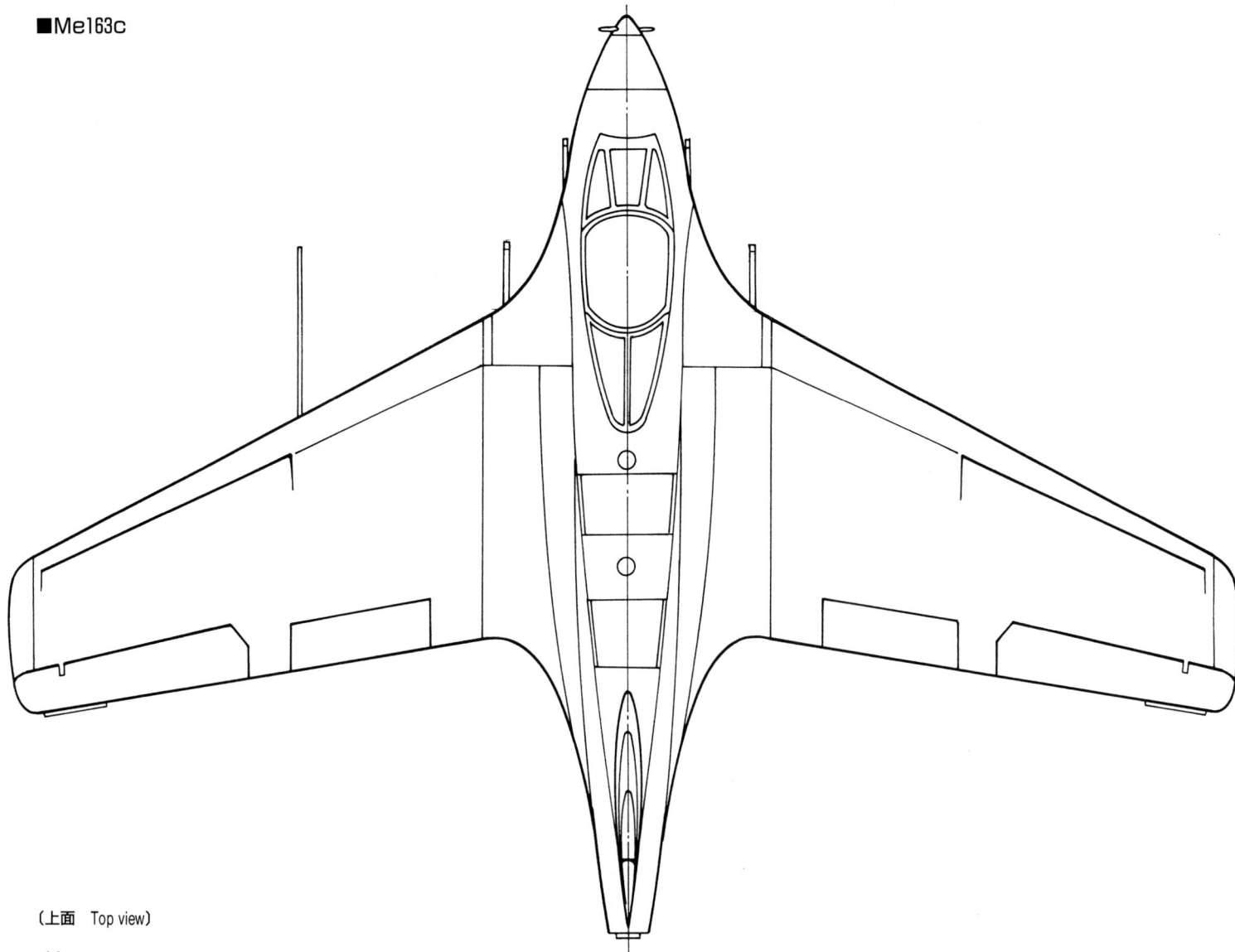

（上面　Top view）

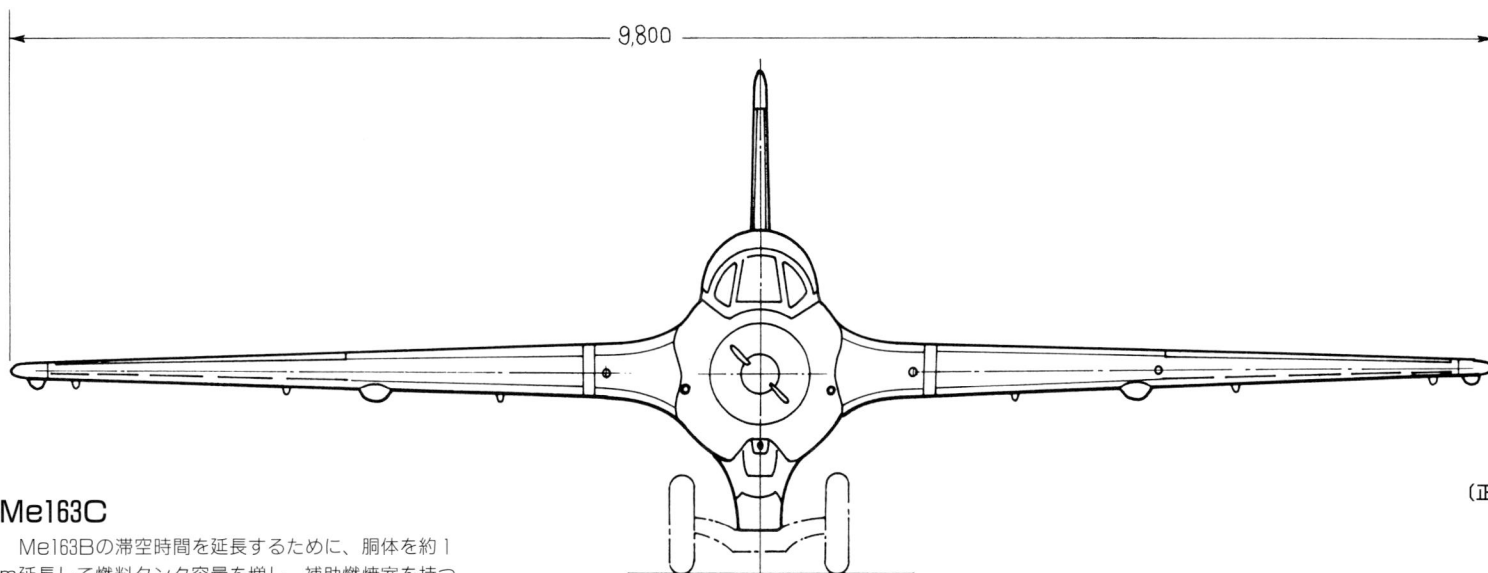

9,800

Me163C

　Me163Bの滞空時間を延長するために、胴体を約1m延長して燃料タンク容量を増し、補助燃焼室を持つHWK109-509Cロケット・モーターを搭載、主翼幅を50cm大きくして、キャノピーも水滴状に変更、武装をMK108 4門に強化するなど実用面の向上を図って計画されたのがMe163Cである。

　これによって、ロケット・モーターの作動時間は12分（Me163Bは約8分）に伸びたが、並行して開発が進められていたMe163D（Me263）のほうが有望視されたため、Me163Cは、1944年夏までに試作機3機が造られただけで終った。

The Me163C made a number of modifications to the B-series with the main goal being to extend the aircraft's maximum time aloft. Among these changes were lengthening the fuselage by one meter in order to allow larger fuel tanks, installing the HWK 109-509C rocket motor, with its auxiliary combustion chamber, widening the wings by 50cm, and installation of a teardrop canopy. In addition, the aircraft's armament was boosted again, to four MK108 30mm cannons.

As a result, the aircraft's maximum time aloft was boosted from eight minutes to 12, but as the performance prospects for the Me163D (later the Me263), which was being developed simultaneously, were considered even better, the series ended with the production of just three prototypes during the summer of 1944.

Me263（Ju248）

　Me163Cと同様、運用上の大きなネックとなっていた滞空時間の短かさ、地上における自力移動能力のなさなど、根本的な問題を解消するために計画されたMe163Dは、1944年5月に原型機が完成した。しかし、この頃のメッサーシュミット社はMe262の開発、生産に手一杯の状況にあり、本機を量産化するほどの余裕はなかった。

　そこで、空軍は本機の開発権を全面的にユンカース社に移し、Ju248と改名することにした。同社では、さらに胴体を真円断面にして延長、コクピットの与圧化、油圧引き込み式の主脚、前脚を改修するなどの手を加え、1944年8月に1号機を完成させた。

　テストの結果、Ju248のモーター作動時間は15分に延び、実用面の向上も明白に認められた。1944年12月23日の会議において、空軍は本機をMe263（メッサーシュミット社の面子を立てるため）の制式名で、緊急大量生産することに決定したが、敗戦までに量産型は1機も完成しなかった。

The Me263 was developed to address the fundamental problems which had plagued the Komet series, specifically its short eight-minute flight time and its inability to move on the ground under its own power. Messerschmitt completed the prototype in May of 1944, but given the demands of the company's full-scale production of the Me262 which was taking place at that time, the company had no resources left to apply to production of the Me263.

As such, the Luftwaffe transferred production rights for the plane to Junkers, renaming the plane the Ju248. Their engineers made further changes to the plane, including rounding and lengthening the fuselage, installing a pressurized cockpit and retractable main gear, and modifying the nose gear, and finished the first pre-production model in August of 1944.

Tests showed the Ju248 to have a maximum flight time of 15 minutes, a vast improvement over its predecessors. At a meeting on December 23, 1944, the Luftwaffe ordered the plane into immediate full production, and decided to formally name it the Me263 (in order to avoid overly damaging Messerschmitt's pride). Nevertheless, Germany surrendered before any production models could be completed.

7,880

3,170

■Me263（Ju248）

①発電機駆動用プロペラ（3翅）
　Propeller to drive generator (3 blades)
②90mm厚防弾ガラス
　90mm bulletproof glass
③与圧式キャビン
　Pressurized cockpit
④MK108 30mm機関砲（弾数40発）
　MK108 30mm machine cannon (40 rounds)
⑤油圧操作引き込み式前脚
　Retractable nose wheel (hydraulically operated)
⑥油圧操作引き込み式主脚
　Retractable main gear (hydraulically operated)
⑦副燃焼管付きヴァルターHWK109-509C
　ロケット・モーター
　Walter HWK 109-509C rocket motor
　(with auxiliary combustion chamber)

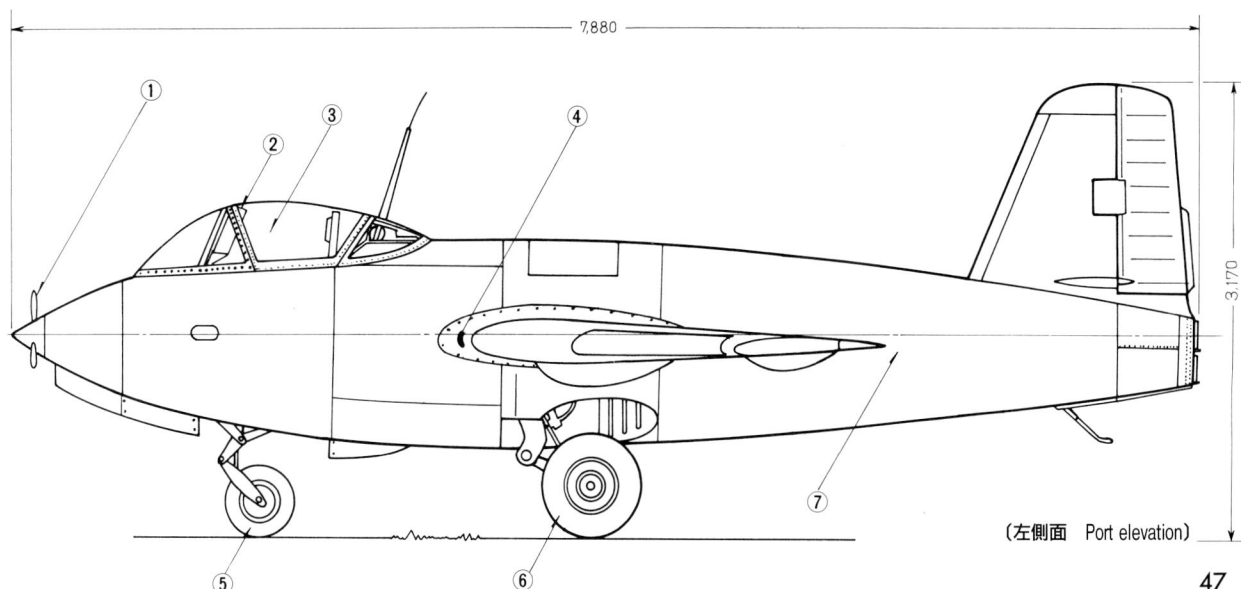

（左側面　Port elevation）

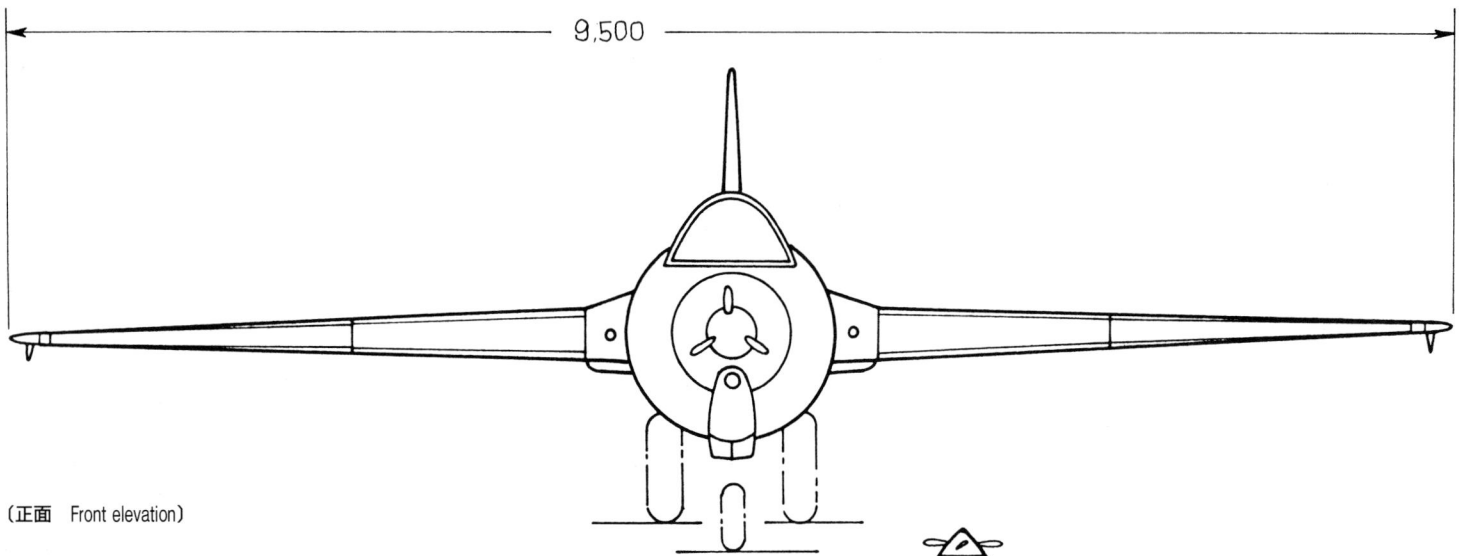

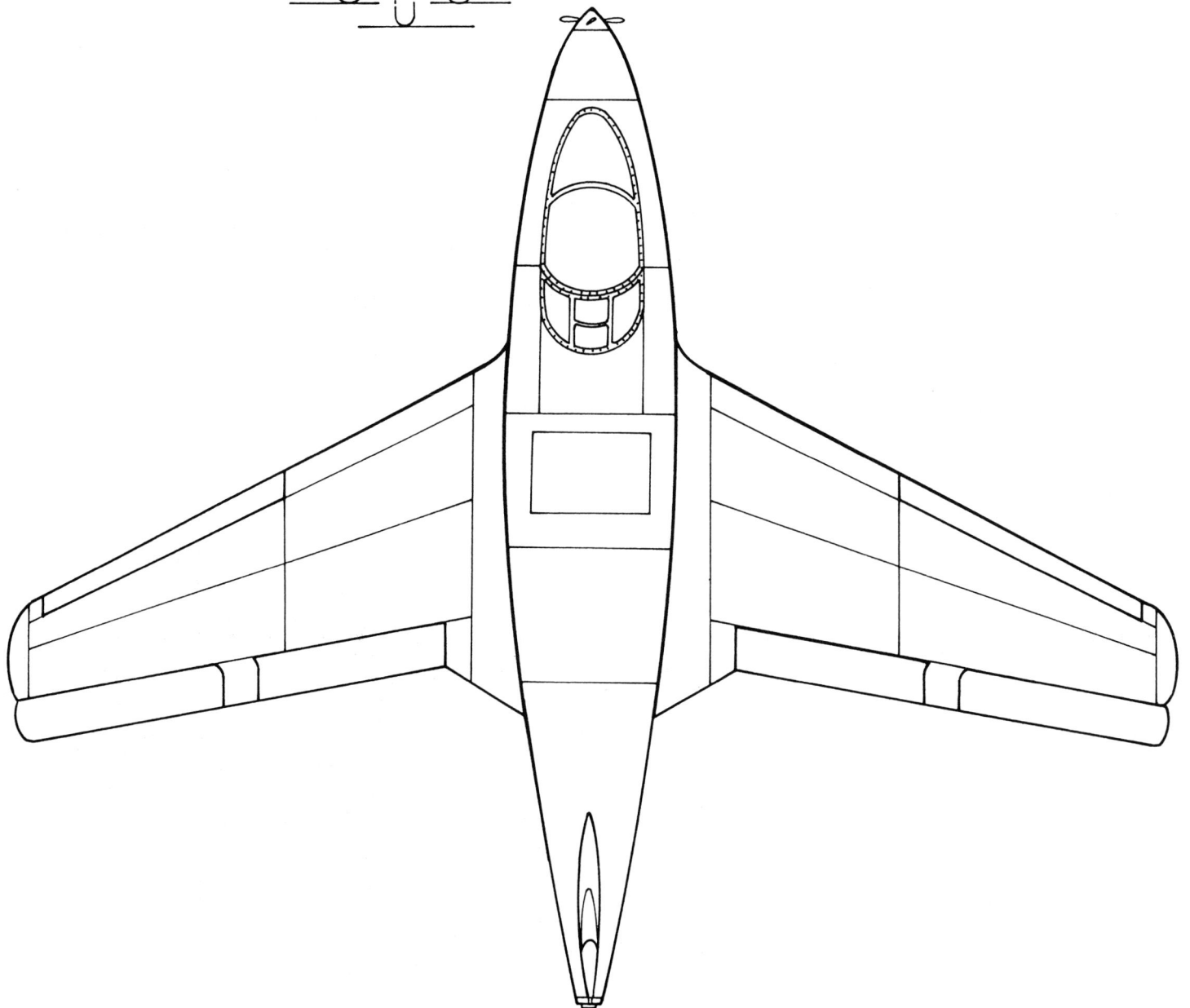

9,500

（正面　Front elevation）

（上面　Top view）

ドイツ空軍国民戦闘機"フォルクスイェーガー" ハインケルHe162A-2"ザラマンダー"

解説／野原 茂

アメリカ陸軍航空隊戦爆連合編隊による情容赦のない猛空襲により、第3帝国の命運も尽きようとしていた1944年9月、ドイツ空軍省は革命機Me262ジェット戦闘機の大量生産を促す一方、BMW003ジェット・エンジン1基を搭載する、より簡易な小型の迎撃戦闘機、いわゆる"Volksjäger"（国民戦闘機）の開発を提示し、絶望の中に一条の光明を見い出そうとした。

『緊急軽量戦闘機計画』と呼ばれた本計画は、戦略物資（アルミ合金）の使用を極力抑さえ、簡素な設計にして、初心者でも容易に乗りこなすことのできる、安定した操縦性を有することが肝要だった。それでいて性能は最高速度750km/h以上、航続時間30分以上が要求され、5日以内に設計案を提出し、短期間のうちに急速大量生産に入れることという、きわめて現実離れした側面を持っていた。

Me262の量産に手一杯のメッサーシュミット社は、とても実現不可能と判断して棄権したが、アラド、ブローム・ウント・フォス、フォッケウルフ、ハインケル、ユンカース、フィーゼラー、ジーベルの7社が応募し、9月15日に設計案審査が行われ、その結果ハインケル社のP.1073案が採用されて、開発契約が交わされた。

P.1073案は、すでに2か月前からハインケル社が自主的に開発を進めていただけに、設計作業はスピーディに進み、2か月後の11月には完了し、並行して機体の組み立ても行われていたため、12月6日には1号機が初飛行にこぎつけるという、驚くべき早さだった。

ハインケルは、本機にHe500の名を冠したかったが、これは認められず、空軍はHe162"Spatz"（すずめ）と命名した。常識的にエンジンを胴体内に収容すると、空力上の処理、艤装面で設計に長時間を要するため、胴体背部にナセルごと載せるという、最も手っとり早く、かつあまり例のない配置とし、必然的に双垂直尾翼となった。

胴体は鋼製骨組みにジュラルミン外皮、主翼は左右一体に作られ、骨組み、外皮とも木製した。排気の影響を受けるため水平尾翼のみは骨組み、外皮ともにジュラルミン製。14°の上反角がついているのが特徴。垂直尾翼は木製だが、方向舵は強度を維持するためジュラルミン製である。

コクピット直後にエンジン吸気口が位置するため、脱出時のパイロットの安全を考慮して、火薬式の射出座席を導入した点が極めて斬新ではあった。

開発期間短縮のため、主脚はBf109Kのそれを流用している。

しかし、簡素な設計は確かだったが、やはり短期開発のツケがまわり、本機の操縦は極めて難しく、とりわけ離着陸時のコツをマスターするには相当の技倆を要するという、皮肉な結果になった。

もっとも、速度、航続距離などは要求を満たしていたので、直ちに大量生産が命じられ、ハインケル社はもとより、ユンカース社、ミッテルヴェルケ社および全国の木工家具工場までを動員してのフル生産態勢が敷かれた。

そして、1945年1月中旬にはハインケル社ロストック、ヒンターブリュール工場から相次いで生産機がロールアウトし、空軍は直ちに既存の戦闘航空団から選抜してHe162への機種改変に着手させた。

最初のHe162部隊となったのは、Fw190を使用していたJG1で、ヘルベルト・イーレフェルト大佐指揮のもと、第I飛行隊が2月12日からパルヒム基地において転換訓練に入った。

幸い、I./JG1はパイロットのレベルが高かったこともあり、わずか1か月半の訓練でHe162をマスターし、3月31日にはデンマーク国境に近いレック基地に展開して実戦配置についた。

しかし、燃料事情などもあって飛行隊が全力出動できる状況にはなく、少数機ずつパトロールのような形で出撃するのが精一杯だった。その結果、連合軍レシプロ戦闘機、爆撃機を断然圧倒する高速（830km/h）を持ちながら、敗戦までの結果は2機撃墜にとどまった。

I./JG1に続き、II./JG1が4月上旬にハインケル社工場のあるロストックに移ってHe162への転換訓練を行い、敗戦4日前の5月4日にレック基地に合流してきたが、実戦出撃するまでには至らず、その後に続くはずだったIII./JG1、1./JG400の改変は実現しなかった。

敗戦までに、ハインケル社は各工場あわせて200機程度、ユンカース社は約30機、ミッテルヴェルケ社は18機以上のHe162を完成させており、さらに地下工場などでは約800機が製作途中だったが、すべては無に帰した。

He162は、いわば戦争という非常時が生み出した機体である。その設計には無理なところもあったが、3か月で完成させるには、あのような形を採らざるを得ない。むしろ量産態勢まで持っていけたことが驚異である。

同じジェット戦闘機でも、Me262とはまるで次元の異なる機体であるが、He162も別な意味でドイツ航空工業の一面を象徴する機体だったと言えよう。

(He162A-2 データ Data)

全幅　Width：7.20m
全長　Length：9.05m
全高　Height：2.60m
主翼面積　Wing area：11.16㎡
自重　Empty weight：2,338kg
全備重量　Loaded weight：2,805kg
エンジン　Powerplant：BMW003E×1
推力　Thrust：800kg
最大速度　Max speed：838km/h
着陸速度　Landing speed：165km/h
実用上昇限度　Service ceiling：12,000m
航続距離　Range：620km
武装　Armament：MG151/20×2
乗員　Crew：1

He162A-2 W.Nr120235

写真/野原 茂、塩飽昌嗣
Photos by Shigeru Nohara,
Masatsugu Shiwaku

インペリアル戦争博物館ランベス

IMPERIAL WAR MUSEUM-LAMBETH

住所　Address : Lambeth Road, London, SE1 6HZ, U. K.
TEL：01-735-8922
開館時間　Admission hours：月～土　10:00～17:50、日　14:00～17:50　From Mon. to Sat. 10:00～17:50,
Sun. 14:00～17:50　Closed Bank Holidays

本機は、JG 1 第 3 中隊に属していた機で、機番号は黄の〝6〟を記入していた。RAEの管轄下で飛行テストを受け、その後はブライズ・ノートン基地の第 6 整備隊によって保存されてきた。1960年代にI.W.M.に移管され、ロンドン市内の本館とダックスフォード基地の別館を交互に移動して展示されていた。1990年11月取材した折には本館にあった。

天井からの吊り下げ式による展示のため、コクピット内部等の状態はわからないが、Revi16Bは付いておらず、計器類の欠落もあると思われる。

以前は、降着装置を下げた状態で吊るしていたが、現在は収納状態となっている。

残念なことに、本機の塗装、マーキングはオリジナルにはほど遠く、単に機番号〝6〟が合ってるだけで、塗装の参考にはならない。表面にやけに光沢があり、グリーンの色調も黄緑が強くて実感を損ねている。いずれ、この辺も含めてしっかりした復元が行われることを期待したい。

This plane (number"6"in yellow) was originally assigned to 3./JG 1. Following testing by the RAE following the war, it was transferred to Braise Norton Air Base and stored. The aircraft was donated to the Imperial War Museum in the 1960s, and since then has been displayed alternately between the main museum in London (Lambeth) and the auxiliary museum in Duxford. This picture was taken at the London museum in November of 1990.

Since the plane is hung from the ceiling, the exact condition of the cockpit cannot be confirmed, but it is definitely missing its Revi 16B gunsight, and much of the other instrumentation is thought to be gone as well.

Previously, the plane was displayed with its landing gear down. For some reason, the gear are now in the up position, making examination of the interior of the bays and fuselage impossible.

Unfortunately, with the exception of the aircraft number ("6"), the plane's markings are not original, and the colors used, though similar, are clearly different from actual Luftwaffe standards.

He162A-2 W.Nr120227

写真／野原 茂
Photos by Shigeru Nohara

イギリス空軍博物館

ROYAL AIR FORCE MUSEUM

住所 Address：Hendon, London, NW9 5LL, U.K
TEL：01-205-2266
開館時間 Admission hours：月〜土 10:00〜18:00, 日 14:00〜18:00 From Mon. to Sat. 10:00〜18:00,
Sun. 14:00〜18:00 Closed Bank Holidays

　レック基地で捕獲され、イギリス本土に運ばれた11機のHe162A-2のうちの1機。JG1の第2中隊に属し、赤の機番号 "2" を付けていた。RAEの管轄下に計26回のべ11時間45分の飛行テストを受けたのち、各基地を転々としながら保存、展示され、1976年にセント・アサン基地において、内部、塗装を含めてオリジナルに近い程度に復元された。その後、RAFヘンドンの空軍博物館に移管され、現在に至っている。

　I.W.M.のW.Nr120235に比較すれば良いほうだが、塗装、マーキングの考証がいまひとつ不正確で、とくに機首先端の赤／白／黒帯、エンジン・ナセル先端の赤塗装はオリジナルにはない。
　コクピット内部は、計器類の多くが失なわれてしまっており、代わりに複製品で代用している。Revi16B照準器も付いていない。

Confiscated at Leck air base and then shipped to the U.K. along with 10 other He162s, this Salamander was originally used by 2./JG 1 and assigned aircraft number "2" in red. The plane was tested by the RAE 26 times for a total flight time of 11 hours and 45 minutes. It was then displayed at numerous U.K. air bases over a period of several years until 1976, when it was completely refurbished inside and out at the St. Athan air base, restoring it to near-original condition. Following this effort, it was transferred to the RAF's Museum in Hendon, where it has been displayed ever since.

The restoration of the aircraft's markings is slightly inaccurate. In particular, the red, white and black markings on the nose, as well as the red marking on the engine nacelle were not present on the original. Most of the original cockpit instrumentation is missing, with replicas installed instead.

He162A-2 W.Nr120230

写真／野原 茂
Photos by Shigeru Nohara

アメリカ国立航空宇宙博物館　ポール・ガーバー保管施設

NATIONAL AIR AND SPACE MUSEUM PAUL. E. GAHBAR PRESERVATION FACILITY

住所 Address：Suitland MD 20746, U.S.A
TEL：202-357-1552
開館日時 Admission：見学は予約確認が必要 By appointment only

　レック基地に進駐してきた連合軍にとって、本機はひと際目立った存在だったに違いない。機首先端に記入された黒／白／赤の第3帝国カラー帯が、指揮官機を示していたからだ。本機こそ、He162を装備した唯一の航空団JG1の司令官ヘルベルト・イーレフェルト大佐（撃墜数132機）乗機だった。

　アメリカ軍の割譲機に入れられた本機は、本国へ送られたのち、他の3機ともどもフリーマン・フィールド基地にて調査、テストされ、その後オハイオ州ライト・フィールド基地に移された。今日、唯一のカラー写真として残るのは、このときに撮られたもの。

　現在は、NASMが保管しており、ポール・ガーバー施設内にて、復元を待って限定展示中。照準器など一部の部品は欠落したままだが、色褪せたとはいえ、オリジナル塗装を維持しているのは貴重。

　なお、本機に付いている垂直尾翼は、本国に輸送中、もしくはテスト中に損傷したためか、W.Nr120222のものと取り替えられており、オリジナルではない。

For the advancing Allied forces taking over Leck air base, this aircraft no doubt stood out from the rest. The black, red and white colors of the Third Reich on the plane's nose indicated the personal aircraft of a commander. This was the actual plane flown by super-ace Obst. Herbert Ihlefeld (132 victories), the *Kommodore* of JG 1, the only unit to use the He162.

The plane was shipped to the U.S. with three other He162s and tested at Freeman Field. Following testing, it was transferred to Wright Field in Ohio. The only existing color photograph of the plane from this period was taken there.

At present, the plane is on limited display and awaiting full restoration at the Paul E. Gahbar Preservation Facility in Silver Hill, Maryland, an arm of the National Air and Space Museum.

While this He162 is missing a few parts, including the gunsight, it is an extremely rare and valuable example of a Salamander in its original colors and markings.

The vertical stabilizers of this plane were damaged either during shipment to the United States, or during flight testing, and have been replaced with those from W.Nr 120222.

51

He162A-2 W.Nr120077

写真／塩飽智彦、紅谷 彰
Photos by Tomohiko Shiwaku,
Akira Beniya

プレーンズ・オブ・フェイム

PLANES OF FAME

住所　Address : Chino Airport, 7000 Merrill Ave. Chino, CA 91710, U.S.A
TEL : 714-597-3722
開館時間　Admission hours : 9:00〜17:00 (daily)

　アメリカ本国に輸送された４機のHe162のうちの１機で、"T2-489" の登録記号を附与され、インディアナ州フリーマン・フィールド、およびカリフォルニア州エドワーズ基地において調査、テストを受けた。その後、基地のオープン・ハウスなどに展示されるなどして各地を転々としたあと、1960年代初め頃に私設航空博物館主エド・マロニー氏に払い下げられた。

　1970年代に経営が悪化し、一時ムービィ・ワールド博物館に転売されたが、その後買い戻して現在は、カリフォルニア州チノ空港に隣接してオープンして

いる "プレーンズ・オブ・フェイム" に展示中。

　本機は、ずっと長い間各国籍標識、尾翼のW.Nrを除いてオリジナル塗装を維持していたが、1980年代に塗り替えられてしまった。機首に描かれた、旧Ⅲ./JG77の飛行隊章（2./JG1の中隊章になっていたとも言われる）、および同左側のパーソナル文字 "Nervenklau"（神経質な盗賊──気難しいジェット・エンジンにひっかけたスラングで、He162のことを指す）は、もとからあった。

　機体コンディションは良好で、コクピット内部のオリジナル度も高い。

Another of the four He162s brought to the United States from Leck, this one was assigned number "T2-489" and tested extensively at Freeman Field in Indiana and Edwards Air Force Base in California. Following testing, the plane was displayed at various bases during open houses and such over a number of years. In the early 1960s, the plane was purchased by Mr. Ed Maloney, who was establishing a private warplane museum.

The plane was sold to the Movie World museum in the 1970s during a financially difficult period for Mr. Maloney's *Planes of Fame* museum, but was eventually repurchased. It is now on public display at the museum, near the airport in Chino, California.

This He162 kept its original markings and coloring scheme for an extended period, but was eventually repainted in the 1980s. The wolf's head emblem of III./JG 77 on the nose (also apparently used by 2./JG 1 just before Germany's surrender) as well as the personal inscription on the left side, *Nervenklau*, ("Nervous Thief" — a term used to describe an uncooperative jet engine and hence, slang for the He162) are said to be original.

Overall, both the fuselage and cockpit of this Salamander are in very good to near-original condition.

He162A-2 W.Nr120223

写真／石戸 宏
Photos by Hiroshi Ishido

フランス航空宇宙博物館

MUSEE DE l'AIR ET DE l'ESPACE

住所　Address : 93350 Le Bourget, France
TEL : 1-838-9111
開館時間　Admission hours : 月〜金 10:00〜18:00、土・日 10:00〜12:00 14:00〜18:00 From Mon. to Fri. 10:00〜18:00, Sat. and Sun. 10:00〜12:00　14:00〜18:00

　アメリカ、イギリス軍に付いてドイツ本土に侵攻してきたフランスも、レック基地のHe162の接収には、しっかりと権利を主張し、7機も本国へ運び込んだ。その後の調査、テストの概要は不明だが、大部分は機体構造を調査しただけでスクラップ処分され、現在パリのル・ブールジュ空港に隣接する航空宇宙博物館に保存、展示中のW.Nr120223が残るのみ。

　フランスに運び込んだ直後に、オリジナル塗装は

すべて落とされてしまったために、機番号やエンブレムの有無、色などは不明で、現在の塗装はオリジナル塗装と全く異なっている。

　コクピット内部の状態などはよくわからないが、欠落している部品が多いようだ。ただ、全体のコンディションはそう悪くない。上記塗装も含めて、一度しっかりした復元を行うべきであろう。

Along with the Americans and British, the French also took part in the seizure of Leck airfield, and they too made sure to lay claim to some of the He162s at the base, shipping no less than seven Salamanders back to France. The details of the testing program are unknown, but following modification, the planes are believed to have been scrapped. The sole exception is W.Nr 120223, which is displayed at the *Musee de l'Air et de l'Espace* adjacent to Le Bourget airport.

As the plane was entirely repainted shortly after its shipment to France, its original colors and markings are a complete mystery. Nevertheless, its current paint scheme is not thought to bear any resemblance to the original.

Details on the condition of the cockpit are unknown, but many parts appear to be missing. Overall, the plane's condition is not too bad, however.

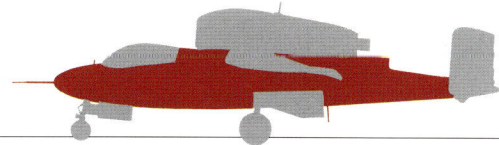

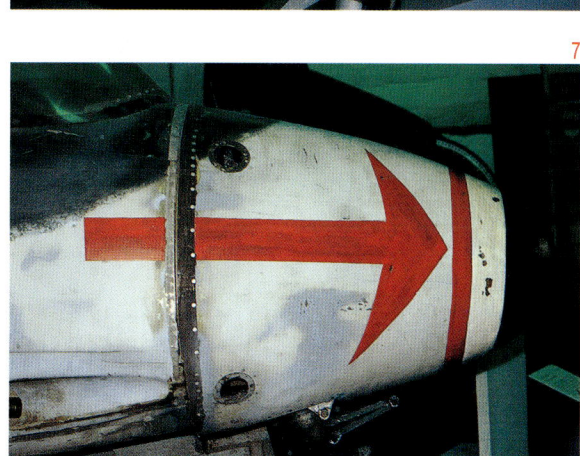

写真1～5：He162A-2の機首部。写真1はフランス
航空宇宙博物館、写真2～4はインペリアル戦争博物館、
写真5はプレーンズ・オブ・フェイムのHe162A-2。
写真6～7：He162のノーズ・コーン。プレーンズ・オ
ブ・フェイムの機体（写真6）は機首先端のピトー管が、
米航空宇宙博物館の機体（写真7）はノーズ・コーン後
方上下にある取り付けボルトのカバーが欠損している。

Photo 1-5: The nose section of the He162 A-2. Photo 1 is
the Salamander in the Musee de l'Air et de l'Espace. Photos 2-4 are of the plane in the Imperial War Museum. Photo
5 is the aircraft displayed in the Planes of Fame Museum.
Photo 6-7: The He162's nose cone. The Planes of Fame
aircraft (photo 6) has lost its nose pitot tube, while the
Smithsonian plane (photo 7) is missing the bolt covers (the
circular openings) from the rear section of the nose cone.

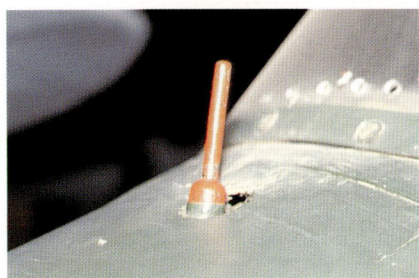

写真8〜9：キャノピー前方の赤い棒は、前脚位置表示棒。脚下げ時は、表示棒が写真のように上方に突き出した状態となる。
写真10：ノーズ・コーン後方にある小パネルは取り付けボルトのカバー。写真7と比較すればわかるように機体によって、このカバーの形状が異なっていることに注目。
写真11：He162A-2の胴体前部左側。
写真12〜14：機首側面下方のMG151/20 20mm機関砲発射口。写真12は右側、写真13、14（MG151/20未装備）は左側の砲口。

Photo 8-9: Close-ups of the position indicator rod for the nose gear. When the nose gear is in the down and locked position, the rod protrudes up in front of the canopy, as shown in the photos.
Photo 10: The bolt cover on the lower-rear portion of the nose cone. Note that the shape of the cover varied slightly from plane to plane (compare this view with photo 7).
Photo 11: The front section of the fuselage of the He162A-2 seen from the left side.
Photo 12-14: Close-ups of the gun ports for the MG151/20 20mm cannon. Photo 12 is from the right side. Photos 13 and 14 are from the left (the cannon is not installed in the plane in these views).

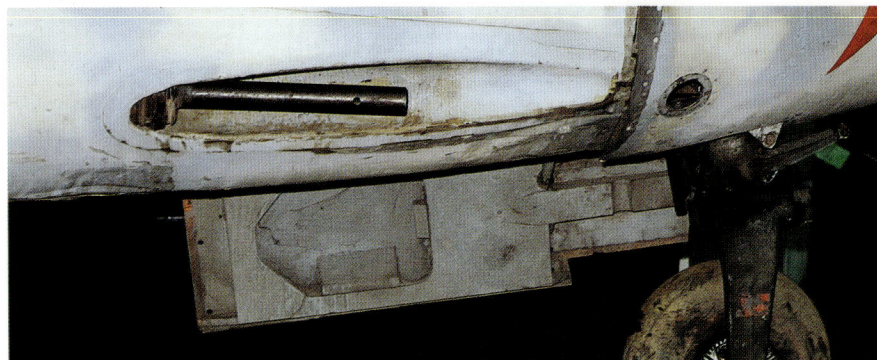
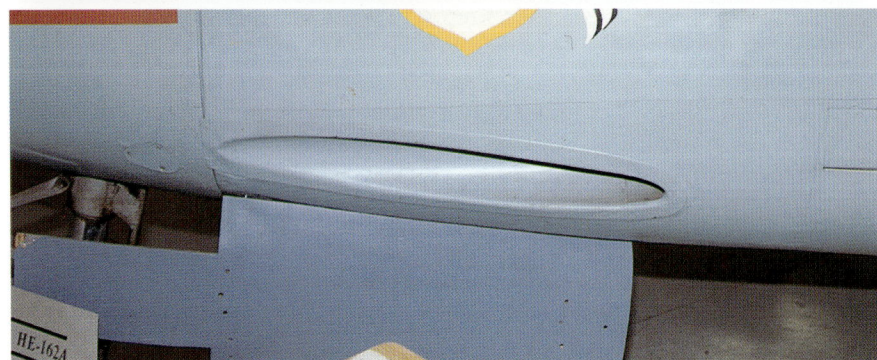

Hier U...

hier Unterbocken   Sauerstoff Anschluss

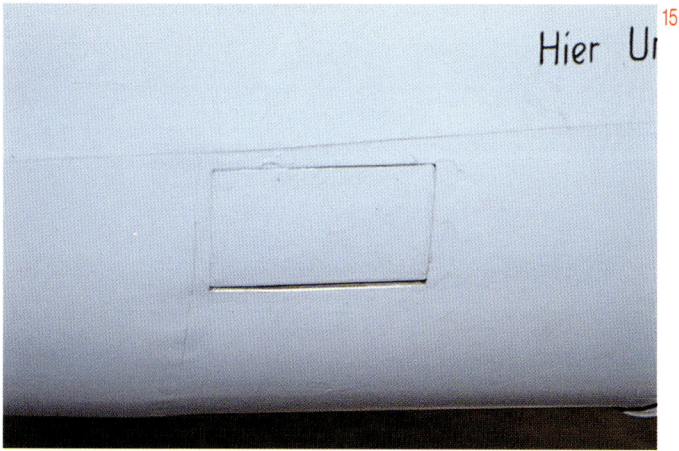

Photo 1, 11／H.Ishido
Photo 2, 19／N.Okazaki
Photo 3, 4, 18／M.Shiwaku
Photo 5, 8〜10, 13〜15, 20, 21／T.Shiwaku
Photo 6, 17／A.Beniya
Photo 7, 12, 16／S.Nohara

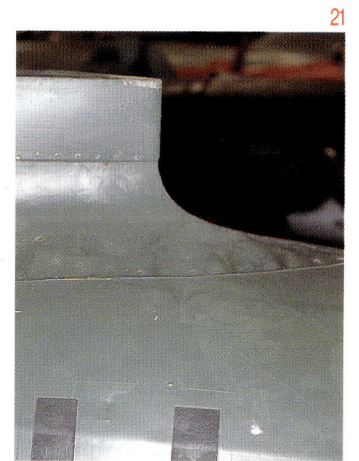

写真15：機首左側のキャノピー下方に設けられた足掛け（長方形の小パネル）。通常は、写真のように外壁と面一だが、つま先で押すと内側に引き込むようになっている。

写真16：前部胴体側面下方に設置された機関砲の着脱／点検ドア。

写真17〜19：胴体左側。

写真20：エンジン・ナセル前部の取り付け部付近（右側）。細長い板とその下方の小さな突起物は、アンテナ空中線の取り付け基部だが、これは、写真のプレーンズ・オブ・フェイムに展示されているHe162のみに見られる。オリジナルなのか、復元時に取り付けられたものかは不明。

写真21：エンジン・ナセル取り付け部の後方。

Photo 15: The footstep on the port side of the fuselage, directly below the canopy (the small, rectangular panel). Normally it is flush with the fuselage as shown in the photo, but when pushed with the toe, it folds into the fuselage.

Photo 16: A view of the inspection and maintenance hatch for the plane's cannons, located on bottom of the fuselage, just aft of the cockpit.

Photo 17-19: Views of the port side of the Salamander.

Photo 20: A close-up of the front edge of the engine mount. The paddle-shaped object jutting out from the base of the mount, as well as the small cone-shaped object below it are mounts for the radio's wire antenna. However, these fittings are only present on the He162 displayed at the Planes of Fame Museum, so it is not known if they are original, or were added when the plane was restored.

Photo 21: The rear portion of the engine mount.

写真22〜25：He162A-2のキャノピー。
写真26：前部固定キャノピー。キャノピー正面下部に見える複数の小さな穴は、コクピット内空気取り入れ口。
写真27〜30：コクピット前部。主計器板を覆う装甲板、その前方に取り付けられた方向舵ペダルの取り付け基部（三本の板状のもの）が見える。残念ながら、装甲板を兼ねた主計器板覆上のRevi16Bは取り外されている。
写真31：後部キャノピーの左側面には悪天候時に使用する開閉式の視認用小窓が設けられている。

Photo 22-25: The canopy of the He162 A-2.
Photo 26: A view of the fixed, forward portion of the canopy.
Photo 27-30: Views of the forward part of the cockpit. The armor plate covering the top of the instrument panel, and in front of that, the mount for the rudder pedals (the three black rods) are visible. The small holes in the canopy visible at the base of its front edge (photos 27 and 28) were to allow air into the cockpit to prevent canopy fogging. Unfortunately, the Revi 16B gunsight which should be mounted on top of the armor plate above the instrument panel has been removed from this plane.
Photo 31: The port side of the canopy had a small port which could be opened for use during inclement weather.

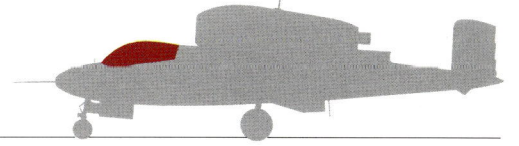

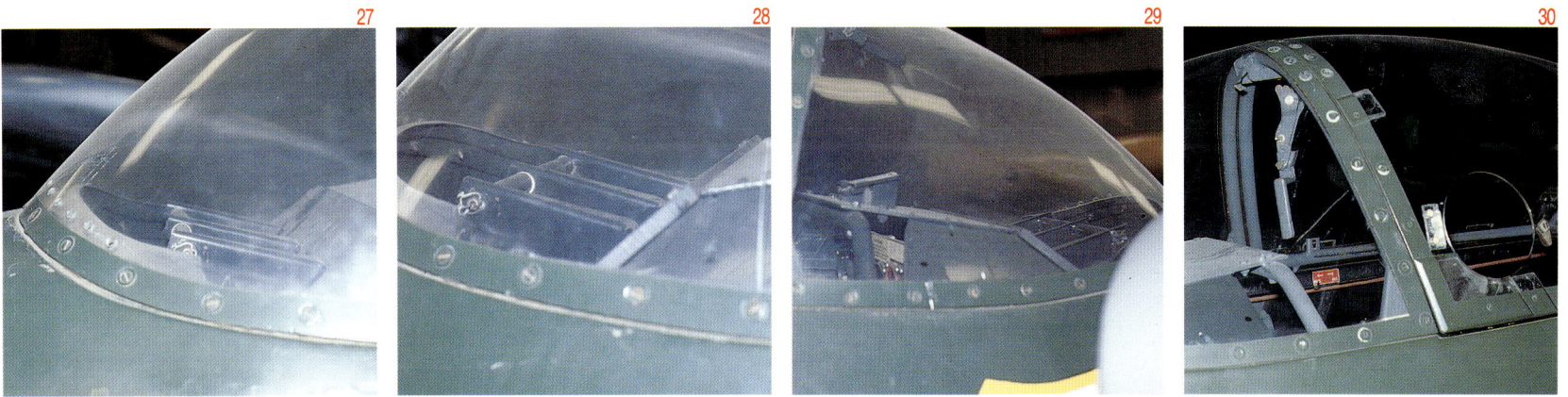

写真32：後部キャノピー後方。He162のキャノピーはドイツ戦闘機としては珍しく上方開閉式。

写真33：主計器板。昇降計はオリジナルとは異なっている。

写真34：He162A-2に装備されたハインケル社製の射出式パイロット・シート。He162以前にハインケル社が開発したジェット戦闘機He280に装備されていた射出シートと基本的に同じものだが、射出システムは圧搾空気式から火薬式に変更されている。

Photo 32: A view of the rear portion of the canopy. The He162's canopy was hinged at the back, unusual for a German fighter.
Photo 33: The main instrument panel. The vertical speed indicator installed on this aircraft is not original.
Photo 34: The Heinkel-manufactured ejection seat installed on the He162 A-2. The seat is essentially the same as the model that Heinkel designed for its earlier jet aircraft, the He280, however the seat's propulsion system was changed from one using compressed air to one using an explosive charge.

Photo 22／H.Ishido
Photo 23, 25～29, 31, 32／T.Shiwaku
Photo 24／A.Beniya
Photo 30, 33／S.Nohara
Photo 34／M.Shiwaku

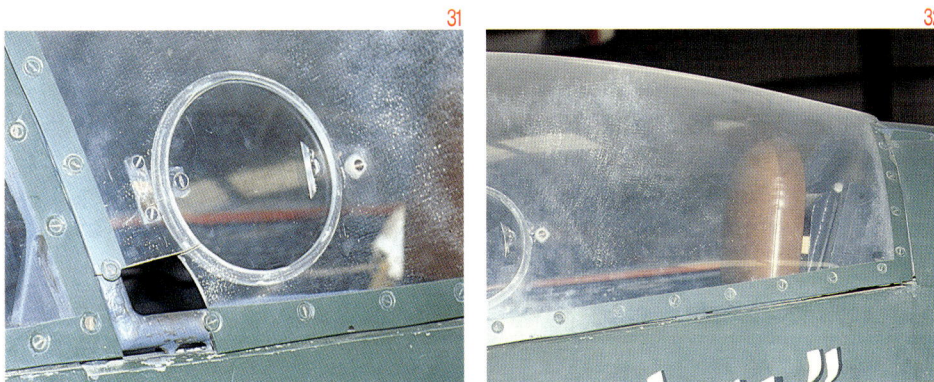

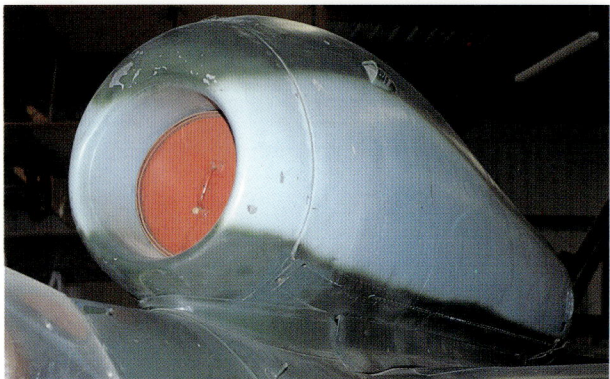

写真35〜41：He162は、エンジン・ナセルを胴体上に配置。このエンジン配置が、He162の特異なスタイルを決定づけたと言っても過言ではない。なお、プレーンズ・オブ・フェイム（写真35、36、39）のHe162は、エンジン・ナセル上のD／Fループ・アンテナが欠損しており、またフランス航空宇宙博物館の展示機（写真37、38、40、41）のループアンテナは代用品である。

Photo 35-41: The He162's engine. The plane in photos 35, 36 and 39 is missing its D/F loop antenna, which should be on top of the engine, while the plane in the other photos has a very crude "replica" antenna installed.

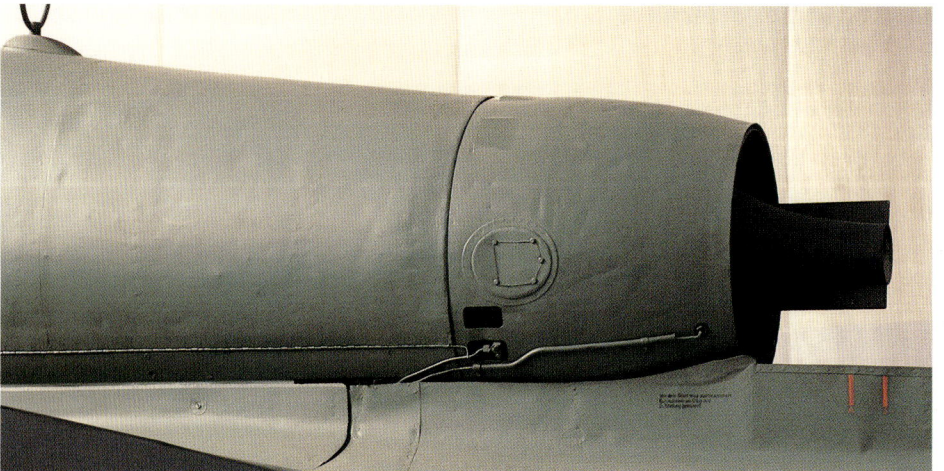

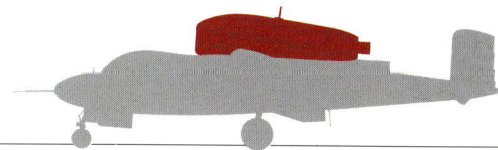

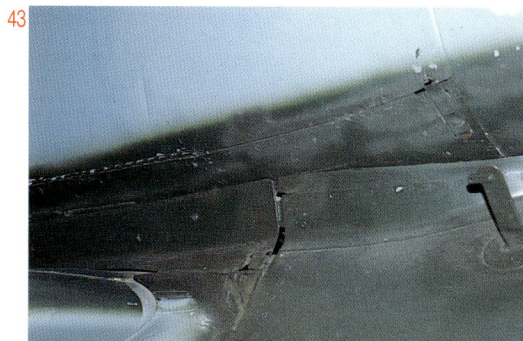

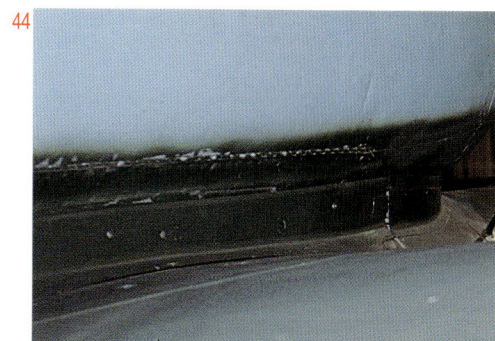

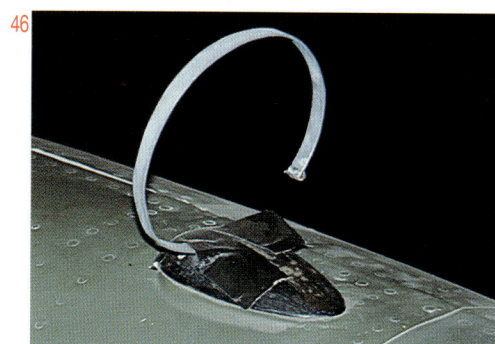

写真42～44：エンジン・ナセルの取り付け部。写真42は左前部、写真43、44は右側方である。エンジン・ナセルは、上面中心線に設けられたスナップ式の止め具を外すことにより左右下方に開閉する。

写真45：エンジン・ナセルの左前部上方に設けられた発電機冷却用のエア・スクープ

写真46：エンジン・ナセル上のFuG16ZY無線器用のD／Fループ・アンテナ。写真の機体は、アンテナが取れてしまったためか、何とガムテープで固定しており、アンテナの右端が外れてしまっている。

写真47：BMW003Eターボジェット・エンジン後部（写真は左側）。

写真48～50：BMW003Eターボジェット・エンジンのノズル部。

Photo 42-44: Close-ups of the engine mount. Photo 42 is taken from the front left side, 43 and 44 are from the right. The engine's panels can be opened to the left, right and rear by operating a snap-type fastener on the top center of the engine.

Photo 45: The cooling air intake scoop for the engine's generator, located on the front port side of the engine.

Photo 46: The FuG16ZY D/F loop antenna for the Salamander's radio, located on top of the engine. The antenna in the photograph apparently was broken and has undergone a very crude repair job using adhesive tape, but the right edge has sprung free.

Photo 47: The rear port side of the BMW003 turbojet engine.

Photo 48-50: Close-ups of the exhaust nozzle of the BMW003 turbojet engine.

51

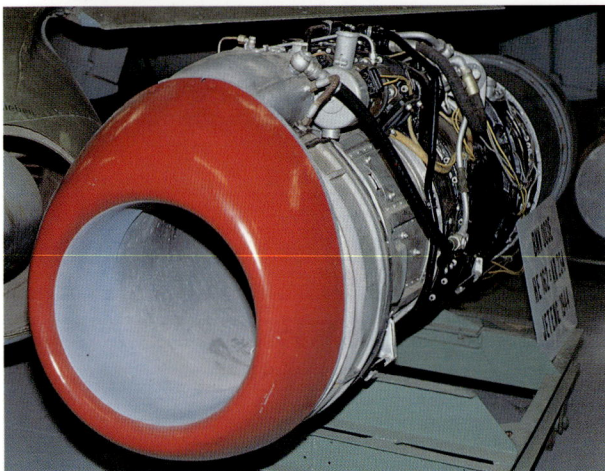

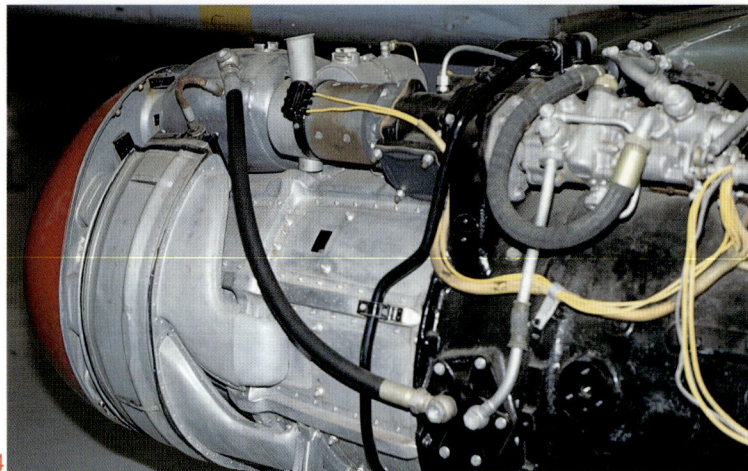

写真51〜52：He162A-2に搭載されたBMW003Eターボジェット・エンジン。BMW003Eは全長3.63m、直径0.69m、重量624kgと小型軽量なエンジンで、推力は800kgである。

写真53〜54：BMW003Eターボジェット・エンジンの前部。

写真55：エンジン前部上に見える銀色の小型タンクは、潤滑油タンク。

Photo 51-52: The BMW003E turbojet engine was 3.63m long, 0.69m in diameter and weighed 624kg, producing 800kg of thrust.
Photo 53-54: Close-ups of the front section of the BMW003E turbojet engine.
Photo 55: The small silver tank visible at the very front of the top of the engine is the oil reservoir.

52

54

53

55

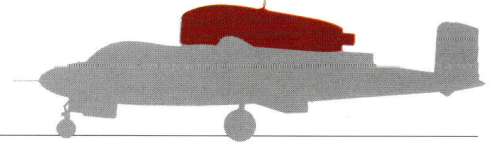

写真56〜57：エンジン前部に取り付けられた潤滑油冷却器。写真57は、冷却器の後部。写真はともに左側。

写真58〜61：BMW003Eエンジンの中央部。エンジン上面には、燃料ポンプ、発電機、ギアハウジング、制御装置、フィルターなどが配置されている。写真58、59は右側、写真60、61は左側。

Photo 56-57: Views of the oil cooler on the front of the engine. Photo 57 is a close-up of the rear of the oil cooler. Both pictures are taken from the left side.

Photo 58-61: Close-ups of the mid-section of the engine. The fuel pump, generator, gear housing, filters and control mechanisms are all mounted on the top of the engine. Photos 58 and 59 are taken from the right side, 60 and 61 are from the left.

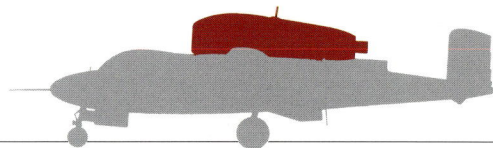

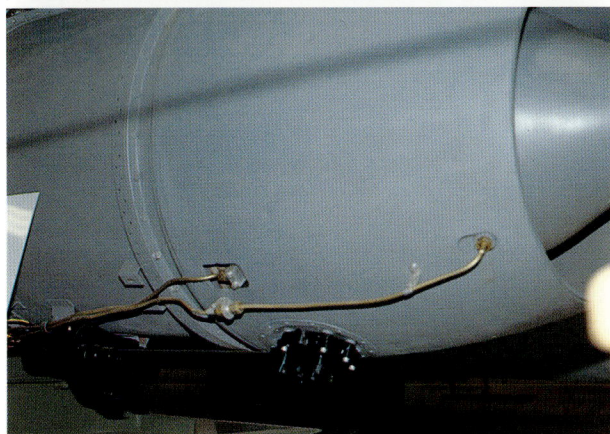

Photo 35, 36, 39, 42〜45, 47, 49, 50, 52〜57, 59, 60〜68／
T.Shiwaku
Photo 37, 38, 40, 41／H.Ishido
Photo 46, 48／S.Nohara
Photo 51, 58／A.Beniya

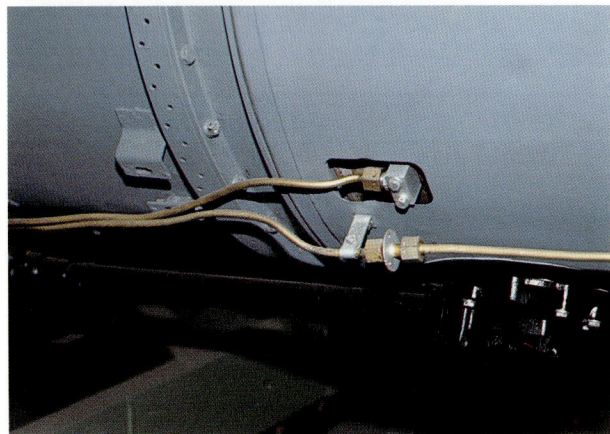

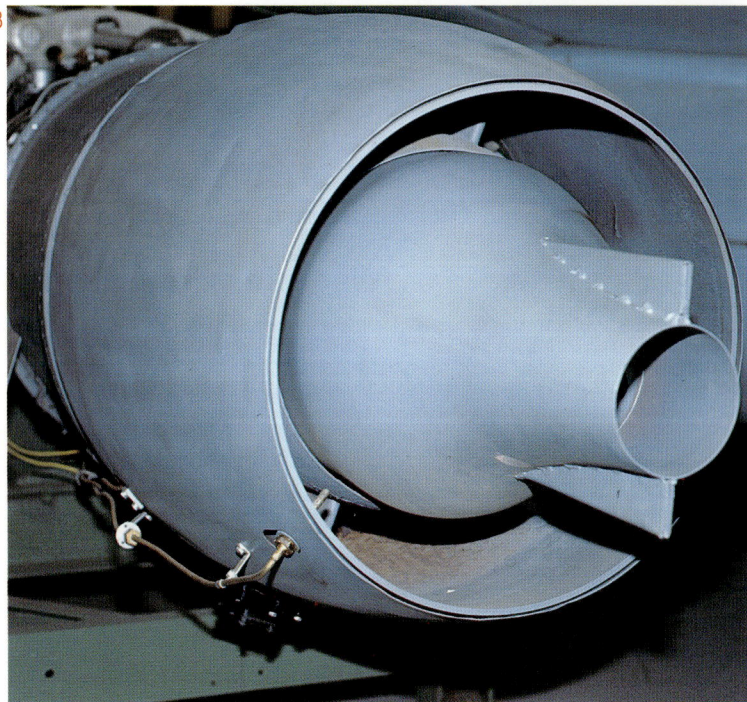

写真62：圧縮器室上部の制御装置、高圧フィルター。
写真63〜64：圧縮器の左側下部。
写真65〜67：エンジン後部下部。下面に取り付けられているコードは、排気温度計測センサーのコード。
写真68：エンジン・ノズル部。内部に見えるノズル・コーンは、離着陸時や飛行状況に応じて、ノズル面積を変えることができるように前後に可動する。

Photo 62: A close-up of the control mechanism and high-pressure filter on top of the compression chamber.
Photo 63-64: Two views of the lower port section of the compression chamber.
Photo 65-67: Three views of the lower port section of the rear of the engine. The piping leading back to the end of the nozzle houses the wiring for the exhaust temperature sensor.
Photo 68: A close-up of the exhaust nozzle. The nozzle cone visible in the center of the engine can move back and forth to adjust power during take-off, landing or other in-flight situations.

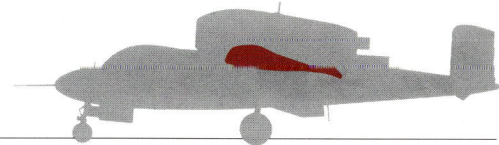

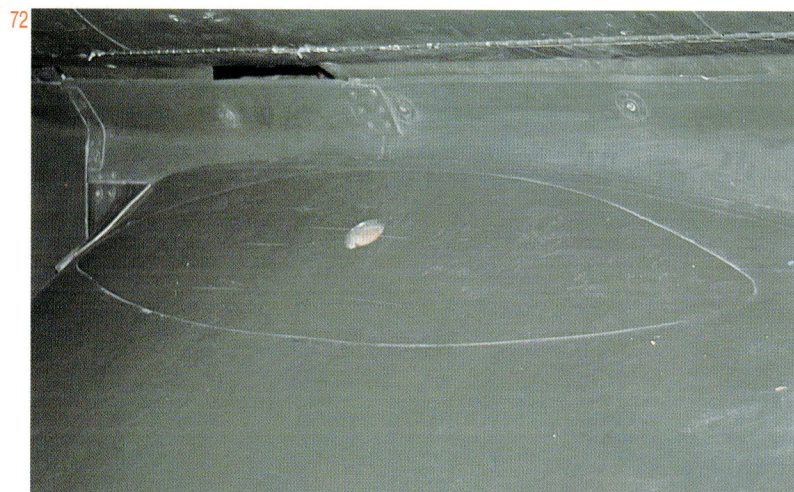

写真69：He162の主翼は、左右一体構造の直線テーパー翼である。Me163B同様、He162も戦略物資（ジュラルミンなど）の使用を最小限におさえた設計を採ったため、主翼は全木製であった。

写真70〜71：ほとんどのHe162は、主翼付け根の前縁に三角形断面のスポイラーが装着されていた（写真70）が、スポイラーが付いていない機体も少数ながら存在する（写真71）。写真は左主翼。

写真72〜73：胴体との主翼付け根上面。

Photo 69: The wings of the He162 were of a one-piece, straight-line tapered type. Like the Me163B, the wings are entirely wooden construction as strategic materials such as duralmin were mostly unavailable to the Germans at this point in the war.

Photo 70-71: Most Salamanders had triangular spoilers on the leading edges of the wings, next to the wing roots (photo 70) but a few which did not also exist (photo 71). The photos are of the port wing.

Photo 72-73: Upper surface views of the wing root of the port wing.

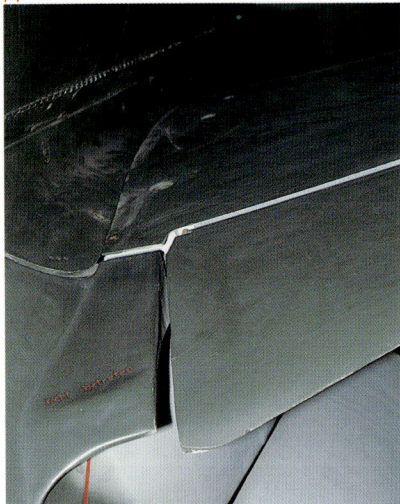

74

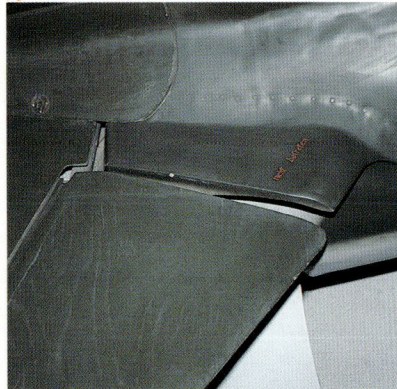

75

76

77

Photo 69／H. Ishido
Photo 70, 72, 74, 75, 77, 79~83／S.Nohara
Photo 71, 73, 76, 78, 84, 86~88／T. Shiwaku
Photo 85／A. Beniya

79

写真74~78：失速を防止するために下方にカーブした主翼付け根後縁のフィレット。写真74は右主翼、写真75~78は左主翼。
写真79~80：主翼後縁内側に設けられたフラップ。
写真81~83：主翼後縁外側の補助翼。写真81は右主翼。写真82、83は左主翼。補助翼後縁の赤い部分は、補助翼のトリム・タブ。
写真84：右主翼下面の補助翼／フラップ作動部付近。
写真85~88：主翼端。横方向安定の向上を図り、主翼端は55°の下反角がつけられている。写真はいずれも左主翼端。

Photo 74-78: The fillet at the trailing edge of the wing roots. The fillet was curved downwards to help prevent speed loss. Photo 74 is of the port side, while photos 75-78 are of the starboard.
Photo 79-80: Views of the flaps on the inboard side of the wings' trailing edges.
Photo 81-83: Views of the ailerons on the outboard side of the wings' trailing edges. Photo 81 is the starboard wing, while photos 82 and 83 are the port. The red strip visible in the center of the ailerons is the trim tab.
Photo 84: A close-up of the control mechanism for the flaps and ailerons on the lower mid-section of the starboard wing.
Photo 85-88: Views of the winglet on the tip of the port wing. Angled downward at 55°, the He162's winglets were meant to improve its lateral stability.

78

80

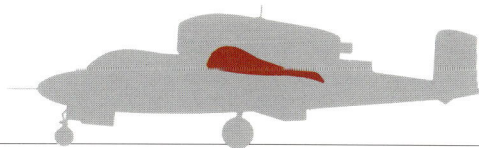

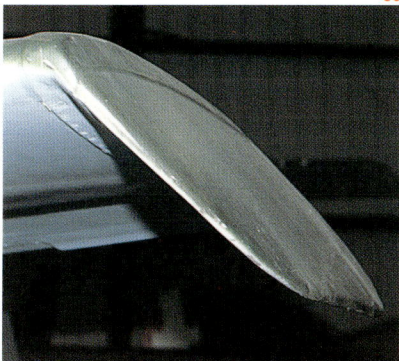

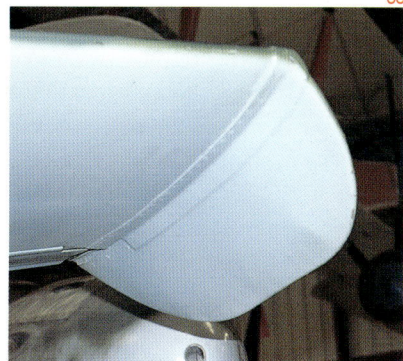

写真89〜92：前脚。前車輪のサイズは380mm×150mm。

写真93：前脚柱。前脚の上げ作動は油圧、下げ作動はスプリングによって行う。

写真94〜95：前脚カバー。写真94は閉じた状態。写真95は開いた状態。

Photo 89-92: The Salamander's nose landing gear. The tire is 380mm × 150mm.

Photo 93: A close-up of the nose gear's strut. The gear was raised via a hydraulic system, and lowered with a spring.

Photo 94-95: The nose gear bay door. Photo 94 shows the closed position, photo 95 is the open position.

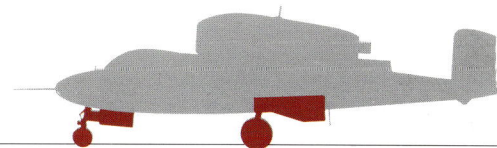

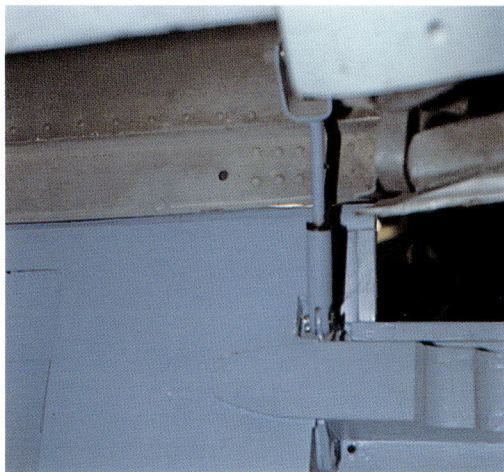

写真96：前脚カバー前部の内側。
写真97：前脚収納部。
写真98〜102：主脚は後方引き込み式。
He162の主脚はBf109Kの主脚をベースに
脚引き込み機構を一部改修したものである。
写真98〜100は左主脚、写真101は右主脚、
写真102は後方から見たところ。

Photo 96: The forward section of the interior of the nose bay door.
Photo 97: A close-up of the nose gear strut mechanism and bay.
Photo 98-102: The main landing gear of the He162. The main gear retract towards the rear of the aircraft. The retraction mechanism is based on a part of the system used by the Bf109K. Photos 98-100 show the port gear, photo 101 is the starboard gear. Photo 102 is taken from the rear.

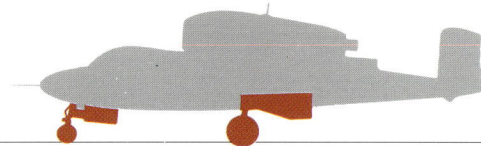

降着装置 LANDING GEAR

103

104

105

写真103～104：主車輪。主車輪はBf109Kと同じ660mm
×190mmサイズの低圧タイヤ。
写真105～106：主脚カバー。写真はともに左主脚カバー
を後方から見たところ。
写真107～108：主脚収納部内。写真はともに左後方から
見たところ。写真では、収納部内前部のオイル・タンク、
オイル・フィルターや油圧シリンダー、ブレーキ支柱な
どが確認できる。

Photo 103-104: The main wheels. The tires used were the
same as that on the Bf109K, a 660mm × 190mm low-
pressure tire.
Photo 105-106: The bay doors for the main gear. Both
photos show the port door from the rear.
Photo 107-108: The interior of the main gear bay. Both
photos are taken from the rear port side. The mechanism
within the bay, including the oil reservoir, oil filter,
hydraulic cylinder and brakes can be clearly seen in the
photos.

106

Photo 89, 90／M.Shiwaku
Photo 91, 93, 96～98, 101～104, 106～108／T.Shiwaku
Photo 92, 99／A.Beniya
Photo 94, 95, 105／S.Nohara
Photo 100／H.Ishido

107

108

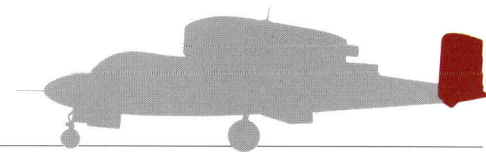

写真109～112：胴体上面にエンジンを配置したため、尾翼は双垂直尾翼形式を採っている。

写真113～116：尾翼付け根付近。水平尾翼は14°の上反角を持つ。

Photo 109-112: Views of the He162's distinctive tail. The aircraft employed a twin-type to avoid control surfaces being in the turbulence caused by the engine mounted on top of the fuselage.

Photo 113-116: Close-ups of the tail mount. The horizontal stabilizer of the Salamander is angled up at 14°.

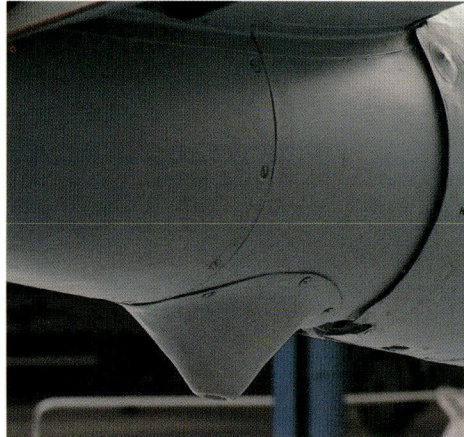

写真117：昇降舵後縁には固定トリム・タブが付く。写真のように細長いトリム・タブのほか、幅広の短かいトリム・タブを付けた機体（写真115参照）もある。

写真118：尾部を右側方から見たところ。

写真119～121：尾部下面に取り付けられている突起物は、離着陸時に尾部と垂直尾翼下部が地面と接触するのを防ぐための保護スキッド。

写真122～123：水平尾翼下面。写真は左水平尾翼。

Photo 117: Fixed trim tabs are installed on the inner edge of the elevators. In addition to the long, narrow type seen in this photo, shorter and broader tabs were also employed (see photo 115).

Photo 118: A view of the underside of the tail taken from the right side.

Photo 119-121: The protrusion on the bottom of the fuselage under the tail is a skid to prevent the tail and fuselage from hitting the ground on take-off or landing.

Photo 122-123: The underside of the horizontal stabilizer. The photos show the port side stabilizer.

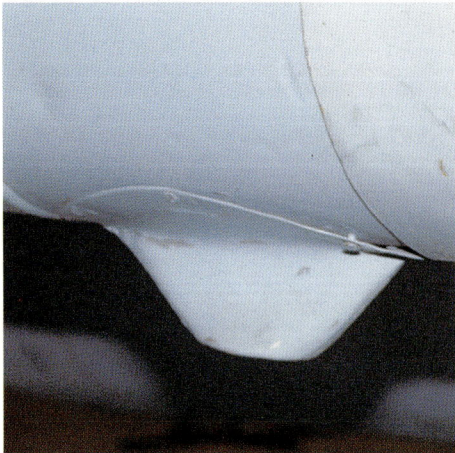

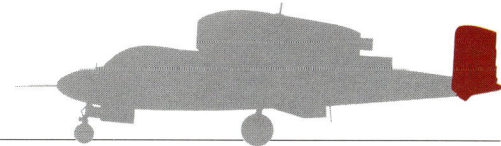

Photo 109／N.Okazaki
Photo 110, 112, 113, 116, 118, 124, 127／S.Nohara
Photo 111／A.Beniya
Photo 114, 117, 120〜123, 125, 126, 128, 129／T.Shiwaku
Photo 115, 119／H.Ishido

写真124〜127：垂直尾翼。写真124は右垂直尾翼の外側、写真125は左垂直尾翼内側、写真126は左垂直尾翼の上部、写真127は右垂直尾翼下部。
写真128〜129：垂直尾翼と水平尾翼の接合部。写真128は左尾翼を前方より、写真129は右尾翼を後方より見たところ。

Photo 124-127: The vertical stabilizer of the He162. Photo 124 shows the outer side of the starboard stabilizer, photo 125 is the interior of the port stabilizer, photo 126 is the top exterior section of the port stabilizer, and photo 127 is the bottom part of the exterior of the starboard stabilizer.
Photo 128-129: Close-ups of the junction between the horizontal and vertical stabilizer. Photo 128 is port side seen from the front. Photo 129 shows the starboard seen from the rear.

He162A-2の迷彩塗装&マーキング

Camouflage & Markings of He162A-2
作図・解説／野原 茂
Illustrations & Commentary by Shigeru Nohara

■RLM81／82／76基本塗装
RLM81／82／76
Standard camouflage scheme

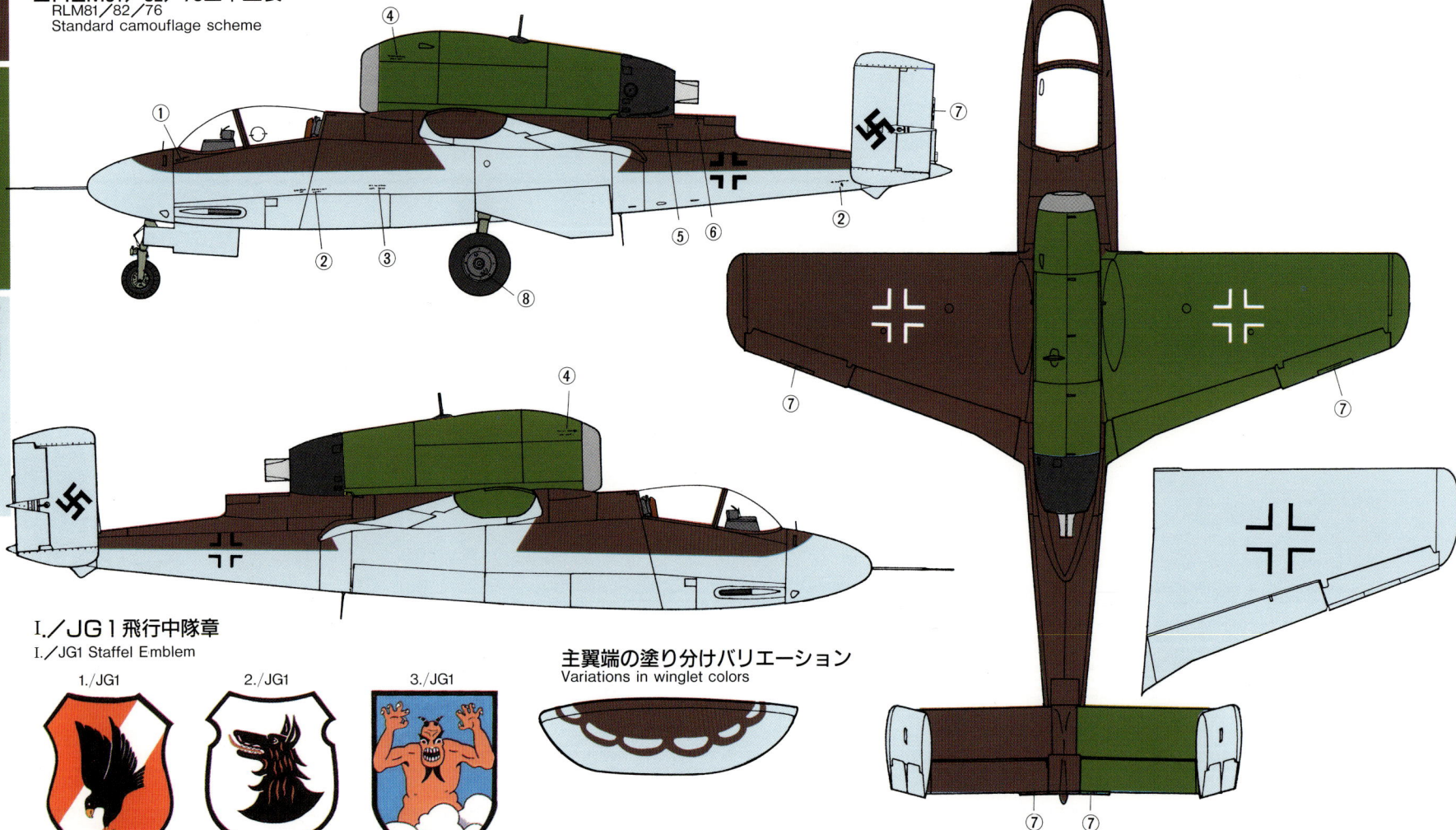

I.／JG1飛行中隊章
I.／JG1 Staffel Emblem

1./JG1　　2./JG1　　3./JG1

主翼端の塗り分けバリエーション
Variations in winglet colors

---

①外部電源接続口表示
Marking for external power supply socket

Auzenbordsteckdose im Bugrädraum

"Auzenbordsteckdose im Bugrädraum"は"外部電源接続口は機首コーン内"という意味。黒文字

Auzenbordsteckdose im Bugrädraum means "External power supply socket located inside of nose cone." Black lettering.

②整備架台位置指示
Maintenance platform location marking

Hier Unterbocken

"Hier Unterbocken"は"ここに下げよ！"という意味。黒文字

Hier Unterbocken means "Lower here." Black lettering.

③酸素供給口表示
Oxygen supply port marking

Sauerstoff Anschluß

"Sauerstoff Anschluß"は"酸素供給口"という意味。黒文字と黒の矢印

Sauerstoff Anschluß means "Oxygen supply port." Black lettering with black arrow.

④エンジン・ナセル開閉時の注意書き
Caution regarding opening of engine nacelle.

Vol dem öffneder der Spannverschlüsse oben Verschlüssel links u. rechts offnen

ドイツ語の注意書きは"開ける前に上部と左右の止め具を外せ！"という意味。白文字

The German marking means "Remove left and right side fasteners on upper side before opening." White lettering.

⑤エンジン・ノズル点検指示
Engine nozzle inspection marking

Vor dem Startmuss Startmnnshaft Kontrollieren ob Düse auf S-Stellung gefahren!

ドイツ語注意書きは"乗員は離陸前にエンジン・ノズルがS位置まで下がっているかをチェックせよ！"という意味。白文字

The German marking means "Aircraft crew should confirm engine nozzle is lowered to S-position before take-off." White lettering.

⑥エンジン・ノズル位置の指示マーク
Engine nozzle position marking

A.S

ノズル位置を示す黒線にA.Sの黒文字

A black line to indicate nozzle position with black A.S lettering.

⑦昇降舵の固定式トリム・タブの注意書き
Caution on fixed trim tabs

Nicht Anfassen

"Nicht Anfassen"は"触わるな！"の意。白または黒文字

Nicht Anfassen means "Don't touch." White or black lettering.

⑧タイヤ整備時の注意書き
Tire maintenance caution

Achtung! Räder nicht teilen bevor reifen luftleer

"Achtung！Räder nicht teilen bevor reifen luftleer"は"注意！ タイヤの空気を抜く前にホイールを外すな"の意。白または赤文字

Achtung! Räder nicht teilen bevor reifen luftleer means "Caution! Do not remove wheels before releasing tire air pressure." White or red lettering.

He162A-2 W.Nr120028　第1戦闘航空団第I飛行隊第1飛行中隊
1945年5月　レック基地／ドイツ

He162A-2 W.Nr120028
1./JG1　May 1945　Leck／Germany

　上面81／82、下面RLM76だが規定塗装と
異なり、RLM76が胴体側面上方まで塗られ
ているのが特徴。機首側面の矢印は赤、機番
号"3"は黒フチ付きの白、胴体側面の国籍
標識は白フチ付きの黒十字。垂直尾翼のハー
ケンクロイツ、W.Nr120028はともに白。

　Upper surfaces are RLM 81/82. Underside
is RLM 76, but aircraft is unique in that RLM
76 extends well up the side of the fuselage,
contrary to official marking scheme. Aircraft
number "3" is white with black border.
National insignia on fuselage is black cross
with white border. Swastika and W.Nr 120028
on vertical stabilizer are white.

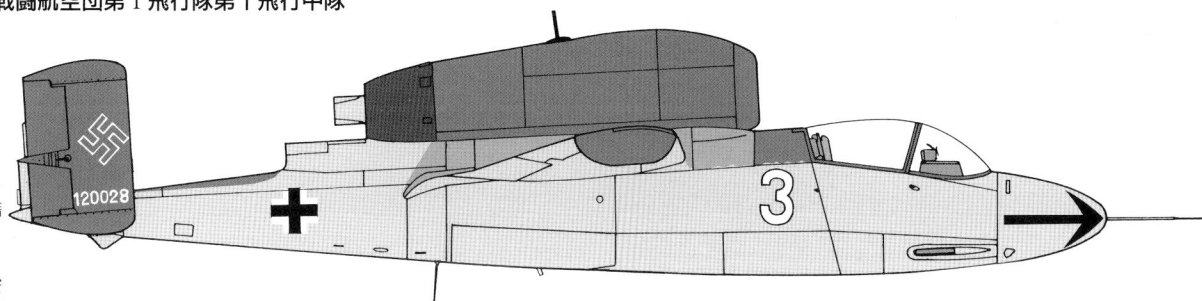

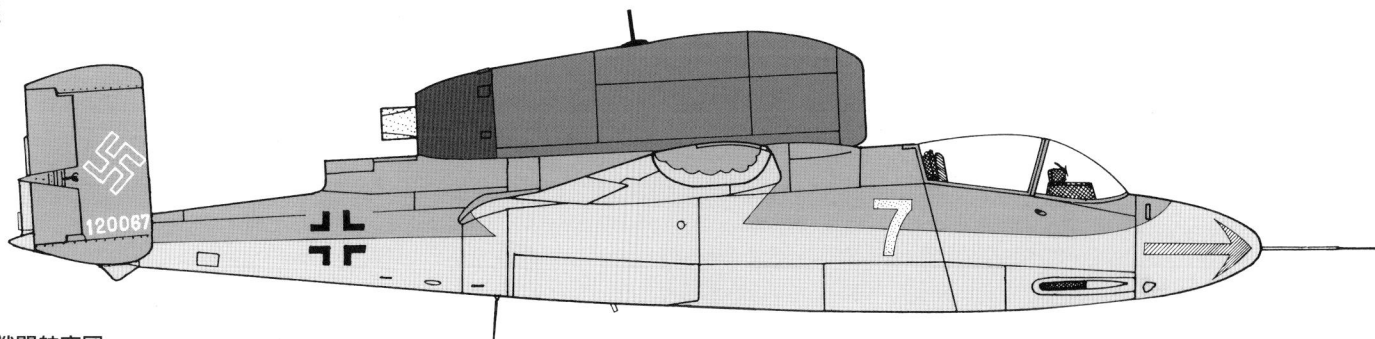

He162A-2 W.Nr120067　第1戦闘航空団
第I飛行隊第3飛行中隊
1945年5月　レック基地／ドイツ

He162A-2 W.Nr120067
3./JG1　May 1945　Leck／Germany

　胴体、主尾翼上面はRLM82、エンジン・
ナセルはRLM81、下面RLM76で規定され
た塗り分けと異なる。主翼、水平尾翼前縁上
面は下面色RLM76が廻り込んだ波状塗り分
けとなっており、機首側面の矢印は赤、機番
号"7"は飛行中隊カラーの黄、垂直尾翼の
ハーケンクロイツは白フチのみ、W.Nr120067
は白。

　Fuselage and upperside of tail are RLM82.
Engine nacelle is RLM 81. Underside is RLM
76 but differs slightly from official marking
scheme. Leading edges of wings, edges of
winglets and horizontal stabilizer have wave
pattern of RLM 76. Arrow on nose is red.
Aircraft number "7" is in yellow, the Staffel
color. Swastika on vertical stabilizer is white
outline only. W.Nr 120067 is white.

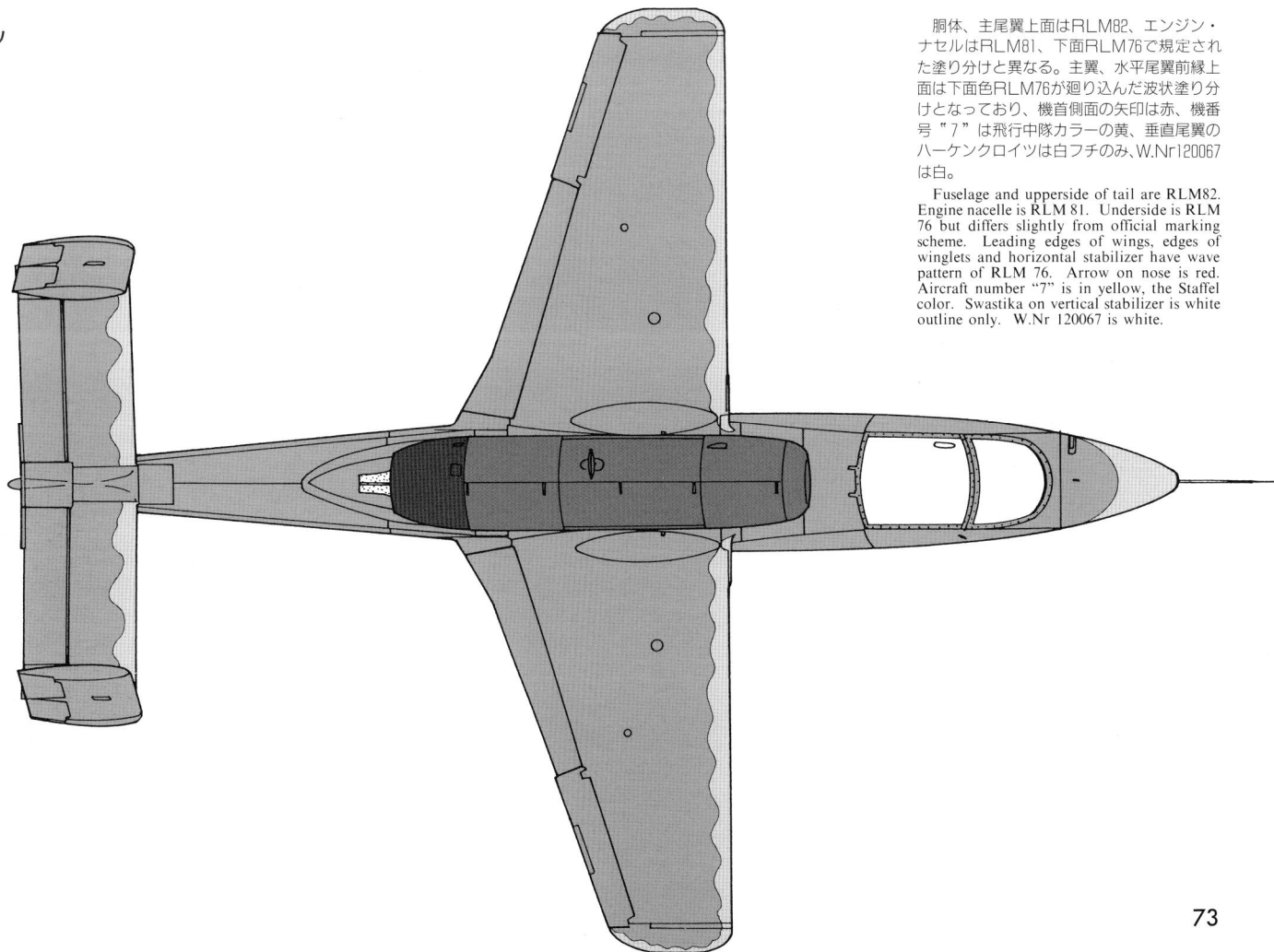

He162A-2 W.Nr120074　第1戦闘航空団第Ⅰ飛行隊第3飛行中隊長エミール・デムート中尉乗機　1945年5月　レック基地／ドイツ
He162A-2 W.Nr120074　Staffelkapitän 3./JG1　Flown by Oblt. Emil Demuth　May 1945　Leck/Germany

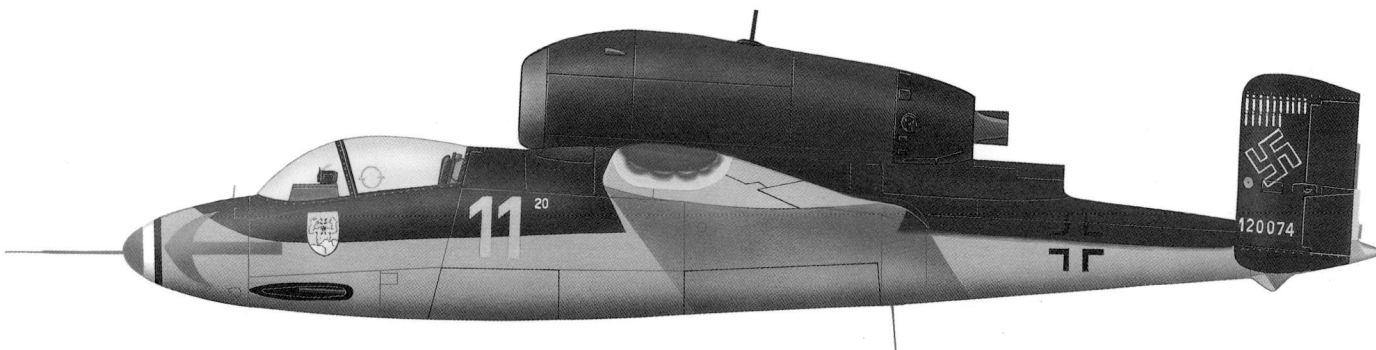

胴体、主尾翼上面はRLM82、エンジン・ナセルはRLM81、ナセル先端は無塗装、下面はRLM76。主翼端上面の塗り分けは下面RLM76が廻り込んだ独特な波状パターン。機首先端は第3帝国カラーを配した赤／白／黒の3色塗装。機首側面には赤の矢印と3./JG1中隊章が付く。機番号 "11" は黄、その後方の数字 "20" は白。垂直尾翼上のハーケンクロイツは白フチのみのタイプ、また、スコアマーク、W.Nr120074は白で記入。

Fuselage and upper surface of wings is RLM 82, engine nacelle is RLM 81, front section of nacelle unpainted, underside is RLM 76. Winglets have unique wave pattern using RLM 76 from underside. Third Reich colors painted on nose in order red, white, black. Red arrow and emblem of 3./JG 1 on side of nose. Aircraft number "11" is yellow, the small "20" aft of it is white. Swastika on vertical stabilizer is white outline only. Kill markings and W.Nr 120074 is in white.

He162A-2 W.Nr120097　第1戦闘航空団第Ⅰ飛行隊第1飛行中隊　1945年5月　レック基地／ドイツ
He162A-2 W.Nr120097　1./JG1　May 1945　Leck/Germany

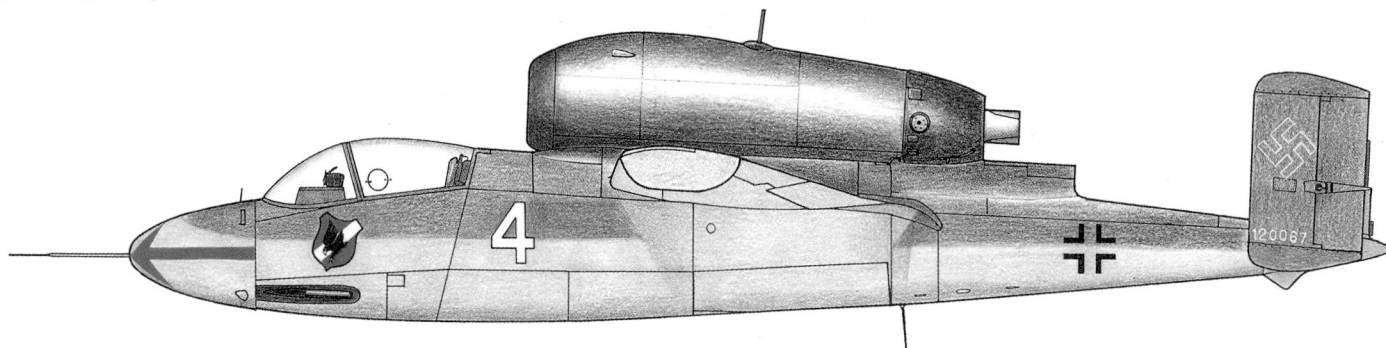

機体上面はRLM82、エンジン・ナセル全体はRLM81、機首の矢印は赤、コクピット横に1./JG1中隊章あり、機番号 "4" は黒フチ付き白。垂直安定板外側もRLM82で、ハーケンクロイツは白フチのみ、W.Nr120097は白で記入。

Upperside of fuselage is RLM 82, engine nacelle is RLM 81, arrow on nose is red, emblem of I./JG 1 below cockpit, aircraft number "4" is white with black border. Outer side of vertical stabilizers is RLM 82, swastika is white outline only. W.Nr 120097 is in white.

He162A-2 W.Nr300027　第1戦闘航空団第Ⅰ飛行隊　1945年5月　レック基地／ドイツ
He162A-2 W.Nr300027　I./JG1　May 1945　Leck/Germany

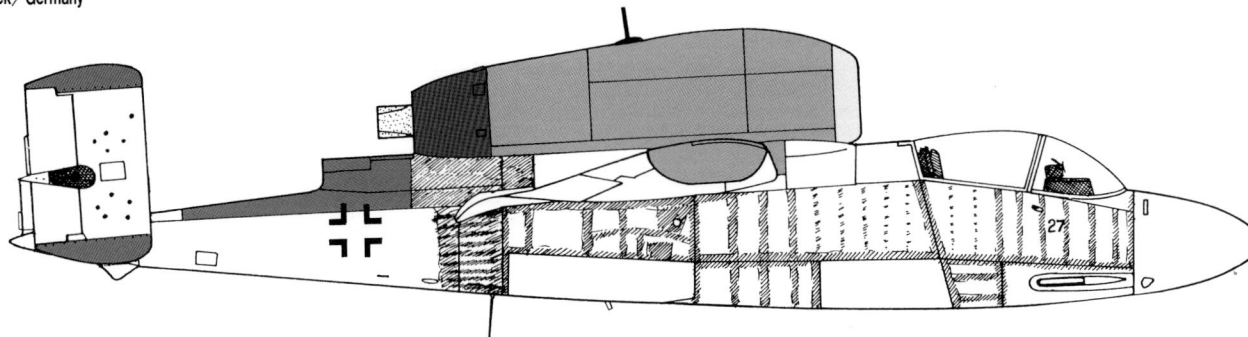

胴体は無塗装で、外板継ぎ目にサーフェイサーを塗布したのみ。胴体後方上面はRLM81、主翼上面、エンジン・ナセルはRLM82、垂直尾翼は上下部のみRLM81で中央部は胴体同様、無塗装。機首側面に記されたW.Nrを示す "27"（下2桁のみ）は黒。胴体側面の国籍標識は黒フチのみ。

Fuselage is unpainted, with surfacer applied at panel joints. Upper part of aft section of fuselage is RLM 81. Upperside of wings and engine nacelle is RLM 82. Upper and lower parts of vertical stabilizers are RLM 81, mid-section is unpainted, like fuselage. "27" on side of nose, indicating last two digits of W.Nr is in black. National insignia on side of fuselage is black outline only.

He162 ディテール・イラスト
DETAIL ILLUSTRATION

作図・解説／野原　茂
Illustrations and Commentary by Shigeru Nohara

胴体構造　FUSELAGE STRUCTURE

He162A-2　胴体内部配置
He162A-2 Interior structure

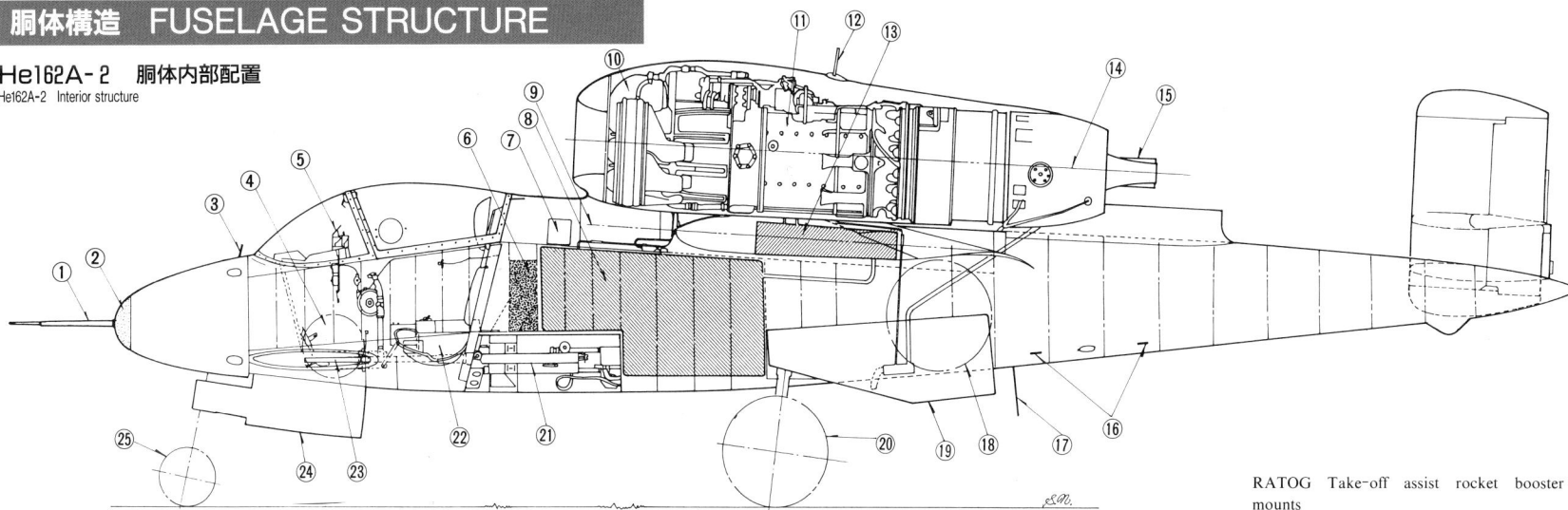

胴体構成および胴枠配置
Fuselage construction and bulkhead layout

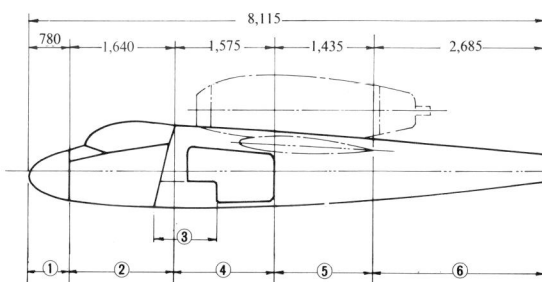

①機首部　Nose Section
②コクピット部　Cockpit Section
③兵装室　Armament Compartment
④燃料タンク部　Fuel Tank Section
⑤中央胴体　Central Fuselage
⑥後部胴体　Aft Fuselage Section

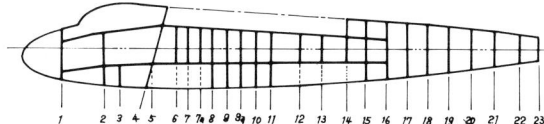

胴体断面図　Fuselage cross-section diagrams

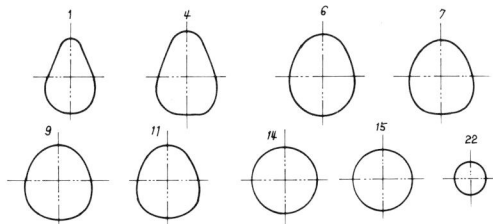

胴体外板構成　Fuselage panel layout

① ピトー管
Pitot tube
② バラスト
Ballast
③ 前脚位置表示棒
Nose gear position indicator
④ 前車輪収納位置
Position of nose gear in retracted position
⑤ Revi16B射撃照準器
Revi 16B reflecting gunsight
⑥ MG151／20 20mm機関砲弾倉（各120発）
Magazine for MG 151/20 20mm machine cannon (120 rounds)
⑦ バッテリー
Battery
⑧ 胴体内燃料タンク（容量635ℓ）
Fuselage fuel tank (635 liters)

⑨ 主翼取り付け角度（＋4°）
Wing mount line (4° upward tilt)
⑩ 潤滑油タンク
Oil reservoir
⑪ BMW003Eターボジェット・エンジン（推力800Kg）
BMW003E turbojet engine (800 kg thrust)
⑫ D／Fループ・アンテナ
D/F loop antenna
⑬ 主翼内燃料タンク（容量325ℓ）
Wing fuel tank (325 liters)
⑭ エンジン推力線
Engine thrust line
⑮ ノズル・コーン
Nozzle cone
⑯ RATOG（離陸補助ロケット・ブースター取り付け金具）
RATOG Take-off assist rocket booster mounts
⑰ FuG25a IFF用ロッド・アンテナ
FuG25a IFF rod antenna
⑱ 主車輪収納位置
Position of main gear in retracted position
⑲ 主脚ドア
Main gear bay door
⑳ 主車輪（660×190mm）
Main gear wheel (660×190mm)
㉑ MG151／20 20mm機関砲
MG151/20 20mm machine cannon
㉒ 火薬式射出座席
Ejection seat
㉓ MG151／20砲身突出部分
Exposed barrel of MG151/20
㉔ 前脚収納ドア
Nose gear bay door
㉕ 前車輪
Nose wheel

主要部品構成
Major components

① ノーズキャップ　Nose cap
② 胴体　Fuselage
③ 尾部コーン　Tail cone
④ 前脚　Nose gear
⑤ 主脚　Main gear
⑥ 水平安定板　Horizontal stabilizer
⑦ 昇降舵　Elevator
⑧ 垂直安定板　Vertical stabilizer
⑨ 方向舵　Rudder
⑩ 主翼　Wing
⑪ 翼端　Winglet
⑫ エルロン　Aileron
⑬ フラップ　Flap
⑭ エンジン　Engine

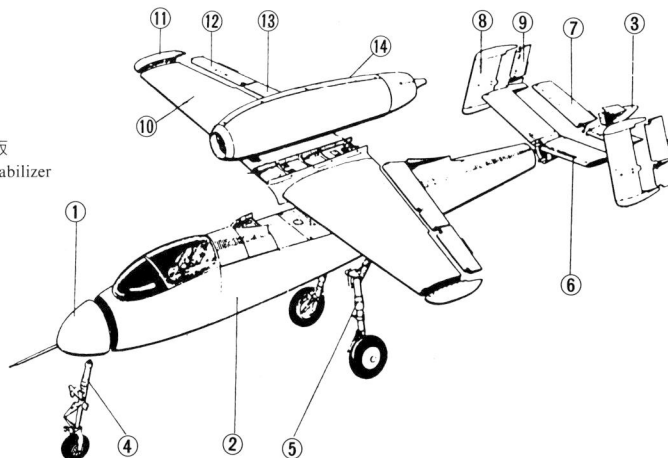

◀主翼付け根の前縁には、失速防止のためスポイラーを装着。ただし、大戦末期時のためか、このスポイラーが付いていない機体も少なくない。(写真／野原　茂)
Spoilers were installed at the root of the wings' leading edges to help prevent speed loss. Nevertheless, many planes lack this part, perhaps due to the turmoil near the end of the war. (Photo by S.Nohara)

◀主翼付け根後縁のフィレット。フィレットが下向きにカーブしているのは、前縁のスポイラー同様、失速防止のためである。(写真／野原　茂)
The fillet at the trailing edge wing root. The fillet is curved downward to help prevent speed loss, like the spoiler on the leading edge. (Photo by S.Nohara)

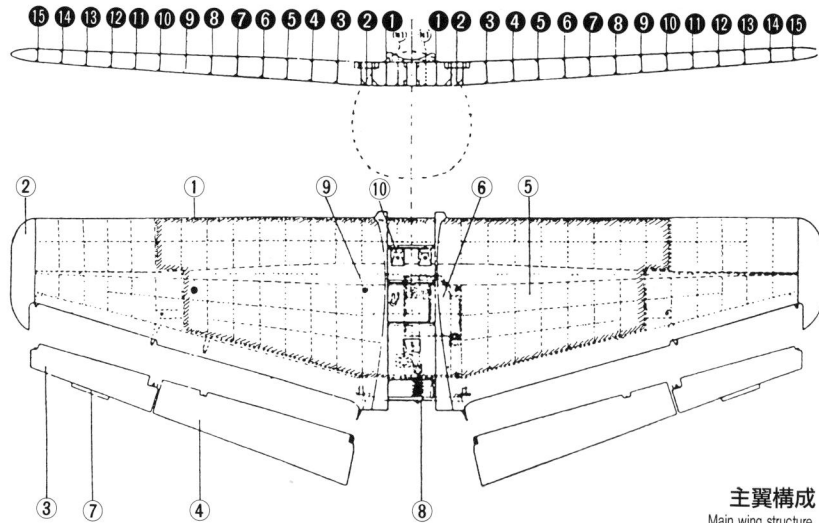

主翼構成
Main wing structure

① 主翼本体　Main Wing
② 翼端　Winglet
③ エルロン　Aileron
④ フラップ　Flap
⑤ 燃料タンク・スペース　Fuel tank space
⑥ 始動燃料タンク・スペース　Engine start fuel tank space
⑦ 固定トリム・タブ　Fixed trim tab
⑧ フラップ用リターン・スプリング　Flap return spring
⑨ 胴体／主翼結合部　Wing / fuselage junction
⑩ 胴体／エンジン結合部　Fuselage / engine junction

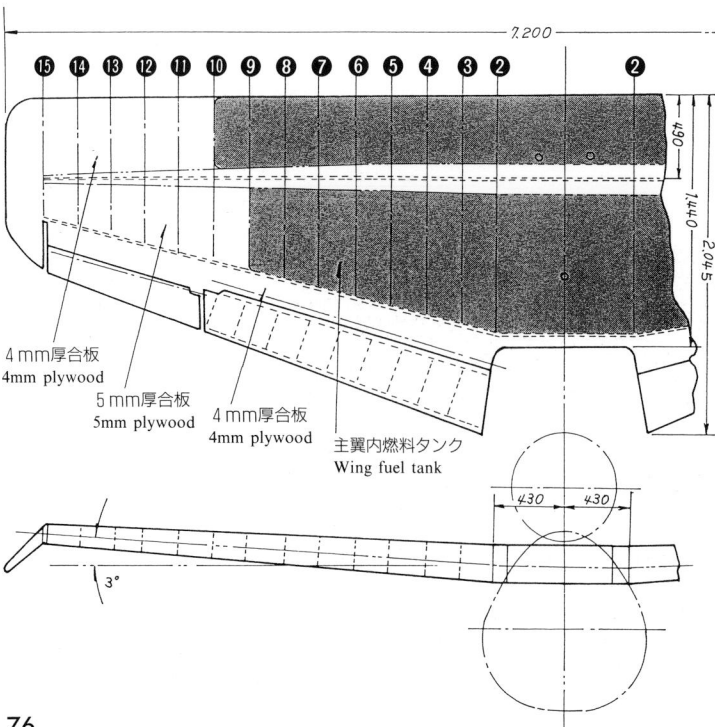

フラップの骨組み
Flap rib structure

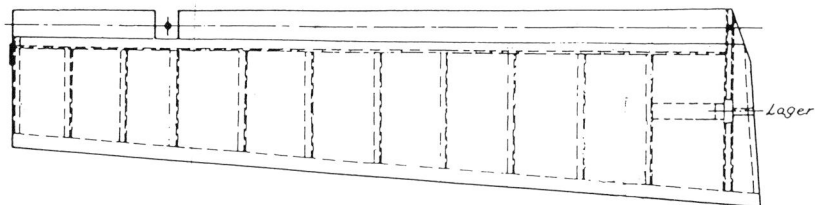

Lager

フラップ第12リブ部の断面
Cross-section at 12th rib

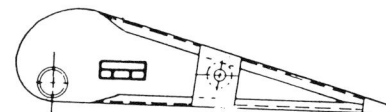

主翼断面形状
Wing cross-section

補助翼部
Aileron section

フラップ部
Flap section

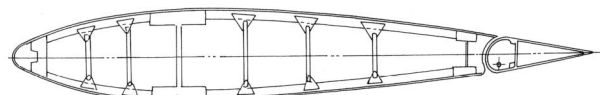

4mm厚合板　4mm plywood
5mm厚合板　5mm plywood
4mm厚合板　4mm plywood
主翼内燃料タンク　Wing fuel tank

斤翼前縁付け根のスポイラー（右主翼）
Leading edge wing root spoilers (starboard wing)

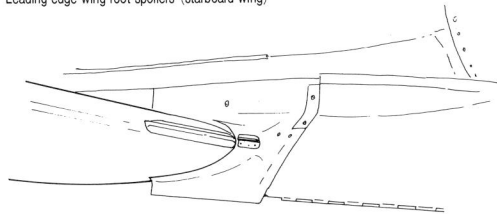

主翼後縁のフィレット（左主翼）
Trailing edge fillets (port wing)

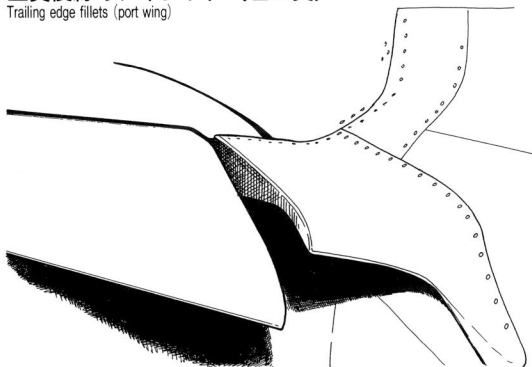

翼端下反角部（左主翼を後方より見る）
Winglets (port wing viewed from behind)

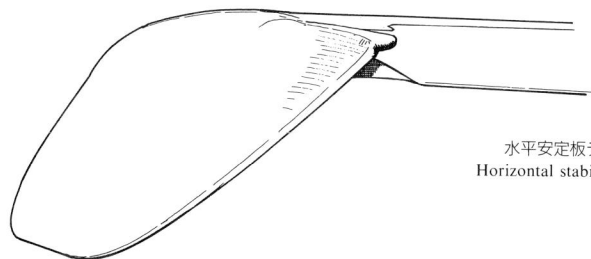

フラップ操作機構
Flap control mechanism

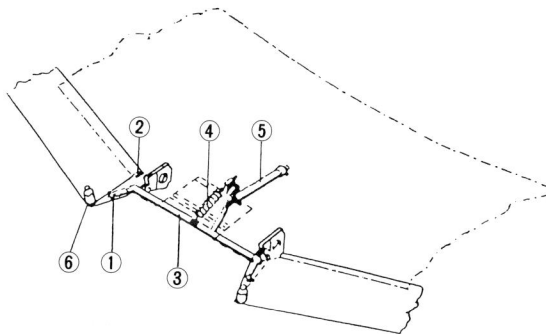

① フォークピース
　Forkpiece
② 静止調整具
　Stationary adjustment
③ ドライブ・シャフト
　Drive shaft
④ リターン・スプリング
　Return spring
⑤ 油圧シリンダー
　Hydraulic cylinder
⑥ スプリング負荷部
　Spring counter-balance

尾翼　TAIL

水平安定板テールフレーム
Horizontal stabilizer tail frame

昇降舵
Elevator

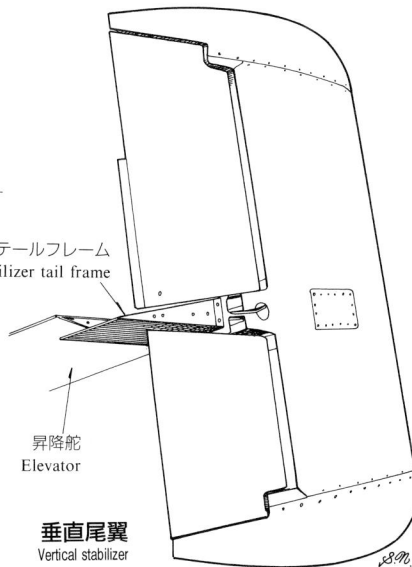

垂直尾翼
Vertical stabilizer

水平尾翼構造
Horizontal stabilizer structure

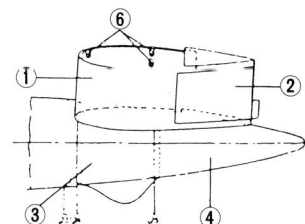

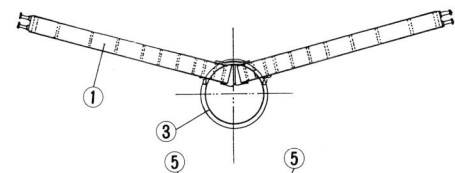

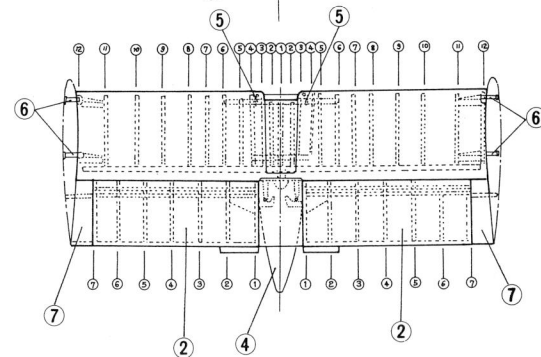

① 水平安定板
　Horizontal stabilizer
② 昇降舵
　Elevator
③ 昇降舵支持架（尾部スキッド付き）
　Tail support brace (with protection skid)
④ 尾部コーン
　Tail cone
⑤ 胴体／水平安定板結合部
　Horizontal stabilizer / fuselage junction
⑥ 垂直安定板取り付け部
　Vertical stabilizer attachment
⑦ 水平安定板テール・フレーム
　Horizontal stabilizer tail frame

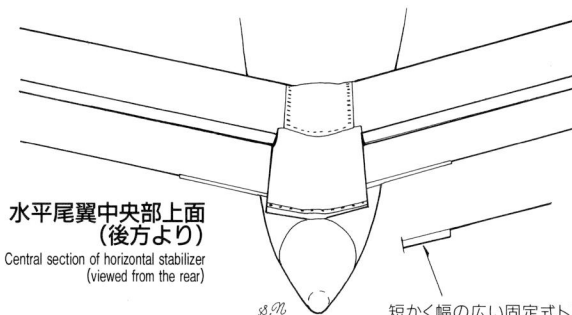

垂直尾翼構造
Vertical stabilizer structure

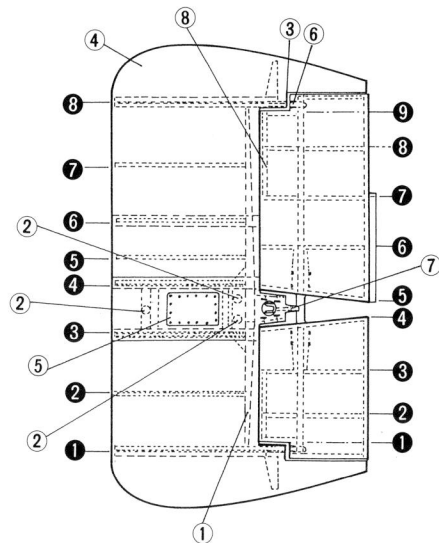

① 主桁
　Main spar
② 垂直安定板取り付け部
　Attachment points
③ ベアリング取り付け部
　Bearing attachment
④ テイル・キャップ
　Tail cap
⑤ 点検パネル
　Inspection panel
⑥ 方向舵取り付け部
　Rudder attachment
⑦ 方向舵操作レバー
　Rudder control lever
⑧ バランスウェイト
　Counterbalance

水平尾翼中央部上面（後方より）
Central section of horizontal stabilizer (viewed from the rear)

短かく幅の広い固定式トリム・タブを付けた機体が多い
Many planes had short and wide trim tabs attached, as shown in the diagram.

◀昇降舵後縁には固定式トリム・タブが装着されている。写真は短く、幅が広いタイプのトリム・タブ。（写真／野原　茂）
Trim tabs attached to the trailing edge of the elevator. The photo shows a plane with the short and wide-type installed (Photo by S.Nohara)

前脚寸法（単位mm）
Nose gear measurements
(units : mm)

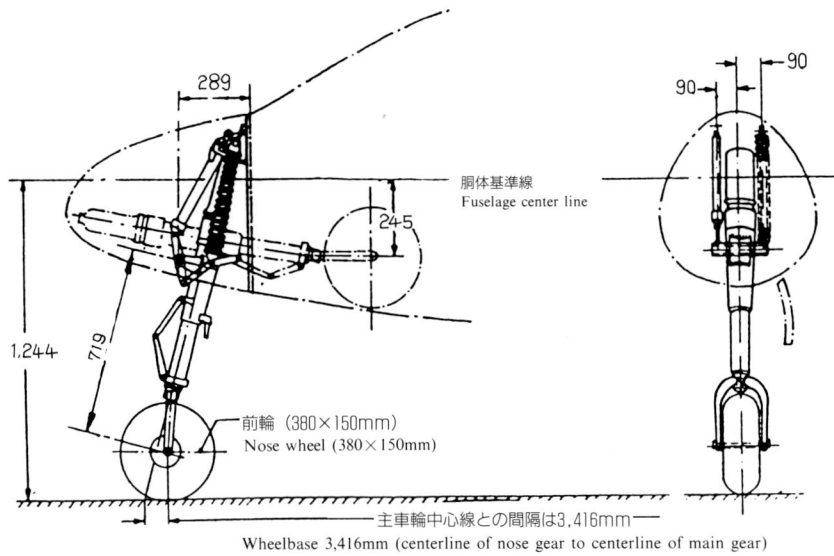

289

90

90

24.5

1,244

719

胴体基準線
Fuselage center line

前輪（380×150mm）
Nose wheel (380×150mm)

主車輪中心線との間隔は3,416mm
Wheelbase 3,416mm (centerline of nose gear to centerline of main gear)

主脚寸法（単位mm）
Main gear measurements (units : mm)

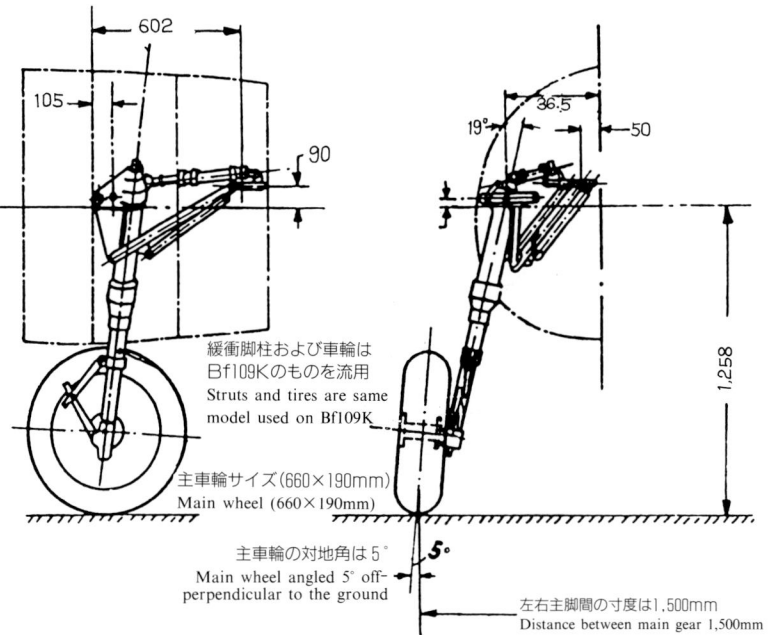

602

105

90

19°

36.5

50

1,258

緩衝脚柱および車輪は
Bf109Kのものを流用
Struts and tires are same
model used on Bf109K

主車輪サイズ（660×190mm）
Main wheel (660×190mm)

主車輪の対地角は5°
Main wheel angled 5° off-
perpendicular to the ground

5°

左右主脚間の寸度は1,500mm
Distance between main gear 1,500mm

主脚構成
Main gear structure

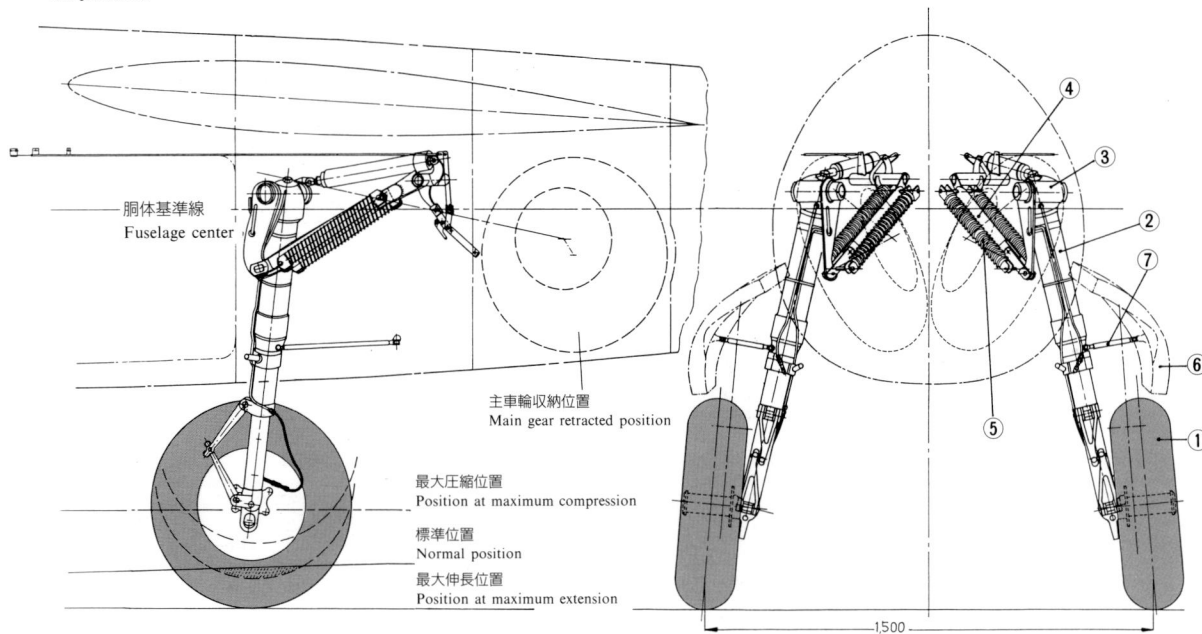

胴体基準線
Fuselage center

主車輪収納位置
Main gear retracted position

最大圧縮位置
Position at maximum compression

標準位置
Normal position

最大伸長位置
Position at maximum extension

1,500

① 主車輪
Main wheel
② 緩衝脚柱
Strut
③ 緩衝脚柱頂部
Strut pivot

④ ブレーキ支柱
Brake support brace
⑤ リターン・スプリング
Return spring

⑥ 主脚収納ドア
Main gear bay door
⑦ 主脚収納ドア開閉アーム
Bay door open / close arm

前脚詳細図
Nose gear detail

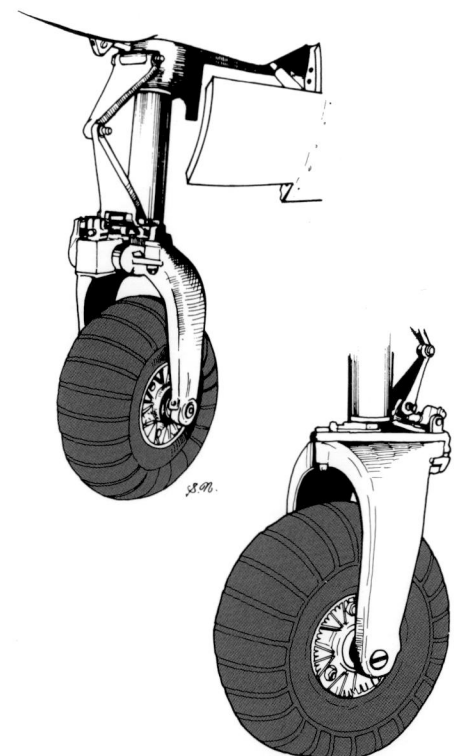

緩衝キ脚杆構造
Main gear strut structure

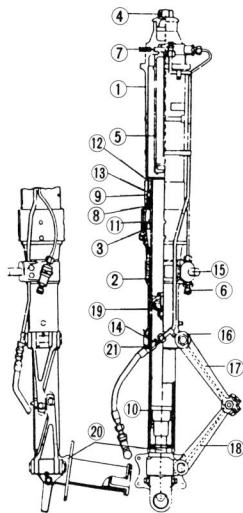

① 上部シリンダー部
Upper cylinder section
② 下部シリンダー部
Lower cylinder section
③ 緊張ナット
Tension nut
④ 固定ナット
Fixed nut
⑤ プランジャー・チューブ
Plunger tube
⑥ 油および空気注入部
Oil / air injection port
⑦ オーバーフロー調整具
Overflow adjustment

⑧ パッキン
Packing
⑨ 圧力リング
Pressure ring
⑩ ピストン・ロッド
Piston rod
⑪ 固定ナット
Fixed nut
⑫ ピストン
Piston
⑬ スロットル・バルブ
Throttle bulb
⑭ ガイド・シャフト
Guide shaft

⑮ 制御ピン取り付け部
Operation pin attachment point
⑯ トルクリンク取り付け部
Torque link attachment point
⑰ トルクリンク
Torque link
⑱ トルクリンク
Torque link
⑲ ピストン・カバー
Piston cover
⑳ 車軸エルボー
Axle elbow
㉑ ストリッパーリング
Stripper ring

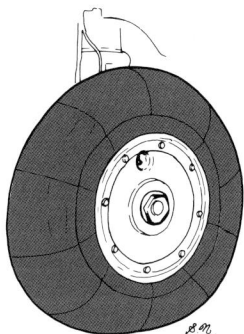

主車輪詳細図
Main wheel hub detail

主車輪部品構成
Main wheel structure

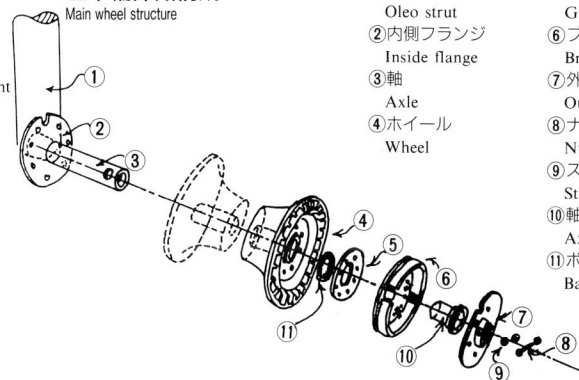

① オレオ支柱
Oleo strut
② 内側フランジ
Inside flange
③ 軸
Axle
④ ホイール
Wheel

⑤ グリース受け
Grease ring
⑥ ブレーキ・ドラム
Brake drum
⑦ 外側フランジ
Outside flange
⑧ ナット＆ボルト
Nut & bolt
⑨ スタッドボルト
Stud bolt
⑩ 軸スリーブ
Axle sleeve
⑪ ボールベアリング
Ball bearings

エンジン　ENGINE

エンジン・ナセル詳細図
Engine nacelle detail

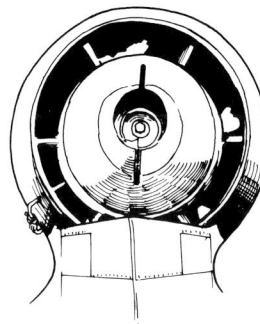
後正面
Rear view

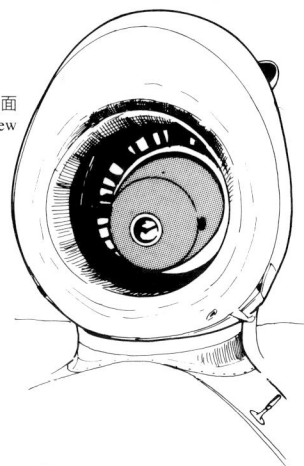
正面
Front view

ノズル部
Nozzle (portside, rear view)

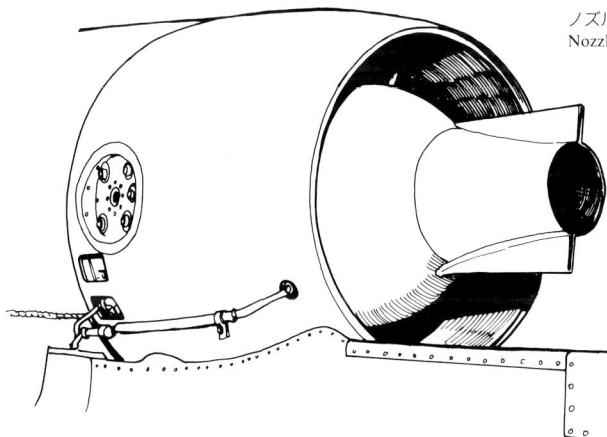

BMW003ターボジェット・エンジン構造図
BMW003 turbojet engine structure

① 潤滑油タンク
Lubricating oil reservoir
② 燃料タンク
Fuel tank
③ 低圧フィルター
Low-pressure filter
④ 燃料ポンプ
Fuel pump
⑤ 制御装置
Control mechanism
⑥ 高圧フィルター
High-pressure filter
⑦ 点火栓
Igniter
⑧ タービン静翼
Stationary turbine
⑨ タービン動翼
Rotating turbine

⑩ 噴流
Exhaust
⑪ 潤滑油冷却器
Oil cooler
⑫ 空気流路
Air flow channel
⑬ 始動モーター
Starter motor
⑭ 空気圧縮器
Air compressor
⑮ 燃料噴射装置
Fuel injection mechanism
⑯ 燃焼ガス
Combustion gas
⑰ ノズル・コーン可動範囲（mm）
Nozzle cone movement range (mm)

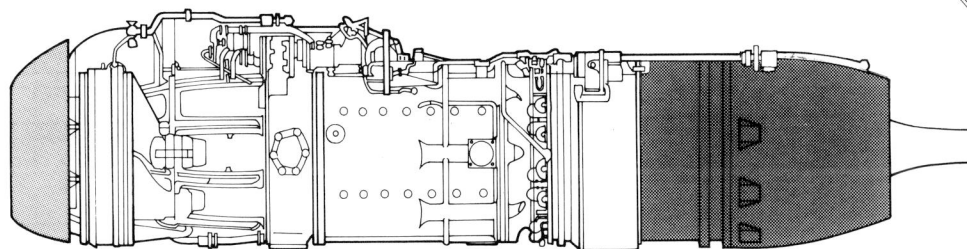

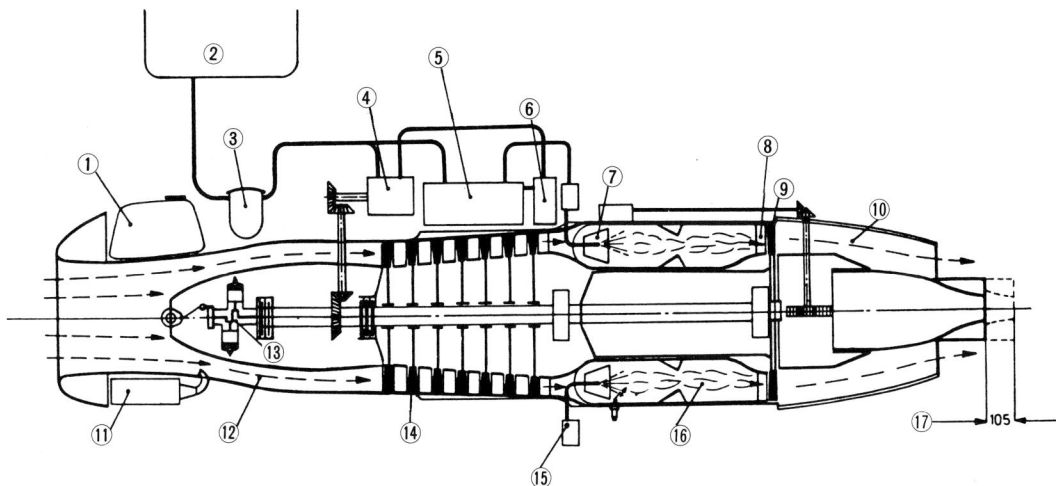

コクピット COCKPIT

ハインケル社製射出座席
Heinkel-manufactured ejection seat

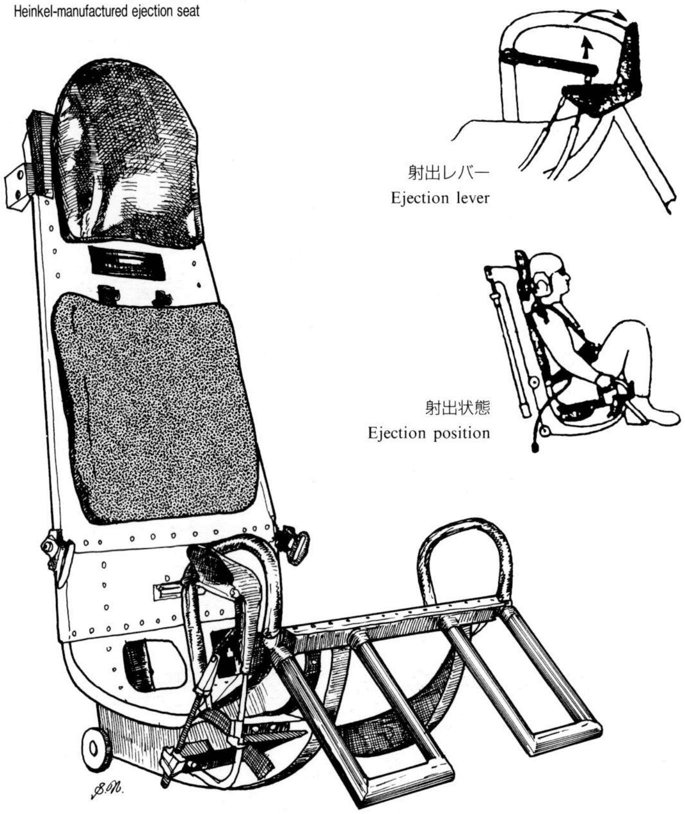

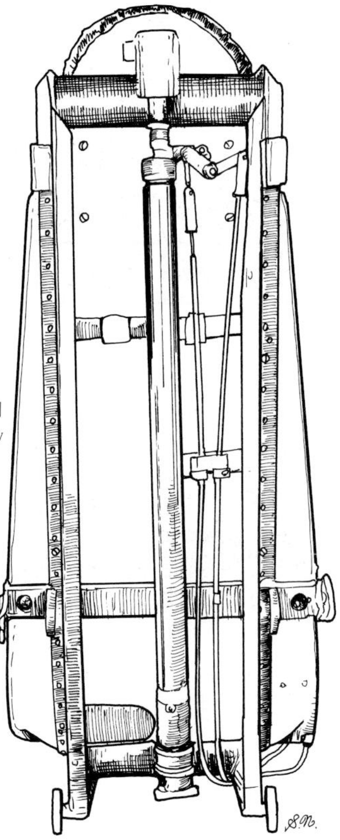

裏側
Rear view

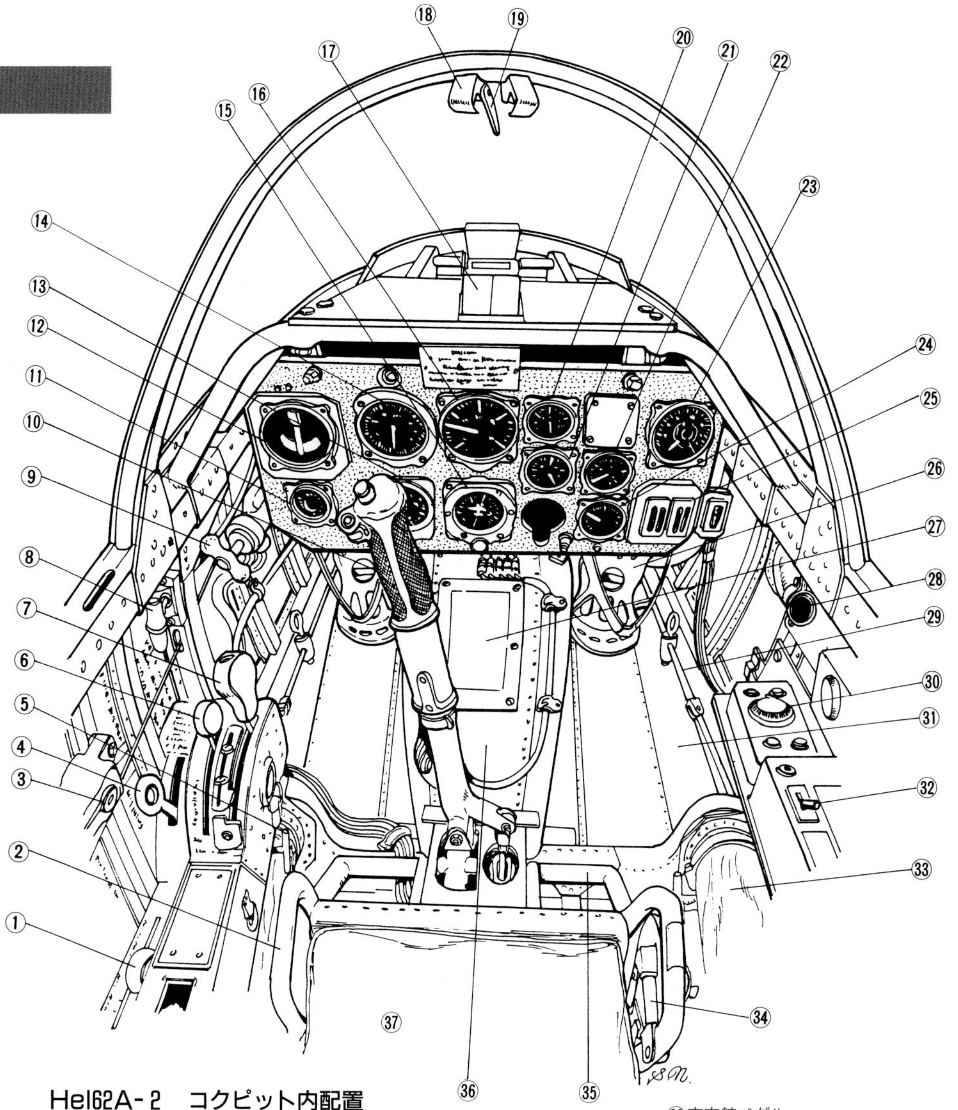

昇降舵操作時の操縦桿の前後可動範囲
Control stick movement range during operation of elevator

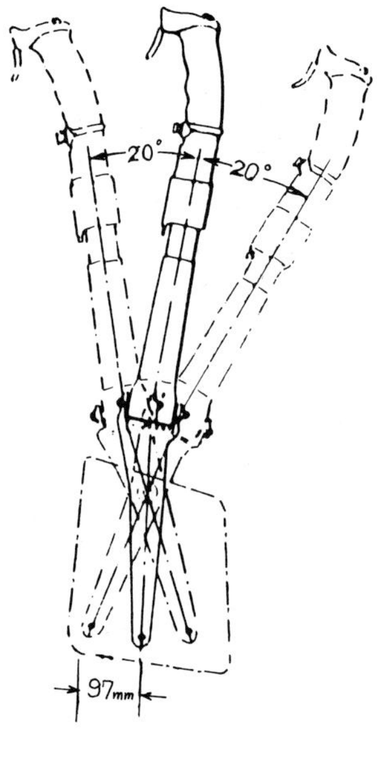

He162A-2 コクピット内配置
He162A-2 Cockpit layout

①昇降舵トリム調節レバー
Elevator trim adjustment lever
②座席ハンドル（射出時使用）
Seat handle (grasped during ejection)
③水平尾翼トリム調節ハンドル
Horizontal stabilizer trim adjustment handle
④脚位置選択レバー
Landing gear position selection lever
⑤機関砲取り付け金具
Machine cannon mount
⑥燃料コック
Fuel valve
⑦スロットル・レバー
Throttle lever
⑧脚操作レバー
Landing gear operation lever
⑨フラップ手動操作ハンドル
Manual flap control lever
⑩操縦桿
Control stick
⑪フラップ角度指示計
Flap angle indicator
⑫旋回計
Turn indicator
⑬高度計
Altimeter
⑭速度計
Airspeed indicator
⑮コンパス
Compass
⑯昇降計
Vertical speed indicator
⑰Revi16B光像式射撃照準器
Revi 16B reflecting-type gun-sight
⑱キャノピー・キャッチ
Canopy catch
⑲キャノピー開閉ハンドル
Canopy latch
⑳ジェット・パイプ温度計
Jet pipe temperature gauge
㉑油圧計
Oil pressure gauge
㉒油量計
Oil gauge
㉓回転計
Tachometer
㉔燃料計
Fuel gauge
㉕機関砲弾消費ゲージ
Ammunition supply gauge
㉖方向舵ペダル
Rudder pedals
㉗前車輪収納状態視認窓
Nose wheel position visual inspection window
㉘信号弾発射筒
Signal flare ejection port
㉙方向舵作動索
Rudder control rod
㉚無線器ダイヤル&選択パネル
Radio control panel
㉛MG151/20ブラスト・チューブ
MG151/20 blast tube
㉜エンジン始動スイッチ&電気回路パネル
Engine start switch & electrical control panel
㉝MG151/20レコイル・スプリング・カバー
MG151/20 recoil spring cover
㉞射出座席操作ハンドル
Ejection lever
㉟射出時用足掛け
Foot rest (used during ejection)
㊱前車輪収納部フェアリング
Nose wheel bay fairing
㊲射出座席（火薬式）
Ejection seat (explosive-powered)

写真１：わずか３か月という驚異的なスピード開発で完成した、He162の原型１号機V1。のちの量産機と異なり、主翼端に下反角はつけられていない。全面RLM02カラー１色の試作機塗装を施している。本機は、２回目のテスト飛行時に、木製主翼の前縁部が接着剤不良で壊われ、墜落して失なわれた。

Photo 1: The V1 prototype of the He162, developed in the amazingly short period of just three months, from initial concept to completed aircraft. It differs from the production model in that it lacks winglets. Typical of test aircraft, it is painted entirely in RLM 02. This aircraft was destroyed in a crash on its second test flight, killing the pilot, when the starboard wing of the aircraft disintegrated during low-level, high-speed testing due the use of defective bonding agents during construction.

写真２～３：デンマーク国境に近いレック基地の滑走路脇に並べられ、連合軍への引き渡しを待つJG1のHe162A-2。ドイツ敗戦２日前の1945年５月６日の撮影で、このとき31機のHe162が連合軍に接収されたといわれており、２個飛行隊の定数よりはずっと少ない数しか保有していなかったようだ。写真２の手前機は、第１飛行中隊所属のW.Nr120097、機番号〝４〟（白）、写真３の右列手前より４機目の機番号〝21〟（白）は、機首先端の黒／白／赤帯からみて、第II飛行隊司令官パウル・ハインリッヒ・デーネ大尉の乗機と思われる。

Photo 2-3: A row of He162 A-2s of JG 1 at the captured Leck airbase near the Danish border awaiting shipment to various Allied countries. This photo was taken two days before the German surrender, on May 6th, 1945. The Allies are said to have captured a total of 31 Salamanders at the base, far less than the number that should have been present to make up the two full *Gruppe* (usually 24-36 planes each) supposed to be stationed there. The aircraft in the foreground (aircraft number "4" in white) is W.Nr 120097, assigned to the 1st *Staffel* of JG 1. The 4th aircraft from the front of the right-side row in photo 3 (aircraft number "21" in white) has the black, white and red markings on its nose of a commander. As such, it is probably the personal aircraft of the *Kommandeur* of II./JG 1, Hptm. Paul-Heinrich Dähne.

写真4～6：レック基地にてアメリカ軍の調査を受ける、JG1航空団司令官ヘルベルト・イーレフェルト大佐の乗機He162A-2、W.Nr120230、機番号 "23"（白）。のちに、本機はアメリカへ輸送される途中、もしくは到着後にW.Nr120222の垂直尾翼に取り替えられ、現在に至る。ナセル先端が白っぽいのは、Jumo 004と同様この部分がエンジン本体と一体になっているためで、無塗装のままにしておく場合が多かった。右主翼端下反角部の白線3本の意味は不明。

Photo 4-6: The personal He162 A-2 (aircraft number "23" in white, W.Nr 120230) of the *Kommodore* of JG 1, Obst. Herbert Ihlefeld, undergoing inspection by U.S. military personnel at Leck. This plane is currently on limited display at the Paul E. Gahbar Preservation Facility in Silver Hill, Maryland, an arm of the National Air and Space Museum. During its shipment to the U.S., or perhaps after it arrived there, its vertical stabilizers were replaced with those of W.Nr 120222. The front edge of the engine nacelle appears whitish in the photograph because it was actually part of the engine itself and was frequently left unpainted, like the Jumo 004. The meaning of the three white lines painted on the outer edge of the right winglet (photo 5) is unknown. The Salamander to this plane's right (in the background of photos 4 & 6) appears to have collapsed landing gear.

写真7～9：1945年10月、アメリカのオハイオ州ライト・フィールド基地にて撮影された、イーレフェルト大佐乗機He162A-2、W.Nr120230、機番号 "23"。垂直尾翼が取り替えられ、エンジンも換装された可能性がある（ナセル先端に塗装が施されている）が、接収当時のコンディションを維持している。正面写真で機体が左に傾いているのは、主脚のオレオ油圧が抜けているため。機首先端の第3帝国カラーを配した指揮官帯は前より黒、白、赤だが、第3中隊長デムート中尉機のそれは赤、白、黒となっており、役職、又は階級の違いを示すものと思われる。

Photo 7-9: The personal He162 A-2 (aircraft number "23" in white, W.Nr 120230) of the *Kommodore* of JG 1, Obst. Herbert Ihlefeld, photographed at Wright Field in Ohio in October of 1945. Its vertical stabilizers have been replaced with those of W.Nr 120222, as can be clearly seen in photo 8, and the front edge of the engine nacelle has been painted (compare with photos 4-6), but otherwise, it seems to be in the same condition as when it was captured at Leck. In the head-on shot (photo 9), the plane is leaning to its left due to insufficient oleo pressure in the main gear. The Third Reich color markings on the nose of the plane are, from the front, black, white and red on this plane, but those on the plane of *Staffel* 3 *Kommandeur* Demuth is in the order red, white, black. The difference in color order is thought to signify differences in rank or assignment.

写真10：胴体、垂直尾翼が無塗装のまま完成した、ユンカース社ベルンブルク工場製のHe162A-2、W.Nr300027。胴体前半部の外板、リベット・ラインに沿った塗り分けは、整形のためのサーフェイサー。コクピット附近は、敗戦を嘆いた工場労働者によって破壊されている。同側面に記入された〝27〟は、W.Nrの末尾2桁。記録によれば、本機はユンカース社で完成した最後の機ということになっている。

Photo 10: An He162 A-2, W.Nr 300027 manufactured by Junkers' Bernburg factory. The fuselage and vertical stabilizers are unpainted. The different color of the panel and rivet lines is due to a coating of surfacer on these parts to smooth the plane's lines and decrease air resistance. The cockpit area of the plane has been severely damaged by workers at the factory upset over Germany's surrender. The "27" marked on the front part of the plane indicates the last two digits of its W.Nr. According to company records, this plane was the last He162 produced by Junkers.

12

写真11：アメリカに運ばれた4機のHe162A-2のうちの1機、もと2./JG1所属のW.Nr120077、機番号 "1"（赤）を前上方よりみる。エンジン・ナセルの塗装がリタッチされてしまっているが、他は接収当時の状態を保っている。コクピット両側に描かれた "Wolfskopf"（狼の頭）エンブレムは、旧III./JG77飛行隊章だったもので、敗戦直前に2./JG1中隊章に適用されたようだ。パーソナル文字 "Nervenklau"（神経質な盗賊）は左側のみに記入されている。現在、本機はカリフォルニア州チノ空港に隣接する、私設航空博物館 "プレーンズ・オブ・フェイム" に保存、展示中。

Photo 11: One of the four He162 A-2s shipped to the United States. This plane (aircraft number "1" in red, W. Nr 120077) was originally assigned to 2./JG 1. Although the engine nacelle has been retouched, the plane is otherwise in the same condition in which it was captured. The *Wolfskopf* (Wolf's head) emblem visible on both sides of the cockpit was originally that of III./JG 77, and appears to have been adopted by 2./JG 1 just before Germany's surrender. The personal marking *Nervenklau* ("Nervous Bandit") appears on the plane's port side only. This aircraft is currently on public display at the privately-owned Planes of Fame museum in Chino, California.

写真12：オーストリアのザルツブルクに近い山中の、岩塩採掘坑道内に設けられたハインケル社の地下工場で、続々と生産されていたHe162Aの胴体部分。写真に写っているだけでも約40機分が確認できる。地上施設の目ぼしいところは、たちまちにして連合軍機の空襲により潰されてしまうため、このような地下工場に中心を移す他はなかった。1945年4月末、アメリカ軍に接収された直後の撮影。

Photo 12: Partially completed He162 fuselages at one of Heinkel's underground factories, a former salt mine in the mountains near Salzburg, Austria. At least 40 assemblies are visible in the photograph. Above-ground aircraft factories were routinely targeted by Allied bombers in the latter part of the war, making such unorthodox facilities necessary. This picture was taken in April of 1945, shortly after the factory's capture by U.S. forces.

13

写真13：戦後の1945年9月、"バトル・オブ・ブリテン週間" と銘打って、ロンドンのハイド・パークで催された捕獲ドイツ機展示会に出展された、もと2./JG1のHe162A-2、W.Nr120086。機番号は消されてしまい、国籍標識も書き直されているため、オリジナルの状態はわからない。本機は、のちにカナダに譲渡され、現在もオンタリオのロッククリフに保存されている。

Photo 13: A captured He162 A-2 (W.Nr 120086) originally of 2./JG 1 on display at Hyde Park in London after Germany's surrender during "Battle of Britain Week" in September of 1945. Its original markings are unknown, as its aircraft number and national insignia have been painted over. This aircraft was eventually handed over to Canadian forces, and is currently preserved in Rockcliffe, Ontario.

14

写真14：本機もイギリスに運ばれた11機のHe162A-2のうちの1機で、もと1./JG1所属のW.Nr120072、機番号 "3"（白）。写真は1945年秋、RAE ファーンボロウ基地にて一般公開された際のものだが、このあと間もない11月9日、本機は飛行テスト中に低空ロールをうった瞬間、垂直尾翼が破壊して墜落、パイロットのロバート・マークス少尉も死亡した。

Photo 14: This He162 A (aircraft number "3" in white, W. Nr 120072), originally assigned to 1./JG 1, is one of the eleven Salamanders shipped to the U.K. This photo was taken in the fall of 1945 during a public exhibition at the RAE's Farnborough Air Base. Shortly thereafter, during a test flight on November 9th, the plane's tail section disintegrated during an attempted low-altitude roll and it crashed, killing the pilot, Flt. Lt. Robert A. Marks.

He162各型変遷
Variations of the He162

作図・解説／野原　茂
Illustrations and Commentary by Shigeru Nohara
図版は1/48&1/72スケール
Diagrams are 1/48&1/72 scale

① 信号弾発射口
　 Gun port for signal flare
② ピトー管
　 Pitot tube
③ 機首コーン取り付けボルト・カバー
　 Nose cone attachment bolt covers
④ 前脚位置表示棒
　 Nose gear position indicator rod
⑤ Revi16B光像式射撃照準器
　 Revi16B reflecting gunsight
⑥ 悪天候時使用窓
　 Observation window for use in inclement weather
⑦ 射出座席
　 Ejection seat
⑧ BMW003Eターボジェット・エンジン
　 BMW003E turbojet engine
⑨ D/Fループ・アンテナ
　 D/F loop antenna

⑩ 前車輪（380×150mm）
　 Nose wheel（380×150mm）
⑪ MG151/20　20mm機関砲（弾数120発）
　 MG151/20　20mm machine cannon（120 rounds）
⑫ 機関砲着脱／点検ドア
　 Armament removal/inspection hatch
⑬ 翼端下反角部
　 Winglet
⑭ 主車輪（660×190mm）
　 Main wheels（660×190mm）
⑮ 主脚収納ドア
　 Main gear bay door
⑯ FuG25a IFF用ロッド・アンテナ
　 FuG25a IFF rod antenna
⑰ 離陸補助ロケット取り付け部
　 Take-off assist rocket mounting points
⑱ 胴体後部保護スキッド
　 Fuselage protection skid

■He162A-2

胴体断面図
Fuselage cross section

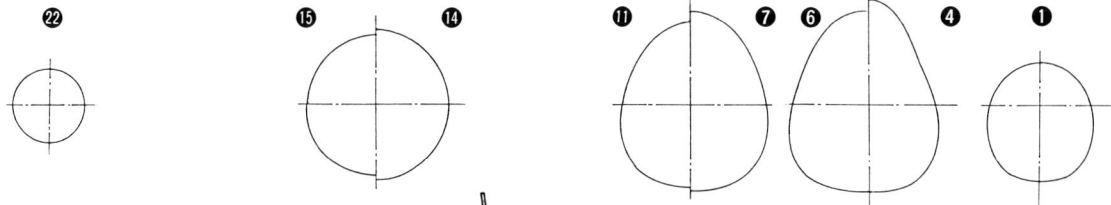

（右側面　Starboard elevation）

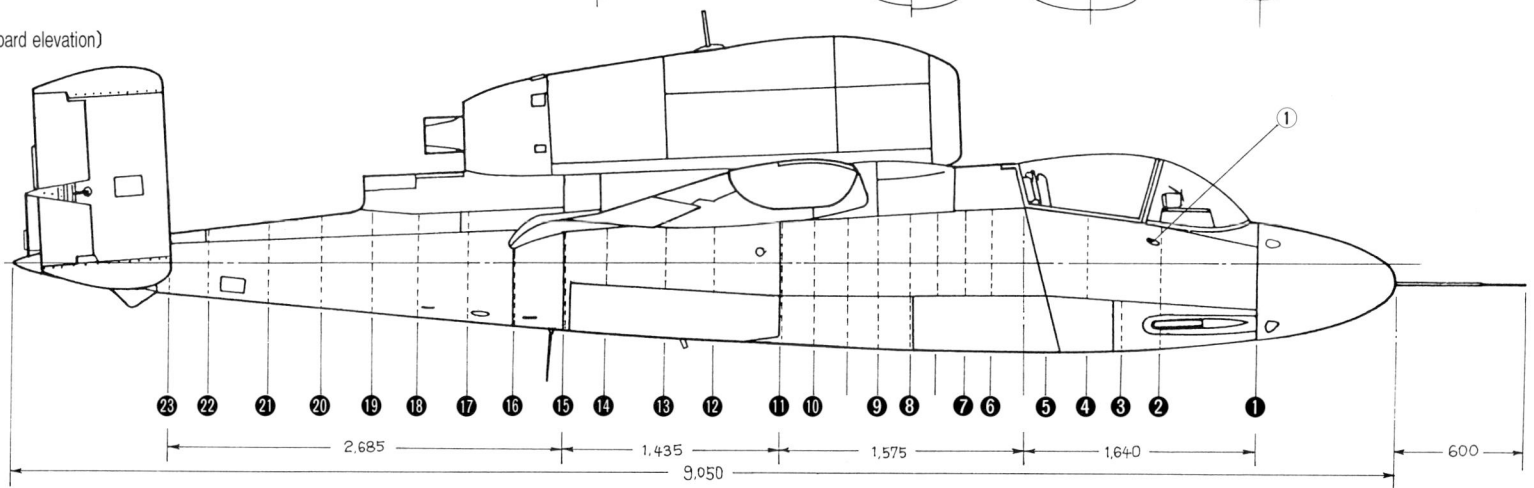

2,685　　　1,435　　　1,575　　　1,640　　　600
9,050

（左側面　Port elevation）

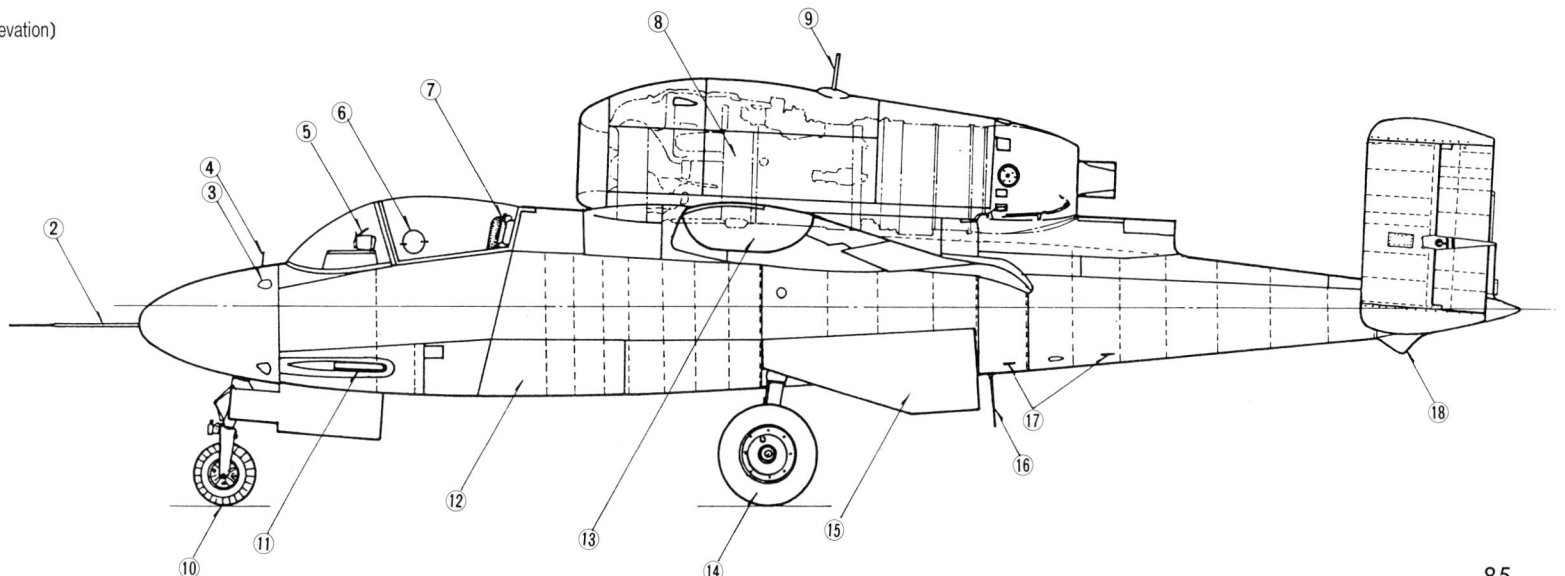

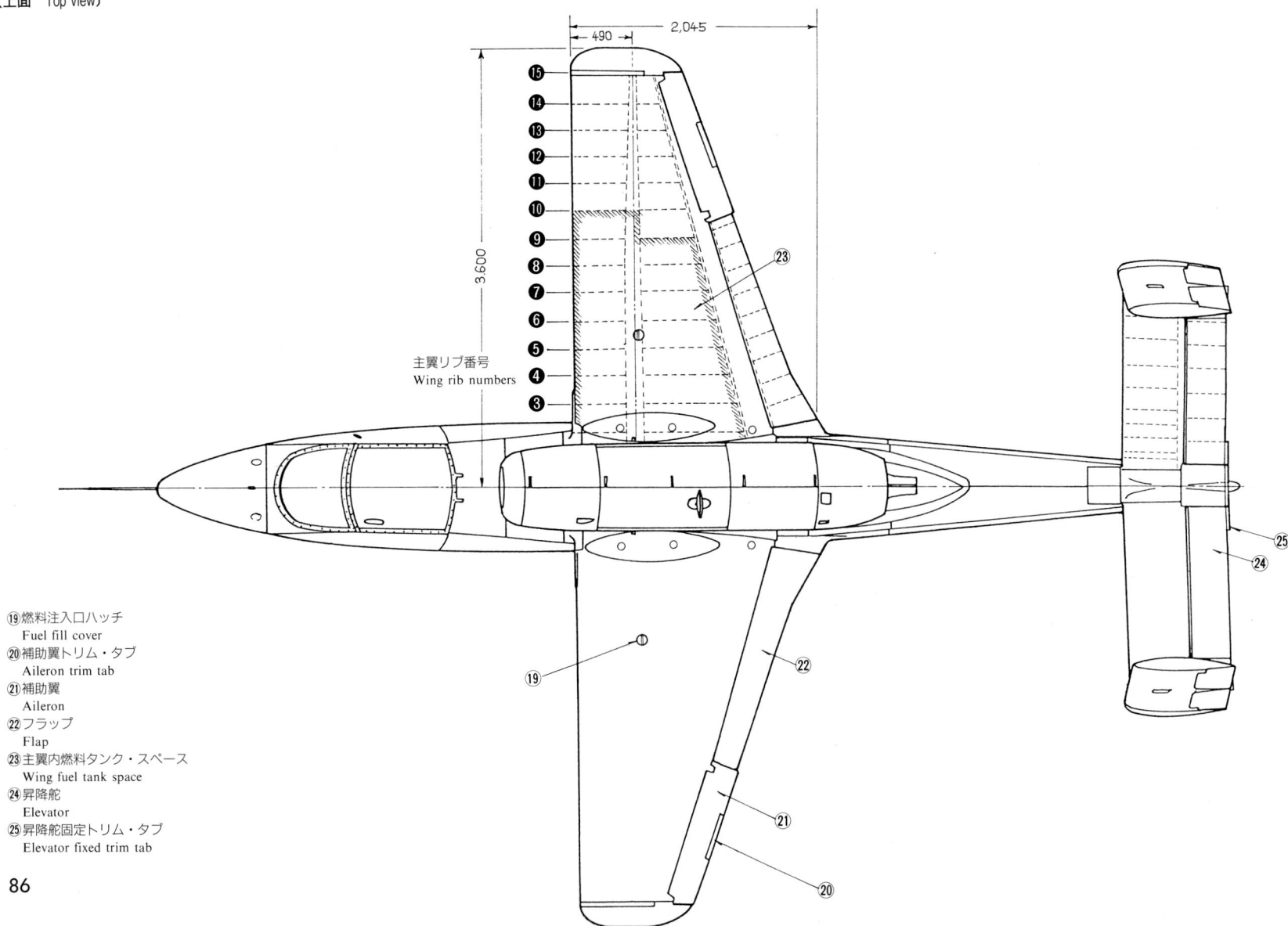

He162A-2

He162の最初の量産型はHe162A-1となる予定だったが、A-1の主武装となるはずだったMK108 30mm機関砲の製造メーカー、ラインメタル・ボルジィヒ社が空襲を受け、同機関砲の供給が難しくなった。そのためA-1の生産は見送られ、代りにMG151/20 20mm機関砲を搭載したHe162A-2が量産されることとなった。

空軍省は、1945年4月までに1,000機生産することを目標にハインケル社のロストック、ヒンターブリュール両工場の他、ユンカース社ベルンブルク工場、ミッテルヴェルケ社ノルトハウゼン工場でも生産が行われ、終戦までに約240機が完成している。

The He162A-1 was intended to be the initial production version of the Salamander, but the manufacturer of the plane's MK108 30mm machine cannons, Rheinmetall Borsig, was bombed by the Allies making supply of the guns impossible. In addition, flight and firing tests had shown that the 30mm weapon was generally too heavy for the Salamander's light airframe. As a result, plans to mass produce the A-1 were suspended, and the A-2, armed with MG151/20, 20mm machine cannons become the first production model.

Hoping to produce 1,000 Salamanders by March of 1945, the Luftwaffe assigned production to Heinkel's Rostock and Hinterbrül factories, as well as to Junkers' Bernberg factory, and Mittelberk's Nordhausen factory. However, by the end of the war, just 240 examples had been completed.

（上面　Top view）

主翼リブ番号
Wing rib numbers

⑲燃料注入口ハッチ
　Fuel fill cover
⑳補助翼トリム・タブ
　Aileron trim tab
㉑補助翼
　Aileron
㉒フラップ
　Flap
㉓主翼内燃料タンク・スペース
　Wing fuel tank space
㉔昇降舵
　Elevator
㉕昇降舵固定トリム・タブ
　Elevator fixed trim tab

86

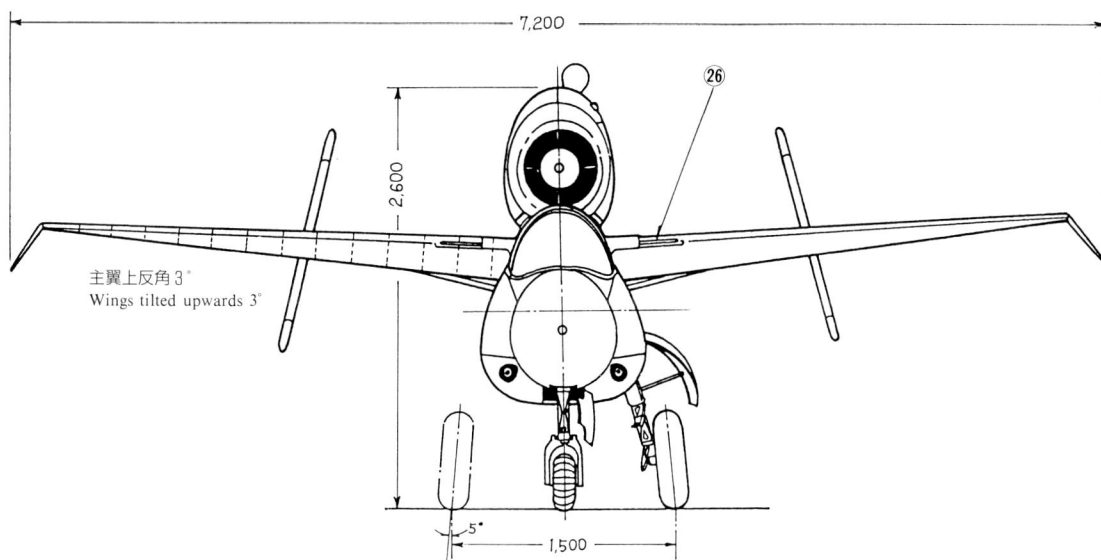

（正面 Front elevation）

7,200

2,600

1,500

5°

主翼上反角3°
Wings tilted upwards 3°

㉖

㉖スポイラー
　Spoiler
㉗MG151/20　20mm機関砲
　MG151/20 20mm machine cannon
㉘空薬莢排出孔
　Empty cases ejection port
㉙主脚収納ドア
　Main gear bay door
㉚FuG25a IFF用ロッド・アンテナ
　FuG25a IFF rod antenna
㉛胴体後部下面保護スキッド
　Fuselage protection skid

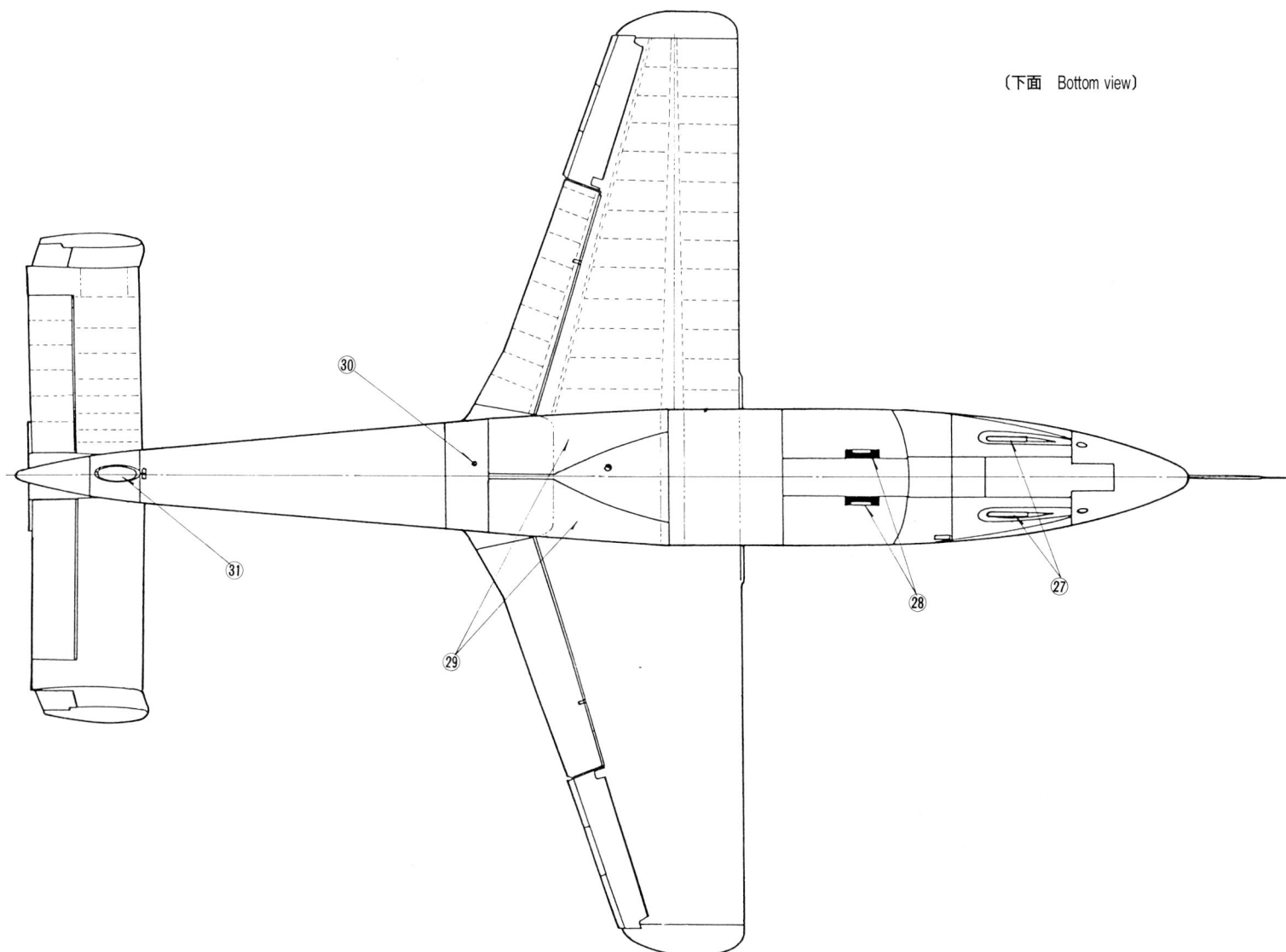

（下面　Bottom view）

㉚

㉛

㉘

㉗

㉙

He162A-10 & He162A-11

　米英軍の大編隊を迎え討つには、1機でも多く戦闘機を生産することが必至となったドイツ空軍は、より簡単に、かつ大量に生産可能な方法としてHe162Aにパルスジェット・エンジンを搭載した簡易型の開発を計画した。As014パルスジェット（推力335kg）を2基搭載したHe162A-10、As044パルスジェット（推力500kg）を1基搭載したHe162A-11の2タイプの案が出されたものの、高空性能に難があるためにこの計画は早々に放棄された。

　In their effort to repel the advancing British and American forces, producing as many fighters as possible became the Luftwaffe's main goal. To that end, they planned two simpler versions of the Salamander with pulse-jet engines which could be produced in greater numbers. Nevertheless, the plans for the He162A-10, with two Argus 109-014 pulse-jets (335kg thrust each), and the He162A-11, with one Argus 109-044 pulse-jet (500kg thrust) were abandoned due to the poor high-altitude performance of the engines.

He162D & He162S

　He162も、他の戦闘機同様にパイロットの操縦訓練用として複座練習機型の生産が計画された。A-2の武装を撤去し、操縦室直後に教官用の後席を新設したHe162D。A-2をベースにタンデム複座とし、垂直尾翼を正方形に近い形状に変更、さらにエンジンを撤去したグライダー練習機He162Sが考案され、He162Dは計画のみで終わったものの、He162Sは終戦までに1機のみ完成した。

　Like any other fighter aircraft, a two-seat trainer version of the Salamander was planned. The He162D was to be an A-2 with the armament removed and an instructor's seat added immediately behind the pilot's. However, the He162D died while still on paper in favor of the He162S, a glider version of the A-2 with the engine removed and a full tandem cockpit. In addition, the aircraft's vertical stabilizers were enlarged, making them almost perfectly square. Only one He162S was built before the German surrender.

①尾翼をV字翼形式に変更
　Tail changed to a V-type
②As014パルスジェット・エンジン（推力335kg）を2基搭載
　Two Argus 109-014 pulse-jet engines (335kg thrust each) installed
③離陸補助ロケット・ブースターを2基着着
　Two take-off assist rockets installed
④As044パルスジェット・エンジン（推力500kg）を1基搭載
　Argus 109-044 pulse-jet engine (500kg thrust) installed
⑤離陸補助ロケット・ブースターを2基装着
　Two take-off assist rockets installed
⑥エンジンをユンカース社製Jumo004Dに換装
　Junkers-manufactured Jumo 004D engine installed
⑦後席（教官用）を新設
　Rear (instructor's) seat installed
⑧エンジンを撤去
　Engine removed
⑨大型の垂直安定板に変更
　Vertical stabilizers enlarged
⑩固定式前脚
　Fixed nose gear
⑪MG151/20を取り外し、砲口部をパネルで塞いでいる
　MG151/20 removed, muzzle ports covered with panels
⑫固定式主脚
　Fixed main gear

■He162A-6

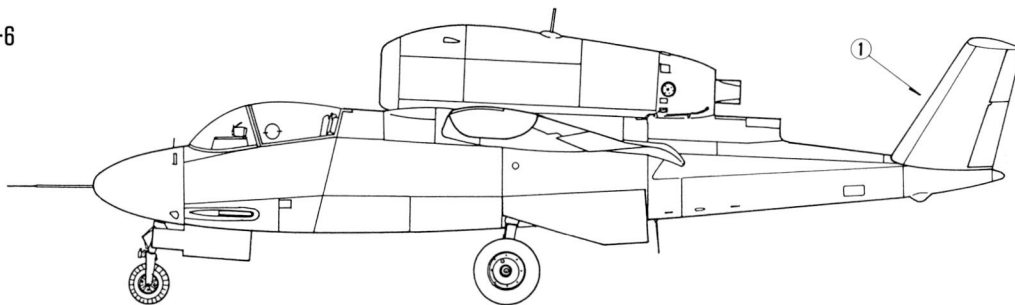

■He162A-10

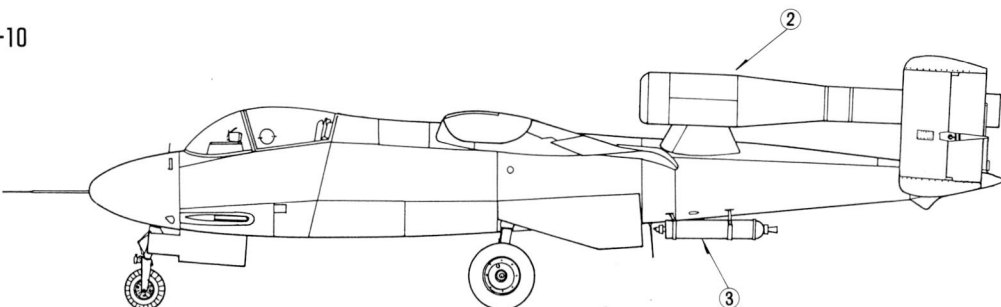

■He162A-11

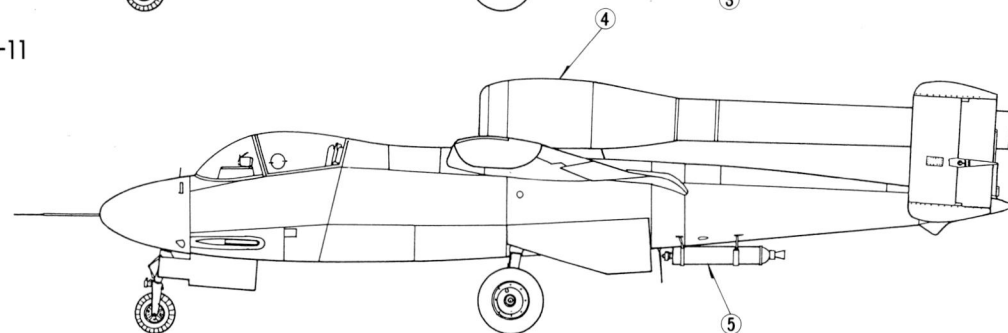

■He162A Jumo004D搭載型
He162A with Jumo 004D Engine

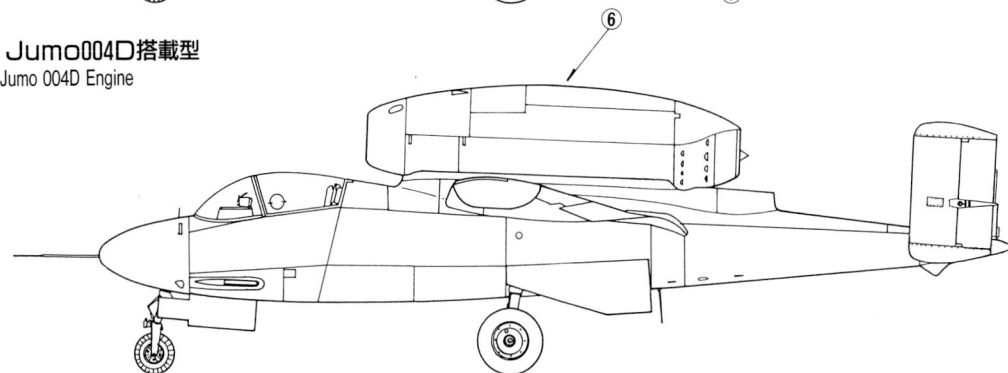

■He162S 複座練習機
He162S Two-seat trainer (glider)

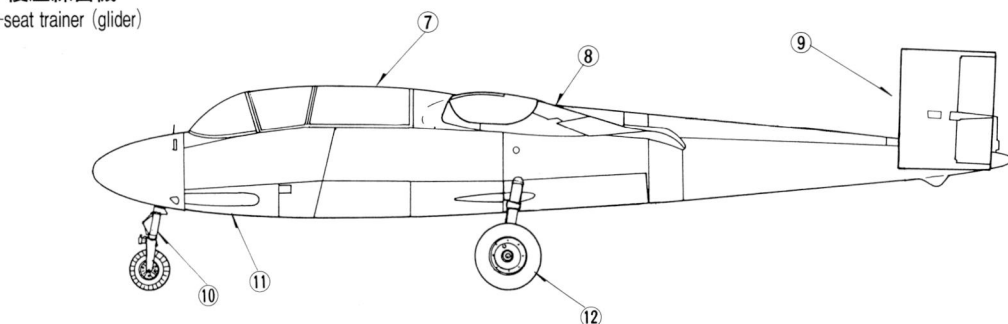

He162B & He162C

超短期間開発機にもかかわらず、He162には量産型A-1、A-2の他にいくつかの発展型、派生型が計画されていた。最も有望視されていたのは、エンジンを第Ⅱ世代のターボジェット・エンジンと呼べる自社製ハインケル・ヒルトHeS011（推力1,300kg）に換装し、さらに主翼は洗練された後退翼（下反角付き）、および前進翼、尾翼はV型形式を採用する案だった。量産に入った場合、前進翼付きはHe162B、後退翼付きはHe162Cとなるはずだったが、HeS011の実用化が遅れたこともあって、終戦までに完成しなかった。

なお、エンジン、主翼はそのままで尾翼をV型形式としたHe162A-6、エンジンをMe262と同じユンカース社製Jumo004Bやジェット／ロケット・エンジン併用のBMW003R（推力2,040kg）に換装する案などもあったが、計画のみで終った。

Despite the fact that the A-1 and A-2 versions of the Salamander were designed and built in an exceedingly short period, a number of other advanced and derivative types were planned as well. The most promising of these were versions which were to employ Heinkel's own second-generation turbojet engine, the HeS011 (1,300kg thrust), in addition to changing the wings to either a swept-forward design, or a rear-swept, gull-wing design while replacing the tail with a V-type. In production, the forward-swept wing version was to be the He162B, while the rear-swept design would be known as the He162C. Nevertheless, development of the HeS011 was delayed and plans were not realized before the end of the war.

A number of other unrealized plans involving the He162 existed as well, including those which left the wings as they were, but changed the tail to a V-type (He162A-6), or those which replaced the engine with the same one used by the Me262, the Jumo 004B. Another involved the use of the jet/rocket BMW003R engine (2,040kg thrust).

■He162D　複座練習機
He162D Two-seat trainer

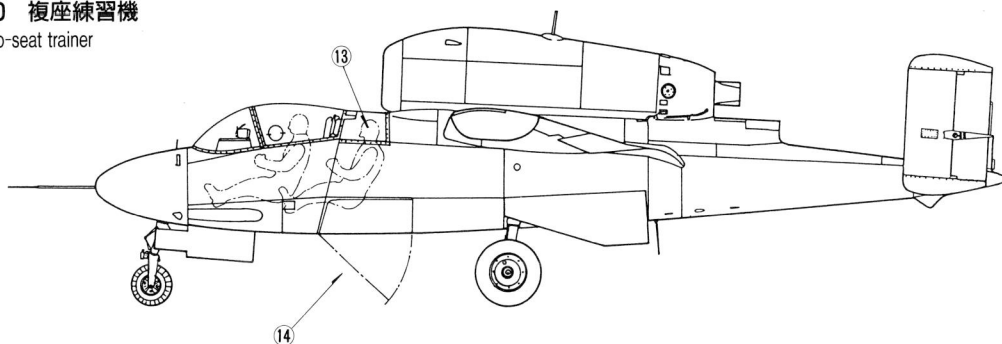

■He162B

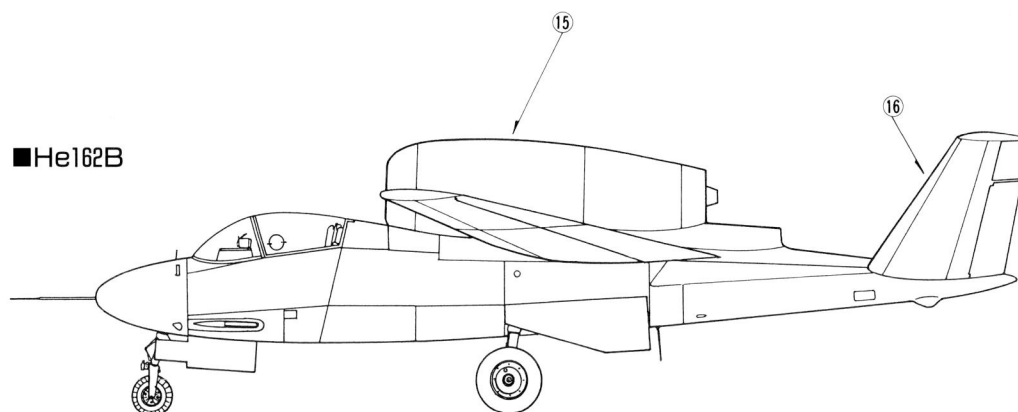

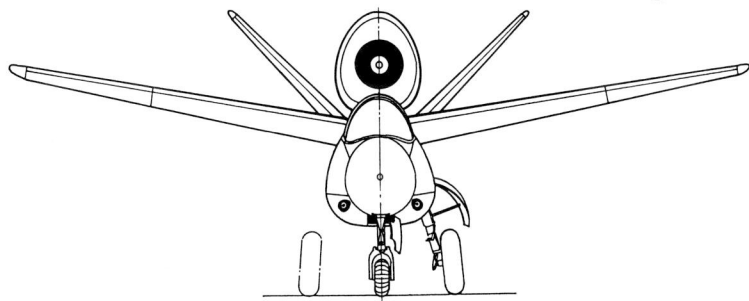

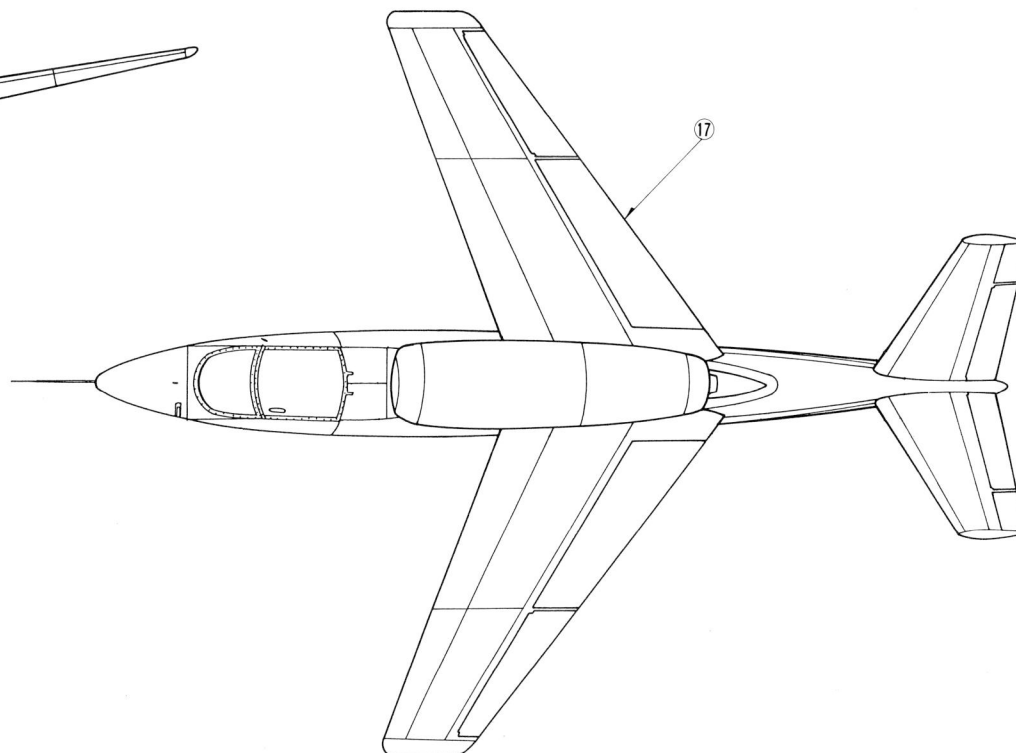

⑬コクピット後方に新たに後席を新設
　Second seat added behind cockpit
⑭後席（教官用）の乗降用ドア
　Rear (instructor's) seat access door
⑮ハインケル社製HeS011ターボジェット・エンジン搭載
　Heinkel-manufactured HeS011 turbojet engine installed
⑯尾翼はV字翼
　Tail changed to V-type
⑰主翼に前進翼を採用
　Wings swept forward

89

■He162C

⑱

⑲

⑳

㉑

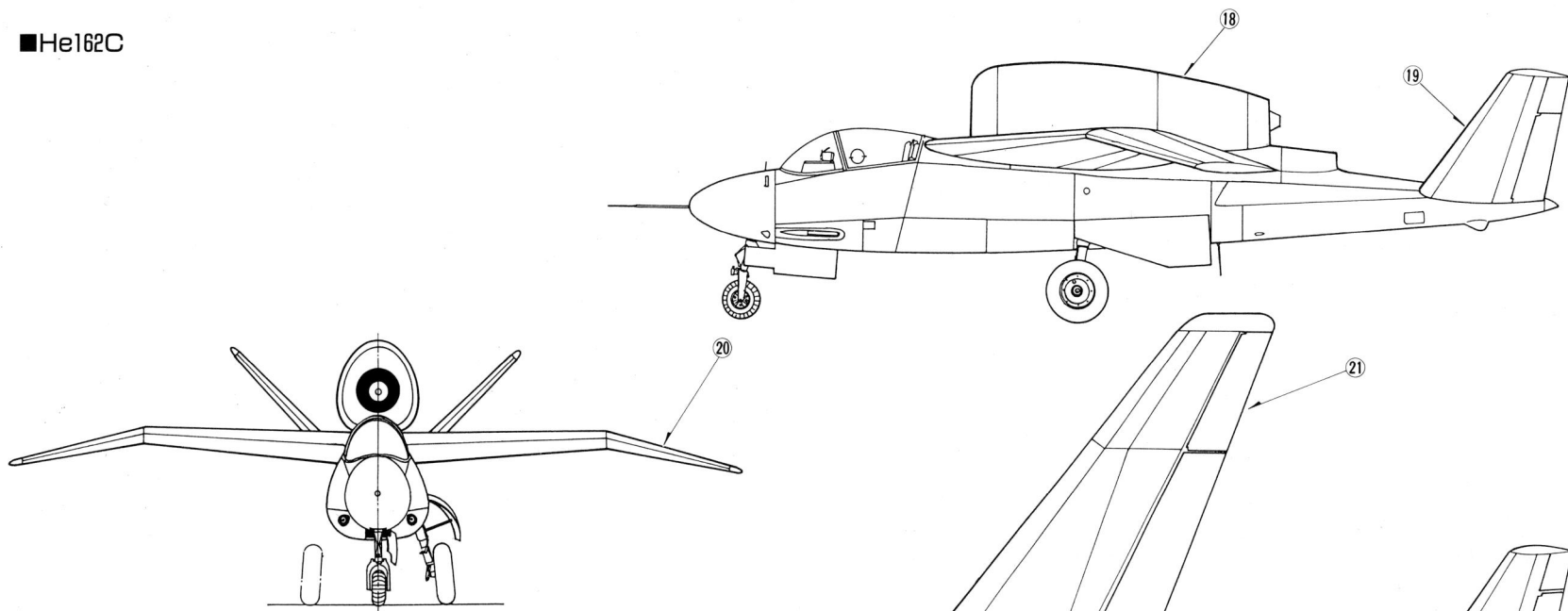

⑱ハインケル社製HeS011ターボジェット・エンジン搭載
　Heinkel-manufactured HeS011 turbojet engine installed
⑲V字形尾翼
　V-type tail
⑳主翼外側には下反角が付く
　Outer section of wings tilted down (gull-type)
㉑主翼は後退翼
　Wing swept back
㉒アラドE377a飛行爆弾
　Arado E377a flying bomb
㉓切り離し式離陸用ドリー
　Detachable take-off dolly

ミステル5

　奇抜な発想で知られる背負い式特殊攻撃機 "ミステル" にもHe162を使用することが計画されていた。これまでのミステルと異なり、爆薬を積んだ子機は既存機からの転用ではなく、アラド社がミステル専用に開発したアラドE377aが用いられる予定だったが、計画のみで終わっている。

The Luftwaffe considered using the He162 as the mother plane for the Mistel 5 (Mistletoe) composite aircraft. The unique and bizarre Mistel concept involved hooking two aircraft together with the lower, larger plane (usually an old Ju88) being used as an unmanned, enormous bomb which would be flown close to its target and then released by a smaller, mother plane (usually a Bf109 or Fw190). However in the case of the Mistel 5, the plan involved using not an old aircraft, but the Arado E377a flying bomb, which was designed especially for the Mistel concept. However, like so many other late-war German plans, the Mistel 5 was never realized.

■ミステル5
Mistel 5

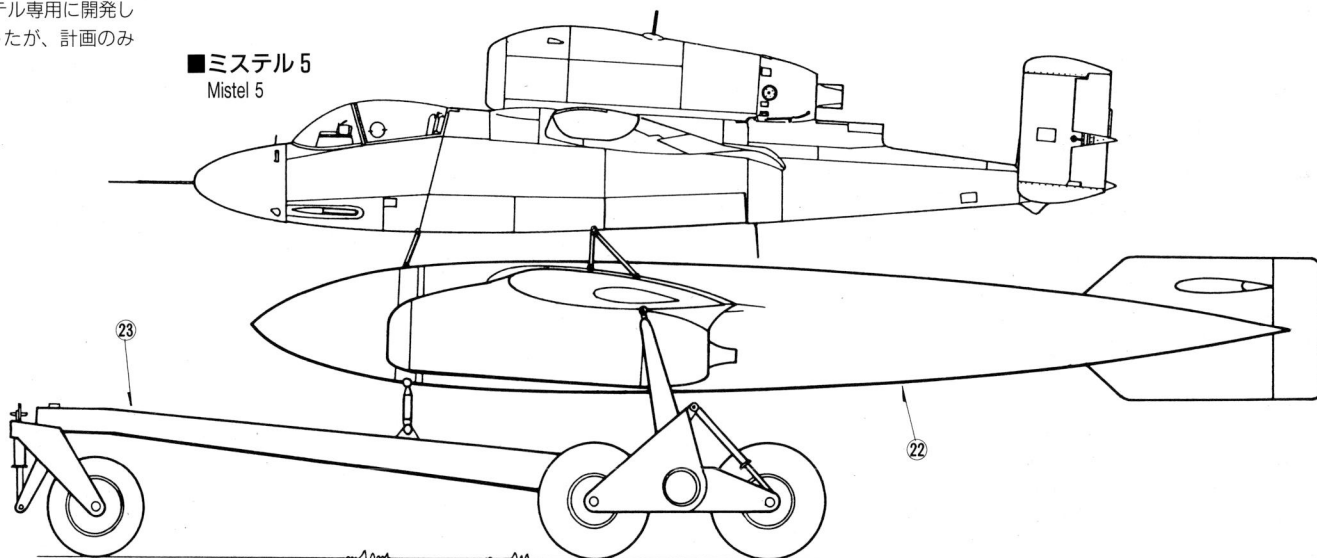

㉓

㉒